THE UNIVERSE LOVES A HAPPY ENDING

Project Credits

Cover Design: Brian Dittmar Design Inc.

Book Production: John McKercher

Hand-drawn illustrations: Carline Vrielink

Developmental Editors: Jude Berman, Sally Castillo, Kiran Rana

Copy Editors: Mark Hoffman, Alexandra Mummery

Managing Editor: Alexandra Mummery

Rights Coordinator: Stephanie Beard

Publisher: Todd Bottorff

THE UNIVERSE LOVES A HAPPY ENDING

Becoming Energy Healers
for the Planet, Organizations and Ourselves

HANS ANDEWEG

An imprint of
Turner Publishing Company

Turner Publishing Company
4507 Charlotte Avenue • Suite 100 • Nashville, Tennessee 37209
www.turnerpublishing.com

U.S. edition and translation © 2016 by Hunter House,
an imprint of Turner Publishing Company

Dutch edition © 2011 by Hans Andeweg
Uitgeverij Juwelenschip, Cothen, The Netherlands
Original title: *Scheppend Leven*

LIBRARY OF CONGRESS CATALOGING-IN-PUBLICATION DATA

Names: Andeweg, Hans.

Title: The universe loves a happy ending : becoming energy healers for the
planet, organizations, and ourselves / Hans Andeweg.

Description: First Edition. | Alameda, CA : Hunter House Publishers, 2013. |
Includes index.

Identifiers: LCCN 2013010344 | ISBN 9780897936699 (trade paper) | ISBN
9780897936705 (ebook) | ISBN 9781681626505 (hardback)

Subjects: LCSH: Mental healing. | Spiritual healing. | Nature, Healing power
of. | Environmental psychology.

Classification: LCC RZ401 .A65 2013 | DDC 615.8/528—dc23
LC record available at http://lccn.loc.gov/2013010344

First Edition

Contents

In 2014 we changed the name of our training from ECOtherapy to ECOintention to avoid confusion with other usages of the word ecotherapy in the United States and elsewhere. Throughout this edition of the book we use our current term, ECOintention.

Important Note

The Universe Loves a Happy Ending is not a scientific book. It is, however, a closely documented account of the author's quest to understand life energy and subtle matter. In doing so, he searched for connections in ancient philosophic traditions and modern scientific theories.

The material in this book is intended to provide a review of information regarding the field of ECOintention. The author has tried to provide the theoretical support for all of the steps he took and every effort has been made to provide accurate and dependable information. However, advances in research are made very quickly, so some of the information may become outdated. Therefore, the publisher, author, and editors, as well as the professionals quoted in the book, cannot be held responsible for any error, omission, or dated material. The author and publisher assume no responsibility for any outcome of applying the information in this book. If you have questions about the application of the information described in this book, consult a professional.

Prologue

These are special times: The climate is changing, there are continual global shifts of power, and major economic and ecological systems seem to be out of balance on our planet. Everything and everyone is affected by these major changes.

I believe we do not need to passively accept these developments, at least in the area of healing the environment. My research and the positive results gained over many years of practice have shown me that each of us is able to help in healing their own environment—and far beyond—on both a small and a large scale. We can *all* be eco-healers; the methods are relatively simple, and everyone can learn them. We are not passive spectators but rather active players on a field of endless possibility. Using our consciousness, we can influence how the world develops; we can make or break the world, unite or divide it. And this is not a fairy tale; I have worked in this field for many years and have seen many practical results that have given me hope for the future of the earth and her inhabitants.

Of the many examples that I could give, the story of the Nizhnesvirsky Reserve in Russia is a particularly good one.

President Michael Gorbachev and the Nizhnesvirsky Reserve

The Russian Nizhnesvirsky Reserve is on the banks of Lake Ladago, two hundred kilometers north of St. Petersburg. It is a magnificent nature reserve with vast forests that alternate with lakes and moors. Elk and wolves make their homes there, and huge flocks of birds use the reserve as a stopover on their long migratory journeys. My first visit was in June of 1994, and I was in the company of some of my colleagues from the Institute for Resonance Therapy, a German company that was developing practical ways of using life energy, and where I was working at the time. We had been invited by Michael Gorbachev, former President of the Soviet Union, who, through his foundation, had informed us that he wanted to have a large Russian nature reserve energetically treated. He let us pick which one.

My work at that time was focused on healing at a distance with energy and intention. Briefly, my research and study had led me to the understanding that life energy and information combine into a *formative force,* a force of mind that is stronger than matter. This formative force is a constructive, center-seeking force that enhances the health and vitality of plants, trees, animals, and all other organisms. We could think of it as the feminine or *yin* force. Through our research we found that it was possible both to explain how the force works and to use it to send energy to distant locations using a map. How this works can be explained using recent scientific discoveries and theories; the most important thing to note, however, is that anyone can learn to do it themselves.

At the Institute we developed techniques for sending life energy and information to remote locations—like communities, parks, small or large ecosystems, and even organizations—where the energy needed balancing or healing. We did this with a map, certain instruments, and dedicated and structured healing intentions. Our first contact with ex-President Gorbachev had been in the spring. One day I found a fax on my desk from Moscow asking for information about our method of healing forests from a distance. We faxed back some information and materials, and soon after that we got the go ahead. I was surprised, both by the quick reaction and by the fact that a man like Gorbachev had no problems with the thought that a large Russian nature reserve of forty thousand hectares could be treated from Germany through a small map.

We chose the Nizhnesvirsky Reserve near St. Petersburg. It had problems with its vitality, and we had the feeling that there were a number of earth power points, places where large amounts of life energy are emerging from the earth. They were important not only for the reserve but for the surrounding area. That last reason appealed to Gorbachev, too.

Gut Feeling

It is interesting that many people—and often those at the top level who have power—don't need a long explanation, discussion, or written briefing to come to a decision. Apart from the fact that they usually don't have much time, "half a word" is enough for them. Gorbachev was like this. People like him trust their feelings and their intuition. Call it instinct or gut feeling, but they somehow sense, even *know*, that something is right and okay.

Whether you prefer intellect or intuition, common sense or feeling, what matters is results. Your theory or method may be ever so attractive, but in the end there must be an improvement of the current situation for it to matter. To help us demonstrate results we had brought in some Czech scientists who would measure the effect of the treatment on the forest according to the methods that were accepted in Europe. They also knew the country, spoke the language, and served as interpreters.

"Everyone Fought Everybody Here"

During the first visit to the Reserve, the staff there made a rather gloomy impression. The foresters, guards, and local researchers hadn't been paid in months, and there wasn't even money for gasoline or diesel fuel for their service vehicles. Large parts of the area were therefore inaccessible to them, and it was widely known that large-scale poaching was occurring. The forest itself also looked shabby. Walking through the dense fir trees we literally and figuratively stumbled onto a battlefield; we saw old foxholes and collapsed trenches everywhere, sometimes covered in rusty barbed wire. In and among the trees were parts of what had once been a truck or a tank. It made a depressed—even forlorn—impression.

"Everyone fought everybody here," said Vasili, one of our guides. "First the Finns fought the Russians, then the Russians fought the Germans, and in the end the Germans fought the Finns." When I wanted to take a look at one of the trenches, he said: "Go ahead, don't be afraid. The landmines have already been taken care of by the elk and the wolves." But he and the other Russians remained at a safe distance while I inspected this gaping scar of the war.

Later they told me that they didn't go near the trenches because of the haunted atmosphere. During lunch we heard that there were two old monasteries in the northern part of the reserve that had been built a few hundred years ago in honor of Alexander Svirsky. This special man had lived there in a small cabin until his death. Many people had turned to him for inspiration and cures for their ailments. Healing powers were attributed to the well next to his cabin, and the Vatican canonized him. The moment we heard this we were enthusiastic. One of the important earth power points we were looking for could be there.

Globally, many holy places, such as churches and monasteries, have been built on these points. Often, several terrestrial energy veins come together at these places. These energy veins can be compared to the acupuncture meridians in our bodies. They transport life energy, or what the Chinese call *ch'i*. There are strong concentrations of terrestrial and cosmic energy in such places, which is why they are also called power points.

One afternoon we used the last of the diesel fuel to visit the monasteries, where we met with another disappointment. They were deserted and dilapidated, with little remaining of their former splendor. One of the monasteries was in ruins, and the other, it turned out, was being used by the Russians as a psychiatric facility.

"Stalin started it," Vasili told us. "He put his prisoners in this monastery. During the German occupation it was a concentration camp, and now it is a psychiatric hospital." We were shocked. On the one hand we had almost certainly just found a power point, but on the other hand it had been "raped" by past events. Instead of emitting positivity and wholeness, it was now the origin of negativity and dissolution. We knew that these compromised veins of energy had an influence on the whole area.

It Works!

We started the energetic treatment of the Nizhnesvirsky Reserve in the summer of 1994 and continued out healing through the autumn of 1997. On a daily basis, life energy and information were sent to the area. The effect was spectacular. Most of the problems in the area were solved. The first change was in the finances. Unexpectedly in the spring of 1995, the management heard that the Nizhnesvirsky Reserve would be the first Russian reserve to be subsidized by the World Wildlife Fund. The money was meant for salaries, new service vehicles, and the development of ecotourism. This was exactly what the Russians wanted!

When I revisited the Reserve in 1995, I found a totally changed situation. All of the people's faces were more cheerful and there was activity everywhere. Among other things, new lodgings were being built for guests. The old building had windows with no glass in them, which meant every morning I was covered in mosquito bites. Now I could sleep like a baby. I was delighted. I was also wondering if the Russians had noticed any effects from our treatment. Of course it was great that there was more money, but it never occurred to me that this was because of the treatment. Before I could ask anybody anything, Vasili and a researcher named Marina came to me smiling and said, "Hans, it works!"

"What works?" I asked, surprised.

"Your treatment. All those dark and nasty energies in the forest are gone. We are not afraid to go past the trenches anymore, and we even go into them. We also feel much better in the whole area."

I was flabbergasted. First because of the effects she described, and secondly because they felt the energetic change so keenly. As it turned out, they were not the only ones. The next day I gave a workshop to explain to employees at the reserve how to perceive the aura of trees. Before my Czech interpreter was able to translate an exercise from English into Russian, the Russians had already completed it. I had never experienced anything like this and was caught off guard, surprised to have run out of subject matter so quickly. This seemed to amuse my hosts. They were obviously tuning in quickly to the changes around them.

The Moment of Truth

A few months later I was given a second chance to show how energy sensing worked. One night while I was on a visit to the Reserve, there was a loud banging on my door. Vasili rushed in with a map of the reserve in his hand. Half awake, I listened to his confused story while he pointed out the window. Through the window I could see a red glow at the horizon. Fire! The reserve was on fire! Vasili pointed to the map, and I understood that I was to point out where the fire was. It took only a moment to understand his predicament, and by now I was wide awake. There were only a few roads through the forest. Taking the wrong one could potentially be disastrous: Any lost time might allow the fire to grow out of control.

My moment of truth in Russia had come. I concentrated on the map as best I could. As my hand moved over it, I felt a soft prickling in my palm that got very strong over a part of the woods north-west of our location. Yes, that was where it was! The fire was there! I indicated the place to Vasili and the other Russians who had gathered around me in the small bedroom.

They understood the message, gave a loud shout, and stormed out into the dark night. I quickly got dressed and was soon ready to go with them to fight the fire. But alas, women and foreign guests were not supposed to take part in such adventures, and I could not join them.

The next morning the men came back, covered in soot and smelling of smoke. They were dead tired but satisfied—and they were beaming. I had shown them the right place, and they had arrived just in time to stop the fire. One after another they embraced me gratefully. It wasn't long before I too was covered in soot and smelling of smoke, but it was delightful, and after that nothing could ever come between us.

Results of the Treatment from a Distance

At the end of 1995, the Czech and Russian scientists monitoring the project concluded that the vitality of the trees in the whole reserve had improved by 10 percent. Because of the excellent results, the people at the Nizhnesvirsky Reserve were more and more pleased with the energetic treatment. They would tease me and say: "If your treatment really works, it would be nice if the monasteries could be renovated." I could only reply that wishes often come true if you focus, and if you and your environment are grounded in your energy. Set a clear goal. Imagine the desired results and even pray for them, if you are so moved.

In January of 1996 their wish became a reality. A generous donor, who remains anonymous, donated money for the renovation of the monasteries. Shortly after, the monasteries rose, like a phoenix, from their ashes. Everyone was deeply moved. The money was considered by many to be a gift from heaven.

In 1997 the project ended. The reserve had developed into one of the best in Russia. The woods were stunning, and there were new accommodations as well as a new service vehicle. As ecotourism increased, the reserve became financially independent. We took our leave in the fall. Everyone was very emotional, but the Russians couldn't resist teasing us by saying, "Hans, if it really works, the holy bones of Alexander Svirsky should come back to the monastery."

These holiest of local relics had disappeared from the monastery when Stalin started to use it for other purposes. Everyone thought that vandals had thrown them away, and nobody was expecting them to return. I could only point once again to the power of their imagination. "Wish for the bones to come back" I told them, "Imagine it happening. Ask for it. Pray, if that appeals to you."

A few months later I received an e-mail from Marina. All it read was: "They found the bones." I couldn't believe my eyes. I later heard that Alexanders Svirsky's bones had been hidden in St. Petersburg for years, awaiting a better day. A lot of attention was paid to their return, which occurred on the same day the monastery was rededicated in the presence of the local people. It was an enormously festive occasion!

Acknowledgments

In large part, this manuscript derives from our work at the Center for ECO-intention: from course materials and training seminars, from questions from the participants and our responses. I often heard myself saying things that were new to me as well. This, in turn, led me to other connections, which are expanded upon in this book.

I would like to thank all the people who have taken a course or been through our training program over the years for their presence, thoughtful remarks, constructive criticism, and, above all, for their interesting and engaging questions. I have learned a lot from, and because of, you.

I owe Felix Erkelens special thanks for his suggestion to revise *In Resonance with Nature*, which led to the writing of this book, which he published in the Netherlands.

My gratitude goes to Rijk Bols, not only for reading and correcting my manuscript but especially for her company, energetic support, and love on my way to my destiny.

The editing of this book has been a lot of work. I am especially grateful to Kiran Rana for his endurance, brilliant suggestions, and painstaking subediting of the manuscript; Alex Mummery for her dedication and for making the manuscript a coherent whole; and Felix Erkelens for his patience, knowledge, and all the hours we spent behind his computer. I think we can all be proud of how *The Universe Loves a Happy Ending* turned out. Good job, team!

The greatest part of my gratitude goes to Linde, Julia, and Philip, through whom I experience energetic guardianship firsthand on a daily basis. Thank you very, very much for helping me to understand the true meaning of this book and that the true meaning of everything is energy. I love you.

Introduction

How My Search Started

One morning I woke up with a headache. Thoughts whizzed through my head. They were accompanied by strange, incoherent feelings and images. I could make neither head nor tail of them, but two sentences arose out of this whirlpool. They forced themselves upon me powerfully:

Life energy plus information generates a formative force.
A formative force plus matter gives a life form.

In those days I performed as a singer-songwriter and dreamed of writing a hit some day. Apparently I dreamt of other things at night, because I couldn't see myself getting into the Top Ten with these lines. Almost every song is about love in some way. Where was the love in these words? This was not the inspiration I was looking for. Nevertheless I decided to write the thoughts down. To my great surprise, as soon as I did that, everything inside me became quiet. The next night I was restless again, and in the morning I had a headache again. More confused thoughts tumbled through my mind; this time, two other lines emerged:

"Becoming conscious leads to a higher state of consciousness."
"The way there is the goal."

I wrote these lines down as well, and immediately a deep silence fell upon me again.

I have written many songs since then, but these four lines have always kept me under their spell. From the moment I wrote them down, I felt a strong urge to uncover their deeper meaning.

The road was a long one. Step by step I started to understand the deep meaning of these words. Slowly all the pieces of the puzzle fell into place, and as they did I saw that together these lines form a fascinating and loving whole. This book is the story of my search.

Resonance Therapy

Although decades have passed since we worked with the Nizhnesvirsky Reserve, I still often think about that experience. It is unforgettable when the energy in forty thousand hectares (150 square miles) of forest visibly changes, the vitality of the trees improves and the mood of the people brightens. Luckily I was not the only one who felt this. The Russians agreed. The Czech research confirmed it. But there was more. The increase in the energy of the reserve not only had a positive effect on the health of the trees but also on the organization and their cash flow.

All of this was in addition to the other positive changes in the area, such as the renovations of the monasteries. This was new: Our treatments had always focused on the health of the forest. Now we had side effects. The deeply felt wishes and goals of the guardians, those in charge of the well-being of the reserve, were fulfilled. Of course one could say that this was a coincidence, but on the other had hand it could be seen as quite remarkable. Thus, by the end of 1997 the thought first arose that the "side" effects were not by chance but that we ourselves can determine the outcome of our energetic work; we can make the future happen.

For me, the Nizhnesvirsky Reserve was the last and largest of a long series of successful projects using resonance therapy. For ten years I had participated in developing this method for healing forests from a distance. We had started out with potted plants, and by the end we were working throughout Europe in large forests, on smaller properties, and even on large English estates.

For the resonance treatment, we used what are called *radionic devices*. The early versions of these devices were developed by Dr. Albert Abrams in the early twentieth century. Originally they were about as large as a cigar box and usually consisted of a detecting plate and several buttons that were used to adjust healing frequencies, but the modern versions contain a computer that runs healing software programs. In almost every case we had positive results, many of which were measured by international scientific institutions and universities. The criteria were, among others, increased vitality, biodiversity, and natural rejuvenation. You can find out more about the history of this practice on the website www .ecointention.com, where there is also a survey of the projects that we have carried out and a summary of the results.

In Resonance with Nature

Something about the process did not feel altogether right to me, however. We had been working as energetic contractors on the principle that "you pay and we do the job." For me it increasingly felt like a shortcoming of our process that the people who were responsible for their sick environments did not heal the environments themselves.

The Russians said the same thing when we left. They were happy with the results but thought it a pity that they had not been able to address the energetic problems of the reserve themselves. Apart from that, and this also applied to the Russians, many customers thought that resonance therapy was a game that only experts could play because of the technology involved. They didn't understand the first thing about it and thought it was a bit weird.

For all these reasons, I left the Institute for Resonance Therapy in 1998 and wrote the book *In Resonance with Nature*. In this book I explain how anyone can sense, interpret, and improve the energy in their house, garden, company, or forest estate without expensive devices, using only their intuition and their own energetic "toolbox" that would contain, for example, homeopathic remedies, colors, music, and symbols that can be used or applied at the location or from a distance.

ECOintention*

After writing the book, I began working with partners to develop courses based on my ideas. The first courses were offered in 1999, and we started providing vocational training for becoming an ECOintention practitioner a few years later. We had started employing a simplified energetic healing method using no devices whatsoever, and our practice of ECOintention emerged from this. ECOintention is applicable to the natural ecological environment and to the manmade world in which economic forces are dominant. Thus it can be applied to nature preserves and other tracts of land, companies, and service organizations, as well as to events such as conferences and concerts. In fact, anything you could describe as an ecological or corporate system, organization, or organism can be addressed via ECOintention.

The effects of ECOintention can be seen and measured in forests and nature preserves that become more vital and healthy, often with increased biodiversity. In organizations it brings higher revenues, more spare time, more satisfied employees, and an improved financial situation. Lasting change and beneficial reorganization may result within complex organizations in a relatively short period of time.

Eco comes from the Greek word *oikos*, which means, among other things, house or home. For our purposes it means home in the broadest sense: house, stable, building, niche, grounds, and also every type of ecosystem including business networks and organizations.

---

* In 2014 we changed the name of our training from ECOtherapy to ECOintention to avoid confusion with other usages of the word ecotherapy in the United States and elsewhere. Throughout this edition of the book we use our current term, ECOintention.

Our view of this home is something that is not static but rather a dynamic living whole that moves organically as it develops, and to represent it we use the metaphor of the wheel. Each entity, every company, every nature preserve, every organization, and every organism—including your own life—can be seen as a wheel on its way to its destination. In this book I have called it the *wheel of life*, though often I just refer to it as the wheel. This wheel has a driver: you, as the creating force in your life, whether you are a farmer, CEO, teacher, project leader, or estate manager. We call this driver the *guardian*.

The foundation of health and vitality in an ecosystem is a harmonious balance between the guardian and their wheel. ECOintention is a method for restoring this balance. It brings the guardian back to the center of their wheel and at the same time strengthens the constructive or vitalizing force of the wheel. This vitalizing force is identical to the formative force I mentioned in the Prologue, a constructive, center-seeking force of the mind that enhances the health and vitality of plants, trees, animals, and all other organisms and is stronger than matter.

Energetic Guardianship

Having worked with over a thousand people over the past several years, I am convinced, as I said earlier, that anyone can learn to bring organizations and nature preserves back to vitality and health from a distance using a map and some simple energetic tools. (Of course some people are more talented at doing so than others, and practice and determination are also important.) That belief gives me hope for the future in a world where natural and cultural equilibriums are more and more unsteady.

ECOintention can be compared to a mechanic fixing a car or other vehicle. After the repair, the guardian can continue the journey to their destination. The ECOintention practitioner's part ends when the car runs smoothly again, the ship is set afloat, or the train is back on track. Once that is done, the guardian can be trained—should be trained—to balance the forces in his wheel himself or herself. Recognizing this made me realize that simplification of the process was necessary and that our understanding and training had to go back into its energetic foundation even more.

That meant addressing questions like: What is the essence of the formative force? What are its most important components? How can a person boost this formative force using only their consciousness, in a so-called technology-free way of healing? What is the simplest way of improving your own health and that of your environment? In other words, how does one "do" energetic guardianship?

Personal Questions and the Relationship to the Great All

Events in the year 2009 brought up a number of questions that gave me doubts about my work with resonance therapy and ECOintention. I felt familiar with the principles of the work and was applying them successfully in my daily life to reach the goals I wanted to attain. Then, all of a sudden, the opposite started to happen. Instead of attaining my goals, I encountered all sorts of disappointments. Why was this happening?

The question was not only to understand, "What is the essence of formative force?" but also, "Why do certain principles work for a while and then all of a sudden stop working?" and "What is the reason for the bad luck I encounter?" And this led me to other questions, like, "Am I going in the right direction?" "Where is my life leading?" and "What is the essence of my life?"

These were questions of a different order, and quite personal at that. How do I create my life? Does everything just happen, or do we create the things happening to us? Does the past push us into the future without any influence from us, or can we "make" the future? Is everything coincidence? I also found myself asking questions about the nature of time. In the years that had passed I had had very little time to do some of the things I wanted to. But how do you make spare time if time flies and is constantly slipping through your fingers? What is time anyhow?

My practice had shown me that ECOintention can enhance the adaptability and self-organization of many systems on a large scale. More than seventy people had graduated as ECOintention practitioners in 2009, keen to start their work on healing oil disasters, damaged coral reefs, and other areas of catastrophe. Why didn't that happen? Wasn't the time right yet? How much longer did we have to wait? How would it continue? How do I continue? What is my destiny? Was the state the earth was in at the moment meaningful? Did it have a purpose, was it predestined?

The Universe Loves a Happy Ending

As I said earlier, this book is also the account of a personal quest, of my search for the answers to all these questions. When I started, I could not have known how my search would end. But as my questions were answered, a coherent whole emerged that connected (quantum) science to universal spiritual laws and offered us practical tools that allowed us to apply our research to our daily lives. We call these results the principles of energetic guardianship, and I explain them in coming chapters. Thus both my quest and this book came to a happy ending.

The Universe Loves a Happy Ending is not a scientific book. It is, however, a closely documented account of my quest, and I have tried to give the theoretical support for all the steps I took. In doing so, I searched for connections in ancient philosophic traditions and modern scientific theories. The symbol and the metaphor of the wheel has been a great help on the way, and it is a central thread that connects the core themes of this book.

How to Approach This Book

Do you want to know what to expect from this book? If so, read the chapter summaries below.

Do you want to start doing energetic work right away? Chapter 14 is your introduction to the principles of energetic guardianship.

If you want to be surprised, skip the rest of this summary and go to Chapter 1. Start your journey there, and let yourself be taken to unknown horizons with an open mind and an open heart.

Note: In the chapter descriptions below, I have summarized my conclusions from my study and practice. Readers may not understand some of the terms and concepts I use or wonder how I arrived at my conclusions; for answers to those questions, please read the full chapter.

Chapters 1, 2, and 3

In Chapter 1 I explain how discoveries from quantum mechanics show us that our beliefs or firm conviction make the world what it is. Matter isn't hard and static but rather "soft" and dynamic. In this context, our consciousness plays a significant, even decisive, role. In essence, everything is energy, information, and consciousness, and everything is possible. This implies that you are able to turn "chance" into good luck or bad luck with your intention.

But is that really so? In Chapter 2 I describe the results of a lot of scientific research that shows that people as well as animals can indeed influence chance. I show that the formative force is built of something called zero-point energy and information from interdependent morphogenetic fields (these terms are explained in the chapter!) and our consciousness gives direction to this force with the help of intention.

I should clarify here that, although the literature contains abundant proof of the force of intention, a formative force is not described in science. I did find evidence for it in old creation myths, and the ancient Chinese knowledge called Wu Ch'i gives a good description and a practical application of it. I describe these in

Chapter 3. Here we also see how the wheel, which embodies the two fundamental forces of creation, originates. These two forces are a feminine, inward-directed formative force and a masculine, outward-directed expansive one. They are also called yin and yang.

The wheel occurs as a metaphor in many cultures. In the East it appears, among others, as a mandala, and in the West as stained glass rose windows or labyrinths. Both of these representations provide more insight into our life path and the journey to our destiny.

Chapter 4, 5, and 6

The formative force, as I described earlier, is a force of mind that is stronger than matter. In Chapter 4 I discuss how to boost its power with your thoughts, both in the presence of the subject and from a distance. Rupert Sheldrake's Theory of Morphic Resonance provides insight into this phenomenon, while making clear how ingrained habits and limiting, firm convictions arise. His theory also explains how you can make contact with your property or business from a distance to get information about both the current situation and the past and influence the development of the whole with your intention.

The morphic field consists entirely of information. The formative force, however, also consists of what in quantum mechanics is called zero-point energy. This is the same as life energy, but how do you make contact with it and how can you influence it?

These subjects are the topic of Chapter 5. I show that by giving something attention, you give it life energy. The condition for this is an open and loving heart. Life energy itself does not come from the heart but from the DNA, which is connected to the zero-point energy field. A loving heart opens our DNA, thus starting the flow of life energy.

Chapters 4 and 5 also show that you can amplify the formative force with your attention and give it direction with your intention. Chapter 6 describes how to apply this with the help of affirmations, using them to confirm your goals and attract your own future. I explain the conditions an affirmation has to meet before it can be effective and also describe a good tool for doing this, Marinus Knoope's Spiral of Creation.

Chapters 7, 8, and 9

The previous chapters describe how to boost the formative force toward attracting a desired future. But is it possible to say something about when your dream will come true and when is the right time for something?

In Chapter 7 I discuss the meaning of time and how we can lengthen or shorten it with our consciousness. We see that time is not made up of static intervals but is dynamic and relative.

Personal integration, achieving goals, and reaching one's destiny are easier when you go with the natural flow. Today, we see time as linear: There is the past, present, and future. In life, however, we see all sorts of rhythms and cycles that suggest that time is cyclical. The Maya calendar has much to say about time cycles and is discussed in Chapter 8.

We also find the connection between the wheel, morphic fields, zero-point energy, space, time, and our consciousness in Chapter 8. The two forces in the wheel form a torus, or donut. This is consistent with the latest discoveries in science, which tell us that the torus is the primal form of matter, the Universe, and space-time. The nature of the torus shows that you are constantly attracting the past you haven't come to terms with. This is an explanation for the obstructions or other disappointments that occur on our life paths.

Chapter 9 describes when to expect such moments and how these periods are connected to the number *phi* and the Fibonacci sequence (0, 1, 1, 2, 3, 5, 8, 13, 21,…). This infinite number is an expression of the Golden Mean and is also related to the rhythmic alternation of the forces in the wheel. There are periods when the formative force works in a more powerful way, when the time is right for inner development. These periods alternate with times to harvest the fruit of this development, when the outward-bound, or expansive, energy is stronger. This discovery gave me insight into the past twenty years of my life, as well as answers to many questions.

Chapters 10, 11, and 12

From the previous chapters, the conclusion may be drawn that the purpose of life is not to make a career or accomplish great things but to realize who you are and where you are going. The road is the goal. It is during the journey that you gain life experience and develop your consciousness. Consciousness leads to a higher consciousness. The question remains: What is consciousness?

This question, the part our consciousness plays, is studied in Chapter 10. There is a connection between the wheel, morphic fields, torsion fields, and consciousness. Everything has consciousness. Consciousness is basic. Developing a higher level of consciousness is the purpose of the Universe.

In Chapter 11 we look at Max Freedom Long's model of Hawaiian Huna spirituality, according to which our self-consciousness consists of three selves, all of which have a different function. The lower self can be compared to body consciousness, the middle self to ego, and the higher self to our connection with the spiritual world. Our task is to become a whole human being. To do so, we must get to know these selves and integrate them into our heart. Huna has a lot in common with the modern knowledge of morphic fields, zero-point energy, and the coherence of the heart (the heart's ability to love) during affirming. Therefore, it gives deeper insight in this process.

At the end of this chapter it becomes clear that you can only reach your destiny by heightening your consciousness and forgiving the past. *Tonglen* is a Buddhist method that uses the heart to transform emotional pain and a burdened past into love. I describe this method in Chapter 12, along with a number of other approaches for handling negative emotions in a positive way.

Chapters 13 and 14

Consciousness is infinite. One consequence of this is that consciousness survives death. In Chapter 13, to answer the question of whether there is life after death, I gratefully use the work of Dutch cardiologist Pim van Lommel. From his work we see that everything has consciousness and that our soul does not cease to exist after our body has died.

Consciousness is the goal of creation. We all come to earth with a script and a destiny. In order to reach our higher goal, we must personally become conscious and cultivate or ennoble our inner world. By healing ourselves, we also heal the world; ever since ancient times our common task has been "*agri cultura*," guarding, cultivating, and ennobling the earth.

If everything has a consciousness, then so does the earth. If everything develops toward its higher goal, then so does the planet. Therefore, is the existing situation a developmental step of our planet toward its destiny? Have we been abusing the earth during the past twenty centuries, or was this way through matter predestined, meaning that a certain guarding, cultivating, and ennobling have taken place after all? The symbol of the cross helps solve this problem. When I found the answer to this great mystery, it made me optimistic about the future.

The book ends in Chapter 14 with the principles of energetic guardianship. With these, anyone can charge his or her wheel energetically and give it direction. Every entity, everything that we can hold in our consciousness and embrace with our heart can be healed by us. We can do more than we think we can. The restriction lies in our fixed conviction of what is or is not possible. Energy, information, time, space, and consciousness are connected. We live in a sea, not only of zero-point energy, but also of time, with endless possibilities.

Together with planet earth, we are on our way to our destiny. We can all create a happy future. Everyone is a god in his or her thoughts. Everyone can start over again at any moment. Everything is possible, and there is always hope.

Everything Is Energy, Everything Is One, Everything Is Possible

Everything is energy, and everything is connected to everything else. The water in the ocean and the clouds in the sky. The trees and the animals. You, me, and the world around us. Everything comes from the same source and returns to it. Everything is one. Thoughts and feelings are energy as well, so everything we think and feel has an influence on everything and everyone on this planet. In this way, we create our own reality, because mind rules over matter.

Everything Is Energy

Is everything energy? *Is* everything united? If I look around right now, I see a laptop and the table on which I'm writing this book, a window, and behind that window a garden with flowers, shrubs, and trees. These are all individual forms and things.

Yes, everything is one, because everything consists of the same matter, but in this "solid" truth I see an incoherent number of phenomena rather than a unified whole. At school I learned that matter is made up of molecules. Molecules consist of atoms. Atoms consist of a nucleus with electrons circling around it. All are parts, fractions, and particles, but at first sight there is no whole, no unity.

Nevertheless, appearances are deceiving. Solid reality turns out to be less solid than it appears. Science has proved that matter is 99.999999999999 percent empty space. That's twelve nines after the decimal point! If you enlarge the nucleus of an atom to the size of a pinhead, the first electron would be at a distance of 160 feet. In between, there is only empty space. That means that the book you are reading now, the chair you sit on, the house you live in, the earth you live on, that so-called solid reality consists for the most part of empty space.

If there is so much empty space, what is left in terms of solid matter? A quick calculation shows us that the solid part of an atom is only 0.00000000001 percent of the whole atom's mass. It is inconceivable that solid objects should consist of so little solid matter. And in fact even this "solid" matter is not solid.

The End of Solid Parts

For a long time after the discovery of molecules and atoms in the seventeenth century, scientists assumed that molecules and atoms consisted of solid particles. But according to quantum physics, developed in the early twentieth century, there are no "particles" per se: Energy is the basis of material reality. Every type of particle is conceived of as a quantum vibration in a field: Electrons are vibrations in electron fields, protons vibrate in a proton field, and so on. Everything is energy, and everything is connected to everything else through fields. At its most elementary level, matter does not show up as isolated little particles; all matter is essentially one and indivisible, a connected, dynamic tissue of vibrating fields of energy. For more on this subject, see Lynne McTaggart's *The Field* and Marja de Vries's *The Whole Elephant Revealed*.

Not only do the atom and solid matter consist mainly of empty space, it is the same in outer space. There are as many stars in the Universe as there are grains of sand on the beaches of the earth combined. These are almost infinitely large numbers, but in between them 99.999999999999 percent of the space is empty. A bit of a waste, all that unused space. Did God lack imagination when he created the Universe, or is there something else going on? The quantum theory researchers discovered the answer: Not only do particles consist of energy, but so does the space between. This is the so-called zero-point energy. Therefore it is true: Everything consists of energy.

Zero-Point Energy

The latest scientific discoveries point more and more to a fundamental primary energy that works throughout the entire Universe and connects everything to everything else. This sea of energy that penetrates everything was first measured by Dr. Harold Puthoff. The experiment was conducted at 0 degrees Kelvin, which is called absolute zero and is the same as −273 degrees Celsius.

If you heat something by adding energy, the molecules move faster and faster. For instance, when heated, water starts bubbling and evaporates. The reverse happens when you cool water down: The molecules move more and more slowly, and the water freezes and solidifies. According to the old scientific model, no molecule, atom, or more elementary particle moves at absolute zero, thus at that temperature it should not be possible to measure any energy whatsoever. Instead of no energy, as expected, Puthoff found what he called "a boiling 'witch's cauldron'" of energy.

The German physicist Max Planck was the first to prove, in 1911, that the empty space between the planets and the atoms is indeed overflowing with energy, which he called zero-point energy. Physicist John Wheeler of Texas University later calculated that the zero-point energy of one cubic centimeter of empty space equals 10^{108} joules. That is more than the energy in all the matter of the Universe. Other researcher's calculations suggest a lower figure. According to the famous American physicist Richard Feynman, the energy density of the vacuum is "only" 10^{95} joules per cubic centimeter. This still means that a glass full of empty space contains enough energy to set the Atlantic Ocean boiling.

In her book *The Field*, Lynne McTaggart gives a survey of scientific discoveries that prove that an energy field that contains everything, connecting everything to everything else, does indeed exist. Consciousness and matter, man and the reality around him—according to her they are all based on the same primary energy. Everything is energy, and according to her, the zero-point energy field is the alpha and the omega, the beginning and the end of our existence.

The Energy with a Thousand Names

If the so-called solid particles of an atom take up 0.000000000001 percent of its volume, and the remaining space is filled with zero-point energy, we could say that matter is totally penetrated with energy. And we immediately see that this is old news. Science has recently "discovered" what ancient cultures have known all along—that energy penetrates matter. Everything comes from this energy and returns to it. It is the source of all life. Each culture has given its own name to it. Therefore it is called "The energy with a thousand names." What are we talking about? Life energy!

Life energy has been known all over the world since antiquity, and almost every culture has a name for this energy. Chinese call it *ch'i,* which is similar to the Greek *pneuma,* the Latin *spiritus vitalis,* the *prana* of yoga, the *mana* of the Kahunas in Hawaii, the Light of the Christians, the *ka* of the ancient Egyptians, and the *ki* in reiki. In our culture you will encounter life energy as the *fluidum* of mesmerists, the *aether* of anthroposophy, the *od* of Reichenbach, and the *orgon* of Wilhelm Reich.

In all cases, they speak of a subtle energy that is universal, which includes all and penetrates everything. This energy is the carrier of the processes of life and connects everything to everything else. Matter is formed by it. Life energy is usually mentioned together with life force. It has healing, magnetic properties.

Zero-Point Energy and Life Energy

Are zero-point energy and life energy really the same? In his book *Tachyonen, Orgonenergie, Skalarwellen* (Tachyon, orgone energy, scalar ways), Marco Bischof gives a well-documented historical overview of the development of the various conceptions of life energy, starting with the Chinese ch'i of 3000 BC and ending with today's quantum mechanics and zero-point energy.

Bischof describes how every culture, depending on its time and place on earth, had a different view on life energy. Because of this, certain aspects of the universal life energy were emphasized more or less so, and he therefore warns us not to group ch'i, ki, ka, prana, mana, and so on together because they are all based on different concepts. According to Bischof there is, however, a common source from which all life energy comes.

Bischof finds that life energy is indeed a different, more subtle energy than the forms of energy we know. We can measure, for instance, chemical energy in gasoline, wind energy, or electromagnetic radiation with devices. But he concludes that life energy is a subtle form of energy that can only be perceived intuitively; it cannot be measured with mechanical devices.

Bischof describes many examples in which life energy is successfully used, thus improving the health of human beings and animals and the yield of crops. His advice to science is to take the existence of life energy seriously as the latest discoveries in Western science also point to a fundamental primal energy that works throughout the Universe, connecting everything to everything else. According to Bischof, the zero-point energy field is the prime source of the universal life energy that has been described, mentioned, and used by every culture in its own way.

Morphic Fields

So we live in a swirling sea of zero-point energy in which everything and everyone bobs up and down. The world is filled with all sorts of life, which appears in many different forms. There is huge diversity, and that makes life fun, rich, surprising, and interesting. But where do these types of life come from? What "forms" them?

There is no easy answer to this question, and science still struggles with the puzzle of how, for instance, a tiny seed grows into a huge tree. How do leaves, branches, flowers, and fruits get their characteristic shapes? Our body forms fifty billion new cells every day, or about five hundred thousand cells a second. How does a cell know that it is situated at the top of our body and that it should form a hair there? How does a cell know that it is part of a toenail? Who or what supervises this? These kinds of questions have to do with what biologists call *morpho-genesis*, the origin of the form (Greek: *morphe* = form; *genesis* = origin). It is one of the great unsolved mysteries of the biological sciences.

For many years scientists thought that this is genetically programmed, but now it appears this is far from the whole truth. Genes determine the sequence of amino acids, the building blocks of protein molecules. Other genes determine the moment in which special proteins are formed. In this way the right protein originates at the right moment during the development of the organism. But it is an ongoing mystery how the characteristic form of the body emerges from these building materials. Your arms and legs are chemically identical, but they have different shapes. While the genes supply the building blocks for the material of the body, the blueprint for the shape or design of the organism is missing. Where is the blueprint? Where is the design? Since the 1920s, some biologists have taken the position that this information is stored in a "morphogenetic" field, which is a self-organizing field that holds blueprints that organize matter, comparable to the way the field around a magnet organizes iron filings.

The English biologist and scientist Rupert Sheldrake has extended this idea to areas outside of biology. Sheldrake thinks that not only organisms but all organizations and ecosystems have an organizing field. He calls all these fields "morphic fields." He has described his theory in a great number of books and publications, supporting his ideas with the results of scientific research.

Sheldrake says there are many different sorts of morphic fields. In plants and animals the fields that are responsible for the development of the body are called morphogenetic fields. Forms of conduct are organized by fields of conduct. A social field organizes and coordinates the conduct of individuals within the social group. An example of this is the way in which shoals of fish or flocks of birds suddenly change direction as a group.

According to Sheldrake, morphic fields contain information: scenarios with step-by-step plans, comparable to the blueprint of a house, as well as instructions that say where to begin. Thus, start with the foundation first, then build the walls, and so on.

A beautiful example is the way arched termite hills are constructed. Two groups of termites start building in different places. Eventually they meet at exactly the same place, high up in the air. There are no termites in charge, running from one hill to the other, directing and coordinating. Both groups build independently, and they follow the blueprint prescribed by the morphic field.

Morphic fields not only contain old information but can also take in new information. A well-known example is "the hundredth monkey phenomenon." The macaque monkey lives on the Japanese island of Koshima. In 1952 scientists fed these monkeys with sweet potatoes that were thrown into the sand. The macaques didn't eat this delicacy because of the dirt. A young monkey found the solution and washed the potatoes in a nearby stream before giving them to its mother. After its mother had also learned the trick, more and more monkeys started to clean the potatoes in the stream. Between 1952 and 1958 a group of around one hundred monkeys started using the washing technique.

One might try to explain this in terms of imitation of a behavior; however, after the hundredth monkey had learned to wash his potatoes, all of a sudden the whole tribe on the island started to do the same. It became even more surprising when colonies of macaques on the other islands and on the mainland suddenly started washing their sweet potatoes. For some unknown reason, the trick had passed on to other monkeys at distant locations. Although there was no exact count, this phenomenon became known as the "hundredth" monkey phenomenon.

Every species of animal, every system, and every organization has a morphic field and therefore has what we might call a collective memory. You can compare this to a big book in which everything is written, including what a species of animal, a group of people, or a company experiences and comes across. In human beings this collective memory is closely related to what the psychologist C.G. Jung called the *collective subconscious*. In esotericism the term *akashic records* is used for the world memory that contains all events since the beginning of time. In a company, everything that has ever happened with the organization is stored in the morphic field of the company. This field is the seat of the company's culture, a way of doing things that is greater than all the workers or employees and that influences them, usually without their knowledge.

The Difference Between Energy and Information

Morphic fields contain information and can be compared to a script that a system can use to organize itself. The field, as it were, informs matter: InFORMation goes into FORM and becomes matter. It is like incarnation, where spirit manifests itself in human form. Information does the same—it becomes form.

However, to read a book, digest the information, and then act on it, you need energy. Sheldrake says nothing about this. In his formative field we only find information, no energy. And interestingly, Lynne McTaggart, in her book *The Field*, only writes about zero-point energy and doesn't mention information. Yet Sheldrake and McTaggart often use the same examples to support their theories.

Many authors treat energy and information as if they were one and the same thing, and that is the cause of much confusion. As we shall see later in this book, practical applications increase if we distinguish between these concepts. Energy and information are different properties.

A radio newscaster gives us information. If we can't hear him or her because the volume is too low, we turn up the radio. At that moment we are adding energy, but that does not change the news, the information itself. You need energy to transfer the information from a speaker to an audience, but the information remains the same, independent of the amount of energy; it only sounds louder or softer. No one would think you were telling a different story if you simply spoke louder.

Energy doesn't just take care of the transfer of information, it also makes information take shape, makes something happen with it. You can buy an excellent book to help you out of a depression, but if you don't have the time or energy to read it, you cannot take in the information. And after that you need time and energy to act on what you have read.

Formative Force

I want to return to the lines that I mentioned earlier:

> *Life energy plus information generates a formative force.*
> *A formative force plus matter generates a life form.*

With the help of the knowledge of zero-point energy, which is the same as the life energy we have known about for ages, and the theory of morphic fields, a few pieces of the puzzle fall into place. We could say that everything is connected to everything else by an unending ocean of zero-point energy, covered by morphic fields of information, acting like a kind of matrix.

From the connection between this life energy and information comes a formative force. If this formative force connects to matter, a life form originates.

This sounds easy, but the existence of such a creative formative force totally contradicts current scientific knowledge. Thermodynamics, a branch of natural science, teaches us that every system tends toward entropy—toward the *loss* of order and structure. Every organism and every system tends to disintegrate sooner or later. Not a very nice thing to look forward to, but luckily you see the opposite if you look around. In nature every ecosystem develops toward greater complexity and a higher degree of biodiversity, increasing the number of plant and animal species. The same is true of societies and highly developed cultures.

The Meaning of Consciousness

This idea of a formative force fascinated me, so I decided to find out if more was known about it. At the same time, I realized that a book or a script, like the information in a morphic field, does nothing of its own accord; it is passive. The information only starts working if someone decides to read the book and act on it. Reading a book is done with your consciousness, otherwise you cannot take in the information. The degree of consciousness is also related to the complexity of the book. For example, you don't ask a child to read about Einstein's Theory of Relativity. On the other hand, every adult can understand the instructions—the script—for putting together an IKEA cupboard. Our consciousness also allows us to choose where to put the cupboard and what to put in it.

Therefore, there are not two but rather three "elements" responsible for the development of life: life energy, information, and consciousness. Life energy has the ability to take shape. Information has the ability to inform and to create form. Both need each other, but neither forms a connection with the other on their own accord. Consciousness brings the two together, and at the moment it does, the formative force originates. Let me explain further…

Consciousness is primary. Energy and information are secondary. A formative force originates from life energy and information, but only when consciousness connects to them. Therefore it is better to speak of a "conscious" formative force. We can therefore say that when a conscious formative force connects to matter, a life form with consciousness is generated.

Having reached this understanding, I turned my thoughts to the other two lines:

Becoming conscious leads to a higher consciousness.
The way is the goal.

Consciousness is the initiator of a formative force that connects to matter and manifests itself as a conscious life form. This consciousness gains experiences during its life in a material form. In human life, experiencing the outer world and interpreting this experience is a process of becoming conscious. If you do this well, you learn something from it. The process of experiencing or learning, in other words of becoming conscious, leads to a higher state of consciousness in the end.

If the way is the goal, it means that the goal in life is the development of ever higher levels of consciousness. This would mean that not only is everything made of energy and information, but also that everything has consciousness and that the development of this consciousness to a higher level is the aim of the Universe.

An Endless Number of Possibilities

The zero-point energy field is not the only discovery stemming from quantum mechanics. When at the beginning of the twentieth century the pioneers of quantum physics got to the essence of what matter is, they were flabbergasted by what they saw. They discovered that the most elementary building blocks of matter sometimes behaved as particles, sometimes as waves, and sometimes as both at the same time. They could appear in all sorts of conditions at the same time until we observed or measured them, and at that moment they changed into something concrete.

It appeared that the researcher influenced the outcome of what he was measuring. If he assumed that light consisted of particles, he perceived particles. If his starting point was light waves, he would find light waves. The wave/particle dualism is one of the most peculiar things in quantum mechanics. According to quantum mechanics, the existence of a wave or a particle depends on your point of view. Therefore, at the most elementary level, nothing is certain.

There is only an endless amount of possibilities. The observer's intention "freezes" something into a particle or wave.

The researchers came to the bewildering conclusion that consciousness creates reality. Einstein then wondered if the moon still exists if we are not looking at it. Time and again, experiments have proven that our consciousness creates the world. Everything consists of a turbulent sea of zero-point energy and information. It is all movement and dynamics, but the moment we look, it "freezes," and a form is laid down. It is as if a motion picture film suddenly stops, and you can only see the frozen image.

From quantum mechanics it appears that we are the ones who make the world static, stationary, and solid. The "solid" truth is what it is because of our firm conviction. It is our firm conviction that the chair we sit on consists of solid matter and that we can safely sit on it without falling through. In essence, reality is totally different from what we see or, more precisely, what we see as *real*. We live in a sea of possibilities, but we affirm our reality with our firm conviction.

Coincidence

Quantum mechanics is among the best researched scientific theories. New experiments prove it correct every time, and so far there has been no experiment that proves otherwise. The implications of this are enormous. If creation is created by our conviction, expectation, and intention, this means that we not only have a huge responsibility for what we do, but we have even more of one for what we think.

Every thought has an influence on us and on our surroundings. A negative thought has a negative effect and a positive one has a positive effect. That means that we have to take care, because this is how we create our reality and future. That is what we call fate. What happens to you and what goes on in your life is coincidental, but it can be good luck or bad luck. If your intention has influence on reality, is it possible to create a positive future by thinking positive thoughts?

Influencing Coincidence— The Power of Intention

2:

Before going on to explore the formative force and the question of whether everything has consciousness, I first wanted to know if scientific research had been done on the influence of our consciousness on reality and on the possibility of influencing coincidence with intention.

Heads or Tails

Our consciousness creates the reality we live in, and our intention influences what is going on in it. The main part of what we see as true is determined by our beliefs. In that sense, you create your own reality and your own future. Life may be a game of chance, but you can create your good luck or bad luck. This sounds interesting, but is there hard evidence to confirm this? Is it, for instance, possible to influence chance—the odds—in our favor by using our intention?

Research done over a number of years shows that this is indeed possible. If you flip a coin there is a fifty percent chance of it coming down heads or tails. Those are the odds. You are influencing the odds if you succeed in turning up more heads than tails or the other way around, and there is ample proof that we are capable of doing so. This proof is the result of a few million tests performed using so-called random number generators.

These devices toss electronic "coins." The statistical division of heads or tails is fifty-fifty if the machines operate undisturbed, but this changes when test subjects try to influence the system with their intention, which leads to more heads than tails or the other way around. These experiments have shown very significant and repeatable results.

In 1997 Jahn and Dunne published the results of twelve years of research on the effect of people on random number generators. In that period they did almost 2.5 million tests and gathered the largest database on earth in this field. Their research showed that almost 66 percent of the test subjects succeeded in influencing the devices in accordance with their intentions, and it made no difference which type of device was used.

Differences Between Men and Women

Two men or two women together often had less success influencing the devices than each of them had individually, but a man and a woman who knew each other had over three and a half times more effect together than each of them had individually.

Men and women who were emotionally involved had the strongest effect, with the joint effect being six times as strong as their individual effects. So it seemed that the effect increased if the emotional bond between the subjects was strong, if they were on the same level or wavelength. In other words, they resonated with each other and together they were strong.

When Dunne analyzed the enormous database further, she found that men generally had more influence on the random number generator, but not necessarily in the direction of their intention. It often happened that they got the opposite result of what they intended. This was different in women: They were less capable of influencing the device, but they got the result they were concentrating on more often. As it turned out, women had better results if they focused their intention but also did other things on the side, whereas men seemed to require greater concentration to achieve success.

The Conductive Influence of Animals

It appears from scientific research that our intention has a constructive influence on reality. Humans can be conscious of this, but what about animals, who have a different kind of or a lower consciousness? Are they also able to focus or project their consciousness and have influence on their surroundings?

French researcher René Peoc'h worked with Jahn's random numbers generators. He did a number of amazing experiments involving baby fowl. Newly hatched chicks, like ducklings, follow the first moving object they encounter. As soon as they were hatched, he confronted the chicks with a little robot that they followed because of the imprint process. The robot was placed outer of the chicken-enclosure and could move about freely, although the route it took was mapped. Inside the robot was a random number generator, which made it move in crisscrossing directions. After a while it became obvious that it was more often closer to the chicks than it would have been if it had chosen its direction randomly. The chicks therefore were capable of "attracting" the robot.

In other experiments Peoc'h kept the chicks in the dark. He put a lit candle on the robot. The chicks were held in a cage that allowed them to see the flame. After a while, these chicks also attracted the robot so that they had more light. Rabbits in a cage were initially frightened of the robot. It then moved away from them; they repelled it. After a few weeks their fear disappeared, and from that moment on, the rabbits tended to attract it.

So, it turns out that it is possible to influence otherwise random processes with intention. Not only can humans do it, alone or in couples, but groups of animals can do it too.

The Effect of Intention and Expectation

Tossing a coin and getting more heads or tails in itself a fairly simple example. You concentrate, and the outcome is one or the other. You can see an immediate result. But what about more complex examples? Can we, for instance, influence the conduct of people, animals, and plants with our intention so that they perform in a preferred way? The fact that this too is possible was shown in the Pygmalion Experiment, conducted at a primary school in San Francisco by psychologist Robert Rosenthal and his colleagues from Harvard University. At the beginning of their experiment they convinced the teachers that certain pupils in their class were promising and would achieve remarkable progress in the following school year.

Rosenthal had ostensibly "found" this with the help of a new test to predict intellectual growth. In every class, the teacher was given the names of the pupils with the highest score. In reality it was an ordinary test, and the names of the pupils with the biggest "chance of growth" were chosen at random.

By the end of the year, the "promising" children had an IQ score that was 15.4 points higher in the first grade and 9.5 points in the second grade, than that of a control group. The "promising" children were also characterized more often by their teacher as nice, adaptive, sweet, curious, and happy. Rosenthal and his colleagues drew the conclusion that the achievements of a pupil are heavily dependent on the expectations of the teacher. Many follow-up studies confirm and support these results.

The intention and the expectation of the teacher, and as a consequence the way in which he or she treats a pupil, has a strong influence on the student's achievements. This has very important consequences. The teacher can, as it were, make or break his student. The same applies to a company leader or manager. The achievements of the staff depend on the intention and expectation of their managers.

However, there is more to it than simple expectation. In the Pygmalion experiment, Rosenthal had convinced the teacher beforehand that some pupils would rise to the occasion. Being convinced is more than just expecting: You could say that one *believes* in it. The expectations of the company leader can only be met if he or she is really convinced that their team is capable of attaining the goal at hand. Has the influence of conviction been researched?

Placebos—Convincing Fake Medicine

Belief not only influences behavior, it can also influence our involuntary bodily processes. Scientific research has shown that expectation and conviction are of enormous influence in medicine. This is shown by the so-called placebo effect. Placebos are fake medicine. Although they contain no real medicine, their healing effect has been proven without a shadow of a doubt. Placebos often work for a wide range of conditions including coughs, mood swings, heart complaints, headaches, seasickness, anxiety, high blood pressure, asthma, depression, colds, stomachaches, skin rashes, rheumatism, fever, insomnia, and all sorts of pain.

The placebo effect is most prevalent in double-blind research, where both the doctor and the patient are convinced that they are working with a powerful new treatment. If the doctor is convinced that the treatment is less effective, the placebo effect will be smaller. In single-blind research, where the doctor knows which patient gets the placebo but the patients themselves don't, the placebos have even less effect. When the patients also know that they are getting placebos the effect is minimal.

In other words, a treatment works best when both the doctor and the patient are convinced that it has a strong healing power. A lesser conviction leads to a smaller placebo effect and to fewer cures.

A remarkable feature of placebos is that patients not only benefit from them, they may also show signs of side effects, including poisoning. In a survey by Benson and Pogge of 67 double-blind research studies of medications in which 3,500 patients were involved, almost one-third of the patients treated with placebos showed all kinds of side effects, including anorexia, nausea, dizziness, and skin rash. Sometimes the side effects were so severe that they required separate medical attention. On top of that, the symptoms turned out to be connected to the expectations of the doctor or the patient regarding the side effects of the medication that was being researched.

These positive and negative effects point to the force of our consciousness, because once again, there was no chemical substance whatsoever in the placebo that could have induced them. The working of the placebo was based on "mental" force alone. In short, if you believe you are going to be ill, you are more likely to be. If you believe you will get better, you probably will. In the same way you can influence a machine like a random number generator or a robot, you can apparently influence all matter around you. If you make the world, then the world is not as it is but rather as you think it is. Your thinking and your deepest convictions determine reality.

Communicating with Plants

A similar conviction appears to play a role in communicating with plants. According to German therapist Dr. Henning von der Osten, anybody can communicate with plants if they are convinced they can, but someone who believes that they can't has no effect.

Henning conducted the same experiment for years during his seminars: He bought two equal-sized pansies in pots and stuck a minus sign on one and a plus sign on the other. The plants were placed next to each other and got the same amount of water. He arranged with his students that everyone would go to both plants once a day and talk to them. It didn't matter if they spoke loudly or softly. What mattered was that the "minus" pansy was insulted and called names, like "you just go and die soon." The "plus" plant was praised and was told, for instance, that it was extremely beautiful. After ten days the "minus" pansies showed signs of weakness—the flowers were smaller and the leaves hung downward—but the other plant thrived. By the end of the course these differences were even greater.

After the course Henning always took both plants home and paid extra attention to the insulted plant. After a week the differences between both plants would disappear. Then something peculiar happened: The pansies that had originally been called names lived longer, became stronger and healthier, and had more beautiful flowers than the plants that were given positive thoughts from the beginning. In this Henning sees a parallel with people. According to him, someone who has suffered pain and distress and saw the crises as a chance for further growth comes further along his path, gets more mature, and leads a more intense and more beautiful life.

After many comparable experiments, Henning came to the conclusion that communicating with plants only works when someone has an inner conviction that they can. Bad-mouthing has no effect if someone thinks it is ridiculous to call a plant names; it only works if the plant is scolded with conviction. The same holds true for positive thoughts. Half-hearted thoughts have no creative force at all and therefore have no effect.

Smart and Stupid Rats

Our convictions and expectations not only have an influence on plants and people but on animals as well. In a classic experiment, Robert Rosenthal and his colleagues from Harvard University used students as researchers and rats as test subjects. The rats came from one homogeneous group but were randomly divided into two groups designated as "clever" and "stupid." They then had to find their way out of a maze. Of course the students expected the clever rats to learn faster than the stupid ones, and that is exactly what they found. In general, the clever rats reacted in the right way 51 percent more often, and they learned 29 percent faster than the so-called stupid rats. These findings were confirmed in other laboratories and with other forms of learning behavior.

In this case also, the expectations of the test subjects were met, because they were convinced that there were clever and stupid rats. It is striking that in all experiments the test subjects were persuaded by a person they trusted: the researcher or the doctor who provided the information about the potential of pupils, the efficacy of a medicine, or the intelligence of rats.

In summary, this means that expectations become reality if the test subject:
- trusts the source of the information
- has inner conviction that the source tells the truth
- acts with the conviction that the goal is realistic and can be realized

The Influence of the Researcher

The effects of coincidence and expectation were systematically studied in the 1960s and have since been proven in hundreds of experiments. Coincidence can be influenced and expectations can be met if we have inner conviction. From experiments, we learn that the person in charge of the research is mainly responsible for this. Their credibility and power of persuasion determine the result. Sometimes it is not even necessary for a researcher to convince their test subjects of something. Their presence alone, on the spot or from a distance, is enough to influence the result of the experiment.

Researcher Charles Honorton proved this by showing that the ability of test subjects to influence random number generators depended more on him than on his test subjects. The test subjects were successful when he was present, but when they were in someone else's charge, there was no effect. According to Honorton, these sorts of effects show that it is difficult to maintain effective boundaries between test subjects and researchers.

Two British parapsychologists researched this effect in the 1950s. Independent of the way in which the research was conducted, one of them, C.W. Fisk, always had significant results while the other, D.J. West, usually was unsuccessful in proving paranormal phenomena. In this experiment, each prepared half of the tests and also gathered the results. The test subjects were unaware that there were two researchers and they never met them. The test assignments were sent to them by mail and returned in the same way. The test subjects under the charge of Fisk had very significant results in demonstrating clairvoyance, but West's test subjects gave him no useful results.

This shows that a researcher in charge of an experiment can have an influence on the outcome. His personality and his inner convictions influence the test subjects in a positive or negative way, even if he is at a distance and they don't know him personally. We can therefore conclude that in an organization the presence and the personality of the manager can probably be influential enough to get good results. Apart from that, it is important that the staff trusts him or her and that he or she is able to convince them that the goals set are feasible.

In his famous 1937 book, *Think and Grow Rich*, Napoleon Hill shows that successful people owe their success mainly to the fact that they were totally convinced that they would be successful. Hill comes to the conclusion that successful people firmly believe in their goal and don't know any better than that they will achieve it. By focusing their intention on a goal, it materializes.

Free Conviction

The multitude of data on the influence of intention unambiguously shows how the researcher influences the results of the research. This even occurs from a distance, and it even happens when the test subjects do not know the researchers.

The same applies to a company. The inner conviction of the head of the organization or guardian is imperative for getting good results. For this it is also important that the co-workers trust the guardian and that he or she can convince them that the goals set are feasible. The guardian needs to believe in his co-workers and has to rely on their abilities and have inner conviction that they, as a team, can get the job done.

We can connect the effects of conviction to the principle of guardianship that I mentioned in the Introduction. A guardian has a very important task. If there is trust from both sides, his or her inner conviction is the foundation of their company's success. This can make or break, unite or divide the whole enterprise. If they silently have the opinion that it is not going to work anyway, it never will, and the way to the future will be paved with obstacles and disappointments. If, on the other hand, they have a firm belief in future success, this conviction will radiate through the whole enterprise and be a positive influence on all aspects of the business.

So every guardian needs to examine their own beliefs and attitudes and ask themselves these questions: Are they optimistic or pessimistic by nature? Do they see the positive or the negative side of things? Are they cautious or daring?

It is not only the managers of companies who are guardians, daily life is full of them. Everyone is the guardian of their own whole, their own "entirety," which includes all the people, animals, or plants and other elements that are in their care. The coach of a soccer team is the guardian of his or her team. A teacher has guardianship of their classroom and pupils, a doctor of their practice and patients. The moment you get on a bus, train, or airplane, the driver or pilot is your guardian. At that moment you are in their care and you surrender to their inner conviction.

I call this surrender "free" conviction. As opposed to your firm convictions, your beliefs, which are always there and form the foundation of your life, there is freedom of choice in free conviction. When you place yourself in the care of a guardian, that is a free conviction. This can have its advantages. If a teacher is convinced that certain pupils will flourish, they most likely will. If the doctor is convinced that they are prescribing the right medicine and you trust them, even a placebo will do the job.

The more consciously you go about it, the better it works and the sooner you will be independent again. It is important to realize that we exercise a strong, molding influence on each other in this way.

Everything Is One

As we explained in Chapter 1, there is an endless sea of zero-point energy and information through which we and everything around us are connected. From numerous experiments we find that our consciousness, intention, conviction, and expectation work in a creative way. Our consciousness records reality and confirms it, time and again. We can put the film on "hold," but we can also press "play" again by changing our convictions. That gets everything moving and makes "miracles" possible.

This model of a connection between man and matter is diametrically opposed to the mechanical view of the world that Newton introduced in the seventeenth century. Modern society is based on that, and our way of thinking is still strongly determined by it. According to Newton, the world consists of many small, independent objects that behave in predictable ways.

The quantum explorers, however, discovered that our connection to matter is crucial. We can no longer describe ourselves as accidental natural phenomena and aloof observers who watch reality from behind a window. We are the lead players in the theater of life, in which we make our own show.

What we say and do matters—it is even essential to the creation of our world. People are no longer disconnected. There is no longer the dualistic "here" and "there," "you" and "me." We are no longer at the periphery of our Universe, on the outside looking in. We can take the place that is rightfully ours at the center of *our* world, at the center of *our* wheel.

Every thought causes a movement in the quantum field. Every observation records something. Every act counts. A minor influence can have great effect on the long term. The development of reality is less predictable than science admits. Even if there are laws in nature, nature itself regularly goes beyond its boundaries. Mother Earth knows the loopholes in the maze of science better than anyone else.

"As Within, So Without"

Our consciousness is indeed the creator of reality. We are not passive spectators but rather active players on a field with endless possibilities. We can make or break the world, divide or unite. In simple terms, we determine how the world develops with our consciousness. Because everything is energetically connected, there is an unbreakable bond between reality and us. There is no separation. Everything is energy and everything is one. The inner and outer worlds are inseparably united. We are one. As above, so below; as within, so without.

From research we know that our brains cannot discern between really seeing something or remembering it. Recordings of the electromagnetic field around the brain with PET and CAT scans show that in both cases—observing and remembering—there is activity in the same parts of the brain. To our brain it doesn't make too much of a difference whether we actually do something or just think about it and imagine doing it. Our body doesn't know the difference, because it reacts to both in the same way.

This phenomenon was first discovered in the 1930s by Dr. Edmund Jacobson. When Jacobson asked his patients to imagine doing certain physical exercises, he saw their bodies react with subtle muscle movements, as if they were actually doing the exercise. Since then, many top athletes have made use of this. In an experiment with bodybuilders, the test subjects, who only imagined lifting the weights, formed almost as much muscular mass as those who really sweated their way through.

Different Worlds

The truth is that everything is possible. The restriction lies in ourselves. According to quantum mechanics, we also have a very limited picture of reality. Through our skin and other senses, our brain takes in four billion bits of information per second, but we only are aware of two thousand bits. O.K., the readers of this book are intelligent and self-conscious, so you probably take in at least four thousand bits per second, but that still doesn't make you much the wiser as it is still only 0.0001 percent of reality, which is a minute fraction of what is happening around you.

There are many different worlds. Dogs can hear tones that are far out of our reach; visual impressions are not as important to them. They live in a world of scents and rely much more on their sense of smell. Insects can see ultraviolet light and birds can perceive electromagnetic fields. All you have to do is get on all fours to see the world of a child, dominated by the legs of tables and chairs.

The Beating of the Heart

Seeing auras and feeling the radiation of plants are not out of the ordinary. In all likelihood, every human being perceives them, but the brain filters them out as irrelevant. Of course perceiving the energy of a plant doesn't really change your world. At most a few hundred bits of information are added to your existing picture of the world. From experience, however, I can tell you that the picture becomes richer and more complete. Instead of stereo, you hear Dolby surround. Instead of black and white TV, you see it in color.

What we conceive of as true is what we see. If we don't have it in our consciousness, then we don't see, hear, feel, or smell it in the world surrounding us. These are the discoveries of quantum mechanics. It is also the most important theme in the work of the late professor Dr. Jan Hendrik van den Berg, a neurologist and former professor in Leiden, The Netherlands, who wrote more than thirty books on the subject in the second half of the previous century. His books have been translated into many languages. Van den Berg calls his work *Metabletica*, the doctrine of changes.

Van den Berg describes how medical science was shaken to its foundations in 1628, when the Englishman William Harvey published his discovery of the circulatory system. In the same publication Harvey also wrote that the beating of the heart can be heard. When he wrote this, everyone was surprised, and many were incredulous because they didn't hear anything. Harvey's observation of the beating heart was challenged, sharply criticized, and even considered ridiculous by the experts of the time.

In his book *The Human Body*, van den Berg describes that before 1628 a beating heart was not known to medical science. Until then it was impossible to hear the beating of a heart. It didn't exist. Only when the concept of the heart as a pump became familiar, could ever-increasing numbers of people hear the beating of the heart.

Van den Berg studied many old medical works going all the way back to Hippocrates, but neither there nor in other important authors from antiquity like Erasistratus and Galenus did he find a description of a beating heart. In some poems from antiquity there is a question of noises made by the heart. A youngster in love hears the world sing if he has his head on the chest of his loved one. But a beating heart is nowhere to be found, nor the description of the heart as a mechanical pump.

Until 1628 the heart was not a mechanical pump but rather a sensitive organ in which feelings were experienced. It was the seat of the soul. This is the heart we mean when we say we should open our heart to connect ourselves to the world. This heart is an energetic heart, connected to the heart chakra in our chest, and not a throbbing muscle. Through this heart we are in contact with material reality, the field of information, and zero-point energy, according to the American HeartMath Institute and scientist Gregg Braden. In the chapters to come I will elaborate on this further.

In short, you could say that humanity had to learn to hear the heart in the seventeenth century and that it has to learn to feel it again at the beginning of the twenty-first century.

You Are a God in the Very Deepest of Your Thoughts…

Our consciousness is at the same time both the creative and the limiting factor in reality. Our mind is stronger than matter. We live in an endless sea of information and energy and we have, at all times, the freedom to create anything of it we want. On the one hand this is frightening, but on the other hand it is a hopeful perspective, because if you can create your world, you can also turn it into something beautiful. You are free to create whatever you want and, because of that, you are one hundred percent responsible for the result and for what that means to the world.

The Dutch poet Willem Kloos started a sonnet in 1885 with the famous words: "Ik ben een God in 't diepst van mijn gedachten" (I am a God in the very deepest of my thoughts). We shall have to get used to the truth of this. In his inaugural address in 1994, for the presidency of South Africa, Nelson Mandela said, quoting Marianne Williamson: "Our greatest fear is not that we are inadequate (…) It is our light, not our darkness, that most frightens us. We ask ourselves: Who am I to be brilliant, gorgeous, talented, and fabulous? Actually, who are you not to be?"

In our deepest thoughts we are all gods and goddesses with an infinite capacity to create. We all have the power of creation to make our dreams come true and to create a fantastic reality with our imagination.

The Forces
in the Wheel of Life

3

In scientific literature I found a lot of proof for the influence of consciousness on processes in material reality. But what about the formative force? I decided to explore this further, and although I found very little information in science about the way in which the formative force works, I did find it in all sorts of ancient creation myths.

In the Beginning

All around the world, the creation myths of very different cultures, religions, and wisdom traditions narrate that there was nothing "in the beginning," only a void. Then the Universe came into existence by means of a sacred sound or a vibration that was received by this void. In some Hindu traditions the Universe originates from pure consciousness and the sound AUM, ringing in the Great Void, the dark, the ocean of pure potential, the proto-substance or the Mother of Creation that creates and feeds all things. In the creation narratives of ancient Japanese and Egyptian cultures, as with the indigenous peoples of North and South America, the first sound is music or a song. In the Bible, the Gospel of St. John says: "In the beginning was the Word...."

Marja de Vries summarizes the universal process of creation as follows in her book *The Whole Elephant Revealed*:

> *The feminine aspect receives the male vibration and thus Light and Life originate, as is told by the myths of creation in a multitude of different symbols. The light and the flow of life energy move, following a pattern of structuring dynamics, that informs itself. This process can be found in the myths of creation under many different names as the co-operation of the Universal Love (life energy) and Sophia, Wisdom (information).*

From the collaboration of these two complementary forces comes the whole Universe with countless light and sound frequencies that are evermore condensing. This culminates in the creation of the physical world—the stars, the planets, and all forms of life, which are still essentially vibrations.

Wu Ch'i, the Cosmic Egg

A sound is a vibration and a word is information. Both inform the proto-ocean of pure potentiality, which is filled with life energy and waiting for what is coming. The beginning of creation can be seen as a connection between life energy and information, resulting in a formative force. This is perhaps best illustrated by the Chinese creation narrative of the Cosmic Egg.

According to an ancient Chinese wisdom tradition from around 3000 BCE, creation begins with *Wu Ch'i* (or *Wuji*), the Cosmic Egg, which "floats" in the eternal, spiritual world. Wu Ch'i is filled with ch'i, life energy, and contains all possibilities within it. It is the mother of the Ten Thousand Things. The Chinese symbolized Wu Ch'i by a circle that is at the same time full and empty, and both moves and stands still.

The Cosmic Egg "floats," as it were, in the spiritual world and is watched by the Gods. It starts dividing after the divine world has fertilized it with a seed (see Figure 3.1) This is the beginning of Creation and the birth of Heaven and Earth, Mind and Matter, Yin and Yang—the two fundamental forces of the Universe. This phase is symbolized by a circle divided into two halves (see Figure 3.2): yang, the

FIGURE 3.1. The fertilized Cosmic Egg Wu Ch'i

FIGURE 3.2. The beginning of creation

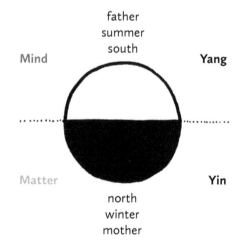

lighter upper part, and yin, the dark lower part. At the upper part we find the Mind and, among other things, the Father, the summer, and the south. At the lower end we find the Mother, the winter, and the north.

Yin and Yang

During the next step in development, the Father and the Mother meet, and fertilization again takes place. This state is called *Tai Ch'i*. According to Chinese wisdom, reality is not static or linear, but rather dynamic and cyclic. Everything is perpetually in motion. The straight line becomes an undulating one, and the mutual fertilization is depicted with a black and a white dot. This drawing is commonly known as the yin-yang symbol (see Figure 3.3). In the adjacent table you can find a classification of different polarities, one of which has a yin and the other a yang character. Some of these polarities are not obvious at first, but they will be elaborated on later in this book.

YANG	YIN
heaven	earth
father	mother
mind	matter
south	north
summer	winter
outer	inner
light	dark
civilisation	culture
prosperity	welfare
quantity	quality
temporary	lasting
intellect	intuition
intelligence	feeling
electric	magnetic
centrifugal	centripetal
noise	silence
explosion	implosion
becoming	being
action	tranquility
hierarchy	holarchy

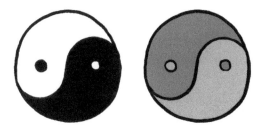

FIGURE 3.3. Two depictions of the yin-yang symbol
In the mind (red), a center-seeking formative force is active (blue)
In the matter (blue), a centrifugal acting force (red) is active

The Origin of the Wheel

The Cosmic Egg goes on dividing. From the Father springs the young father, the Son, and from the Mother the young mother, the Daughter. From the summer comes the young summer, the spring. From the winter comes the young winter, autumn. Spring is connected to the east, because that is where the sun rises. Autumn is connected to the west, because that is where the sun sets. The second division is symbolized by a vertical line.

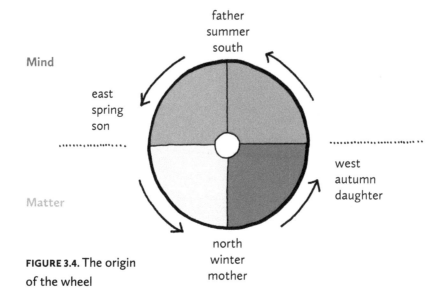

FIGURE 3.4. The origin of the wheel

Thus, the egg is divided into four equal parts, the four quarters of the compass, the four seasons, the four phases of the moon, the four parts of the day, the four elements, and so on. Four is the number of stability and wholeness, and the circle with the isosceles cross (a cross in which all arms are of equal length; see Figure 3.4) is thus one of the oldest symbols of harmony and wholeness that can be found anywhere in the world. We find it, for instance, in the Celtic cross, also known as the sun wheel.

The four major elements—earth, water, air, and fire—split up into ever more elements. The Chinese call these the Ten Thousand Things. In this way the image emerges of a cake with wedges or of a wheel. The center or axle of this wheel is the gate to the world of the Gods. Here is the seat of the eternal, unchangeable Self, and here we find our destiny.

The Cycle of Creation

So this cycle, according to the ancient Chinese, is how creation begins. For a long time I wondered why the development of the seasons is counterclockwise, against time, and why the quarters of the compass are upside down. From the summer comes the young summer, the spring. Instead of the seasons following each other, we see rejuvenation. That is unnatural. In a normal compass, north is at the top, south is below, east is to the right, and west is to the left. I gave it a lot of thought and had almost given up on it, when I suddenly understood that this is the key to understanding the way in which the formative force works.

The formative force that originates in the life energy of the Cosmic Egg and the information from the seed is the engine behind the Cycle of Creation. Creation comes forth from the mind. The formative force, therefore, has its origin in the mind, shown at the top of the drawing. It rotates counterclockwise, to the left, and against time. We will see later on that because of this there is also a connection to the future.

During the Cycle of Creation, the information from the morphic field condenses counterclockwise to the center of the wheel. Until that moment the information has not taken solid shape and the shape exists in the mind only.

The formative force and the Cycle of Creation are symbolized by a blue, counterclockwise or left-turning spiral (see Figure 3.5).

FIGURE 3.5. The Cycle of Creation

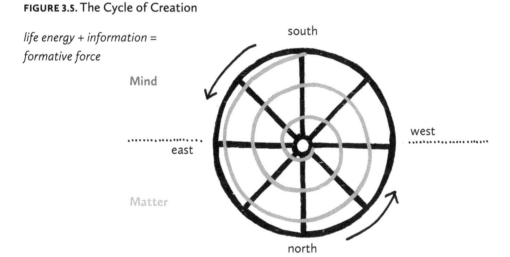

The Cycle of Decay

The Cycle of Decay

After arriving at the center of the wheel, the formative force connects to matter, and from this connection material life originates. This is the birth of the material world with fixed forms. This is preceded by a reversing of the poles: inner becomes outer, invisible becomes visible, subtle matter becomes gross matter, and so on. In this way the world as we know it, where north is at the top and south is below, comes into existence. And everything goes clockwise, to the right, with the flow of time.

In the outer, material world, the cycle of creation also changes poles and is, from that moment on, known as the Cycle of Decay. The counterclockwise, inward-directed formative force becomes an outward-directed, expansive force. This centrifugal force hurls everything outward.

The expansive force and the Cycle of Decay are symbolized by a red, clockwise or right-turning spiral (see Figure 3.6).

FIGURE 3.6. The Cycle of Decay

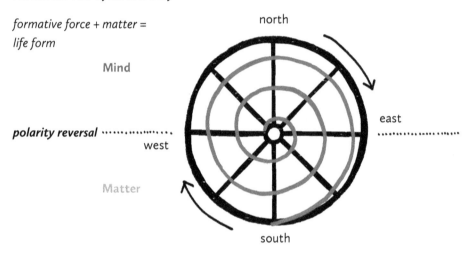

formative force + matter =
life form

Mind

polarity reversal ·················
west

Matter

north

east

south

Two Forces in the Wheel

The image of the wheel thus becomes a metaphor for creation. Two forces are at work in the wheel: a center-seeking (centripetal) formative force that is connected to the cycle of creation, and a center-fleeing (centrifugal) expansive force that is connected to the Cycle of Decay (see Figure 3.7 on the next page).

The centrifugal force is well known. It has been thoroughly studied in physics, makes use of common energy sources like petrol and electricity, and is the force that propels all vehicles. It is the masculine, extrovert force that we are very familiar with in the West, and it is connected to the intellect and the ego. It has a yang character and works in matter, which is yin.

The center-seeking formative force attracts everything from the center. This force is more hidden, less studied, less known. It is based on ch'i, life energy, and works in a constructive way, creating and integrating. It is the life force that takes care of all processes of life, and it is described by many ancient cultures. This formative force manifests itself as a receptive, feminine force of being, which we find

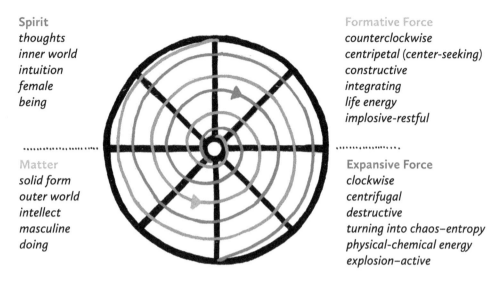

Spirit
thoughts
inner world
intuition
female
being

Formative Force
counterclockwise
centripetal (center-seeking)
constructive
integrating
life energy
implosive-restful

Matter
solid form
outer world
intellect
masculine
doing

Expansive Force
clockwise
centrifugal
destructive
turning into chaos–entropy
physical-chemical energy
explosion–active

FIGURE 3.7. The wheel with the two forces

in the silence. It is connected to intuition and to our inner beings. The formative force has a yin character and works in the mind, which is yang.

The centrifugal expansive force is projected outward and works in the external world. You connect to it by focusing your attention outward.

The center-seeking formative force is aimed inward and works in the inner world; you connect to it by focusing your attention inward.

The Law of Dynamic Balance

In the wheel, both forces are in balance. Nevertheless, mind over matter applies, meaning that the mind is stronger than matter. The feminine formative force is stronger than the masculine expansive force, because the solid form always comes from thought. Everything you see around you has first been thought about. Everything is preceded by a cycle of origin. After that, it reveals itself in the material world as a solid form, or life form, and the Cycle of Decay sets in. The feminine formative force is therefore essential to every development.

In her book, *The Whole Elephant Revealed*, Marja de Vries describes the law of dynamic balance. According to this law, everything in the Universe is derived from two active dynamic principles. In fact, these are the only two forces in the Universe. They are often described as the "feminine" and the "masculine" principles. The masculine principle or force—expansion—is outer-directed, and the feminine principle or force—contraction—is inner-directed.

The feminine, inward-bound force is not only the opposite aspect of the outward-bound masculine force, but at the same time it also forms the connection, union, and integration of these apparent opposites so that they form a whole together. If both forces cooperate, a balance is created. This balance is not static but dynamic. There is a perpetual interaction and a certain amount of imbalance between the two forces, and this imbalance is necessary for development, for growth. Marja de Vries concludes that evolutionary development is optimal when the feminine, integrating principle is stronger than the masculine principle.

It took a while before I realized the consequences of this. "Mind force" or "mental force" is stronger than any material force. It is even stronger than atomic force. That is quite something! Everyone is free to think, but no thought is without consequences. What you think is almost more important than what you do! This offers many positive possibilities if you handle it with consciousness.

Humankind and Its Wheels

According to tradition, the wheel is a metaphor for wholeness, a whole. It symbolizes a harmonic connection between heaven and earth, mind and matter. The wheel can represent the Universe and at the same time every entity in it. For example, your life, the company you own, or the company you work in. As a human being, you are born in your wheel, your life. It is your task to get to the center of your wheel, because that is where your destiny lies and where you will find your everlasting, unchanged self connected with your higher goal.

FIGURE 3.8. The Shri-yantra

The wheel is found as a symbol in many cultures. The word *mandala* comes from Sanskrit, meaning "wheel" or "holy circle." Many mandalas consist of circles around a shared center. The center symbolizes the center of creation and the everlasting, unchanging self of man. There are many different mandalas. Tibetan mandalas often show the Buddha in the center. On the periphery of the mandala we see the gods of the upper world and the underworld, all of whom have the greater goal of creation in mind and who coach or guide people on their paths in life.

The medicine wheel of the Indians is another example. The Shri-yantra (see Figure 3.8) is a holy symbol from Hinduism and Buddhism.

It is a wheel with a symbol in it that is made up of nine triangles. This forms a complex drawing with a lot of little triangles. Every triangle is part of the Nine Fold Path of Buddhist initiation leading to the center. If you have taken the next step on the path, another gate or triangle opens up, so to speak.

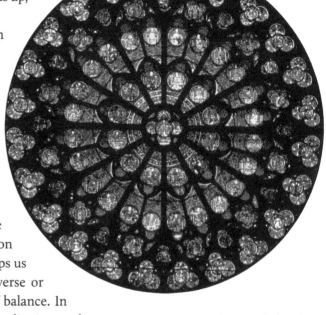

In Western culture we see the wheel in the rose windows found in many major churches and cathedrals (see Figure 3.9). At the center is Christ as the representative of God on earth. Around him are the twelve apostles. The rose is the symbol of love. In combination with Christ, this wheel depicts the all-inclusive love of God.

The mandala, the medicine wheel, the sun wheel, and the rose window are examples of wheels that symbolize creation in harmony. The wheel is a whole. It helps us connect to the largest whole, the Universe or the "whole world," when we are out of balance. In some spiritual traditions this is done by meditating on these wheels or mandalas and by taking in their wholeness.

FIGURE 3.9. A rose window in the cathedral at Chartres

The Flywheel

In many cultures the wheel symbolizes the Universe, with the destiny of our life path at the center. But even if you don't want to seek your destiny or a higher goal, the center is a good place to be. If the wheel symbolizes your whole, your life, or your business, you will have an overview of that whole from the center, and you will be in a place of rest, with no motion. If, on the contrary, you are on the periphery, you are flung about, and your grip on the wheel is tenuous. There, life is not in your own hands. There is a lot of motion and commotion, everything is sped up and time flies.

But how do you get to the center of your wheel? In our modern society, the emphasis is on growth and expansion. Our attention is constantly drawn outward by advertising and news about events in the world. We are constantly seduced by new products and invitations to travel to unknown destinations for a holiday. All kinds of entertainment distract us, day and night. In this way, we are constantly led away from our destiny and from our higher goal. It is not important who you are but rather what you have. Collectively, we are positioned more toward the outer edge of the wheel than at the center.

Luckily, the wheel itself shows us how to reach the center. As a matter of fact, it is very simple. The answer is introspection, by changing our focus from the outer to the inner world. It is about inner guidance: Your inner voice leads you to your destiny. If you listen to it, you automatically connect to the formative force that is directed inward, which leads you to the center of the wheel. The outer and inner worlds then come into alignment, and coincidences will go your way in a direction that is naturally yours.

However, this does not happen automatically. Our way of thinking is usually dominated by our rational mind, which constantly confronts us with questions, arguments, and "yes, buts." As it turns out, this merry-go-round of thoughts, called "the analyzer" by some, can be slowed down with the help of relaxation and meditative techniques. These practices scale down the part the intellect plays in our lives and makes more space available in our consciousness for intuition. This is important because contact with the formative force is made through intuition. In fact, the formative force is literally beyond our intellect.

The Path to Your Destiny

But does that mean that from now on everybody should sit on a mat and meditate all day? Does that fit in with our Western society? Daily life would come to an immediate standstill. For a while that might be fun, but the land must be ploughed, food must be harvested, bread must be baked. Who will do that? Or is there another way to reach our destiny?

The ancient symbol of the labyrinth offers an answer to this question.

The labyrinth is also a wheel, and it symbolizes humanity's path in life to our destiny and the eternal, unchanging self in the center. It should not be confused with a maze. In a maze there are cul-de-sacs in which you can get lost. Not so in a labyrinth. Just keep following the path, and you will always arrive at the center. The labyrinth is therefore a very hopeful metaphor for life: Whatever happens, keep moving, keep living, walk on, and you will always reach your destiny.

Labyrinths have been found all over the world, and were used by many ancient cultures. For example, both the Vikings in Scandinavia and the Aboriginals in Australia used/use this symbol. In his classic work, *Through the Labyrinth*, Hermann Kern gives a survey of the locations of labyrinths throughout the world and shows how almost all peoples use this symbol to gain insight into their questions about life. In contrast to the mandala, the rose window, and other wheels that stand still and with which you connect by means of meditation, you *walk* through a labyrinth. We may see many pictures of labyrinths, but a real labyrinth is on the floor and invites you to step in and start on your way. You can take a question or a problem with you. While you are walking in a meditative way through the labyrinth, the solution usually comes to you.

Today, many farmers in the Netherlands and Germany make some extra money by growing a corn maze or labyrinth in one of their fields. The corn is planted in such a way that after a few months, a true labyrinth has grown. Because of the height of the corn, you cannot see where you are, which is often exciting. In the center of German corn labyrinths, one is usually welcomed by the farmer's wife, who treats you to a grilled sausage and a glass of beer. It may not be the ultimate goal you imagine, but as long as the stomach is the way to a man's heart, visitors will surely have the feeling that they have reached their goal for that day!

The Labyrinth of Chartres

The best known and certainly one of the most beautiful labyrinths is in the Cathédrale Notre-Dame de Chartres in France. It usually has chairs on it, but every Friday these are taken away and you can walk through it.

The labyrinth is marked in black lines on the floor. You can see a miniature version of it in Figure 3.10. The entrance to the labyrinth is at the bottom of the circle. Symbolically, this means that you come out of the spiritual world and step into creation, into your whole. After that, you start off to your destination, the higher goal or the center. If you follow the path shown in Figure 3.10, you will see that you pass the center quite soon after you start on your way in

FIGURE 3.10. The labyrinth in the cathedral at Chartres as viewed from above

life. This suggests that we should—or might—all get an early idea of where our path is leading.

After that the journey really begins, and after walking the long and turning path, you finally reach the center of the wheel. As you progress, you alternately turn right, or clockwise, and then you turn left, counterclockwise.

Turning right in the wheel means being in connection with the outer-directed, right-turning, expansive force. Turning left means connecting to the left-turning, inward-bound, formative force. Just for the fun of it, I once colored those parts of the labyrinth where you walk clockwise in red and the parts that you walk counterclockwise in blue. The result is fascinating (see Figure 3.11). You can see that the labyrinth shows perfect harmony between yin and yang, clockwise and counterclockwise, inward- and outward-bound.

FIGURE 3.11. The labyrinth in the Cathédrale Notre-Dame de Chartres showing the two forces

Red: the right-turning, outer-directed, expansive force, and blue: the left-turning, inward-directed, formative force.

This suggests that we don't reach our destiny by only focusing our attention inward and meditating all day. And we don't reach it only by actively creating and building in the material world either. It suggests that the path is about harmony between the two forces and their rhythmic interchange. Every action and every piece of work in the outer world is followed by a period of introspection and reflection in the inner world. It is necessary to think about events in daily life and to let your feelings speak. In this way you become aware of your actions, and every step you take is in harmony with and brings you closer to your goal. Making your way through the labyrinth makes the process conscious. In the end, this leads to higher consciousness in the center.

A Hopeful Symbol

The labyrinth in Chartres shows in a beautiful way how you reach your destiny by a combination of inward- and outward-directed movement or effort. You make the same movement all the time: You walk to the right, toward a certain goal in the outer world; once you get there you absorb it and then you literally turn your back to it and return practically the same way, turning left, going inward. As you do that, you think about what this encounter, this particular experience in your life, means to you. The moment you understand, you are ready for the next step in the outer world. You turn again and walk on to the right. If you don't understand how it works, the event will repeat itself, and will you have to go back to the start as many times as it takes until you become conscious of the deeper meaning of the event.

You can experience the labyrinth yourself by going to Chartres, but you can also enlarge the drawing of the labyrinth to a tabloid size (two 8½ × 11 sheets of paper joined together) and run your index finger along the path in labyrinth. An exciting journey awaits you if you choose a quiet moment for it and relax your mind. In this way you can experience much of the quality of the labyrinth.

The last part of the labyrinth is very special. After having walked practically the whole path, you find yourself walking the whole perimeter in the final part of the labyrinth. In doing so you turn right. Most people have the experience that this longest stretch of the labyrinth takes ages! There seems to be no end to it. Symbolically, this means that toward the end of your path in life, or at the end of a great cycle in your life, you are at the perimeter of the wheel, focused on the outer world, and are farthest from your destination. At this point you may feel strange, feel that you are completely lost, or feel that you cannot make heads or tails of what is going on and are at your wits' end. Whatever were you thinking when you started out on this path?!

The beautiful and hopeful thing about the labyrinth is that it shows you that this long walk on the perimeter is necessary to get to the center. Suddenly, there is an end to this long stretch. The path bends to the right abruptly and behold: Your destination and higher goal are in front of you. You make for it straight away. After this, there is a short period of reflection and action in the outer world, and before you know it you have come to the end of your journey.

Summary

Every organism, every organization, and every ecosystem or company system can be compared to a wheel. Both forces in the wheel, the center-seeking, or centripetal, force and the center-fleeing, or centrifugal, force, are in balance. If however, you want to grow, change, and fulfill your destiny, the feminine, inward-bound force must be the stronger one. This force is responsible for the Cycle of Creation, in which the spirit condenses, step by step, to connect to gross matter at the center of the wheel. The formative force is based on life energy and information. This energy comes from the zero-point energy field. The information is stored in a morphic field.

The wheel has consciousness by way of a conductor: you, whether as the creating force of your life, the CEO of a company, or the manager or leader of a project. In our terms, the guardian.

We have now seen that there really is a formative force. This "force of mind" is said to have an even stronger effect than the physical forces we know. Results of scientific research show quite clearly that we can influence reality and the direction of our wheel with our intention, expectation, and conviction—in short, with our consciousness. Not much is known about the mechanism, or formative force, that causes this effect. And certainly not about how this formative force works on a large scale.

Morphic Fields and
Perception from a Distance

4

We now know that we can get into contact with the formative force by focusing our attention inward. If we quiet our thinking, we can make contact with the formative force through our intuition.

The next question becomes how to consciously make contact with the morphic and zero-point energy fields. I decided to further explore this by reading more about the morphic fields and to see if there is a connection with the metaphor of the wheel.

The Whole Is More Than the Sum of Its Parts

Over the last few hundred years, science, in search of the secret of life, has analyzed matter and split it up into ever-smaller parts. Rupert Sheldrake, and with him many other modern scientists, believe that we cannot understand life and the Universe by splitting it up more and more, just as we cannot understand an architect by taking apart a house they designed brick by brick or understand a painter by analyzing the paint in their paintings. These scientists feel that we can only understand the thoughts, concepts, or ideas of such enterprises by studying them holistically.

According to Sheldrake, the Universe is an enormously complex, living whole. He calls it a *holon*, from the Greek for "whole." Sheldrake looks upon the Universe, our solar system, and earth as holistic, as built from holons. Holons have different levels of complexity. They are united in a holarchy, where every entity is at the same time part of a larger, more complex holon (see Figure 4.1 on the next page).

Atoms, for instance, are wholes. Molecules are wholes built from atoms, crystals are wholes built from molecules. The same applies to cells in cell tissue, cell tissue in organs, organs in organisms, organisms in communities, communities in ecosystems, ecosystems on earth, earth in the solar system, the solar system in the Milky Way, and so on.

Every system is a whole built from components, which in its turn is part of a larger whole. At every level, the whole is more than the sum of its parts. One and

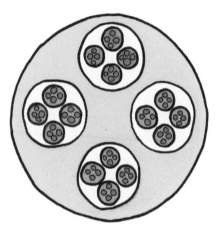

FIGURE 4.1. An example of a holarchy
The red circles are cells. Together, these form tissues (the orange circles). From these tissues organs are made (the yellow circles). An organism is built out of cells, tissues, and organs. This is the green circle.

one makes three applies here. Sheldrake takes the view that every whole is organized by a morphic field, and this field is organized in the same way as a holarchy.

You can imagine a holarchy made up of circles. Every circle is a holon, but is at the same time part of a larger whole. Figure 4.2 uses inverted triangles to show another way to depict a holarchy and a morphic field.

A morphic field can be compared to a bookcase. On the bottom shelf you find the template that organizes the overall structure of the case. The information for the building of the second shelf can be found on the one below it. On the top shelf you will find the script for the whole organism. From bottom to top, the scripts get more and more complex because the entirety is getting larger and larger. Nevertheless, the higher level always aligns with the previous one.

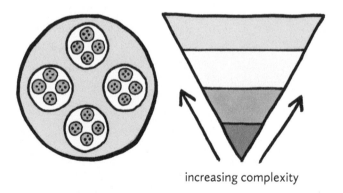

increasing complexity

FIGURE 4.2. A morphic field is organized in the same way as a holarchy.
The smallest whole, cells for example, lie at the bottom, and the whole with the greatest complexity, the body, lies on top.

In other words, on the bottom shelf we find the information to learn how to count. One level above are the scripts with which you learn to do arithmetic. Then you learn about mathematics, and after that a higher level of mathematics, and in the end you are at the top of the triangle at the level of Einstein. To be able to do that well, you must have taken in and integrated the information found on all previous levels.

Holarchy Versus Hierarchy

A holarchy is the opposite of a hierarchy, in which there is a "boss" at the top. A good example of a hierarchy is the army, where an order is an order and talking back is not allowed. In a holarchy, instead of a top-down structure we have a bottom-up structure. Here the larger whole rests, as it were, on the smallest component and needs all the support it can get from the underlying layers so it doesn't lose its balance. This is only possible if there is optimal exchange and cooperation between the levels, with information going back and forth. The top continuously needs to be in touch with the base. This is the opposite of how it works in a hierarchy, which is based on a one-way "trickle down" of information (see Figure 4.3).

A holarchy is based on cooperation, and from this cooperation comes surplus value. A single golden plover cannot cross the Atlantic Ocean by itself. The distance of 1,000 miles is too far for a nonstop flight. They do not have enough energy

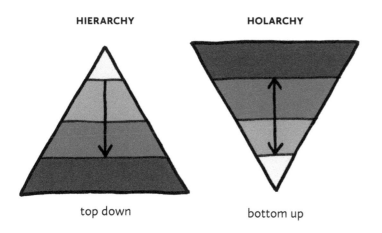

HIERARCHY

HOLARCHY

top down

bottom up

FIGURE 4.3. Holarchy versus Hierarchy
In a hierarchy, information mostly flows from the top to the bottom: The top is in charge. A holarchy is characterized by cooperation and a good, clear two-way exchange of information.

and stamina to do so. A *group* of golden plovers, however, can do so because of the efficiency they gain by flying in a V-formation.

In a hierarchy, the main stream of information flows from the top to the bottom. The top is in charge. Cooperation is characteristic of a holarchy. Good and clear communication—exchange of information—is a condition for cooperation. This means that the morphic field not only organizes the various components of a holarchy but also takes care of the communication between these parts.

In the extremely fast coordination in a shoal of fish or a flock of birds, morphic fields seem to play a role. Using film shots, a reaction velocity of 38 milliseconds has been calculated in a flock of birds, which is far too fast for a "normal" communication between anywhere from hundreds to tens of thousands of birds that have an average distance between them of often more than sixty feet. The birds no longer behave as separate individuals but as a coherent entirety with a group consciousness.

Morphic Resonance

Dr. Sheldrake believes that contact with morphic fields is accessed by means of morphic resonance, also called form resonance. What is morphic resonance?

Everything is energy, including matter, and energy vibrates. Every octave corresponds with a step of condensation from the subtlest energy to matter. Matter can be called coagulated vibration, and light is incomprehensively diluted sound (see Figure 4.4). Every organism, organization, ecosystem, or company system therefore has its own unique vibration.

You are in resonance with something or someone if you are both on the same wavelength. You then have the feeling that you "click," and there is a flow between you. You understand each other effortlessly—a simple word is all it takes. You may feel as one. It is lovely if you can cooperate in such a way, because then you amplify each other.

If you resonate, you are not only figuratively on the same wavelength but literally as well. Take two equal tuning forks, hit one, and then deaden it. You will still hear the sound because the fork you didn't strike is now vibrating. With tuning forks, we are speaking of acoustic resonance. Rupert Sheldrake speaks of morphic resonance. Acoustic resonance is based on the transfer of a mechanical force by vibrations through air. Morphic resonance is about the transfer of information between morphic fields. The force of the morphic resonance grows larger as the similarity between objects increases.

FIGURE 4.4. Resonance
*Everything consists of energy that vibrates. Everything
has a unique vibration. Equal vibrations amplify each
other, and that is called resonance.*

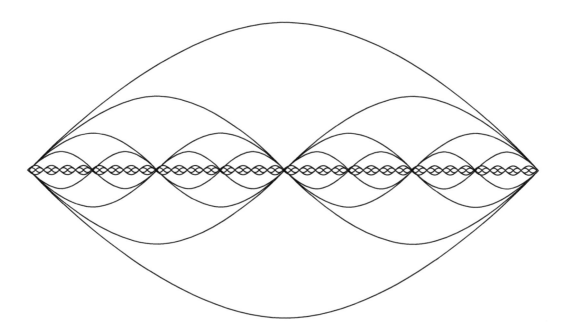

An Explanation for the Potato-Washing Trick

I shall provide a few examples to make morphic resonance clear. All macaque monkeys are similar. Therefore they all resonate with the macaque morphic field. This allows us to explain the phenomenon of the "hundredth monkey" and the spreading of the potato-washing trick of this species.

The first time a macaque discovered how to clean a potato, the trick was stored in the morphic field. The new information was imprinted lightly, so to speak, in the script. Nevertheless, it became easier for another monkey to clean a potato also, because every monkey resonates with the same field, helping the trick to sink in. The behavior was confirmed by repetition.

Every time a potato was washed, the text was written in bolder letters. This made the solution to the problem more and more accessible, with the result being that the cleaning of a potato became increasingly easy for the other macaques to learn. The solution to the problem had become a blueprint and came to them spontaneously.

The distance between the islands didn't influence this transfer of information. According to Sheldrake, the morphic field of the macaque is present everywhere, and thus the monkeys on the other islands could make use of the experience of their fellow monkeys. The power of the information is determined by the number of times the conduct is repeated. That is peculiar, because the fields that physics usually describes, like the gravitational and electromagnetic fields, weaken as distance from their source increases. In morphic fields that is not the case. Therefore we are dealing with a totally new kind of field that probably also exists outside of time and space.

The Presence of the Past

Experiments done in the United States with rats who had to find the exit to a maze showed similar results. Every new generation of rats found the exit sooner than the previous one. This is logical because the solution to the problem of the labyrinth was stored in the rats' morphic field and was accessible for other rats through morphic resonance.

To make sure that the adopted conduct was not inherited, the same experiment was done again years later in England and Scotland with inexperienced rats from other groups. The English and Scottish rats took up the thread where their American colleagues had left off: They set a record time and then improved on it. This too is understandable, because according to the Theory of Morphic Resonance, the right route became present in the form field once the first rat found the exit. Every rat after that one had confirmed this. This shows that time does not influence the information in a morphic field.

That the information in morphic fields doesn't get lost is also shown in the revolutionary research done by the German chemical company Ciba-Geigy in the early 1990s. Looking for new methods of bioengineering, researchers subjected the genes in seeds of wheat, corn, and ferns to electric fields. All sorts of unknown plants sprouted from the treated seeds. Nobody recognized them, except for some paleontologists who were renowned for their knowledge of fossils. They drew the amazing conclusion that the sprouts were prototypes of wheat, corn, and ferns that had long been extinct. After chemical analysis it turned out that the genetic material of these proto-plants was the same as that of the seeds that had been treated. The prototype, therefore, could not be explained by changes in the genetic material. This proved that the prototype was not stored in the genes but outside of them, in morphic fields. Ciba-Geigy had to stop the research because of the enormous fuss in the media.

Learning Capability

From the above, we see that morphic fields are not restricted in space and that they store and exchange information through morphic resonance. New experiences are stored in a script. If something has happened once, the likelihood that it will happen again is greater. If the new behavior repeats itself, it replaces the old text—it gets into the book in bolder letters, as it were. The new behavior gets priority, which means in practice that more and more individuals of a species spontaneously "get" a new idea or show a new behavior. The behavior is confirmed with every repetition, with the result that the new text becomes part of the blueprint after some time.

If a person develops a new behavior, for example operating a computer, the "how" and "what" is stored in the morphic field. Other people can learn from it, because they are connected to the shared human morphic field by morphic resonance. In this way, it becomes increasingly easy to handle a computer. We see that this is indeed the case in young children. They operate computers completely intuitively, without a manual and without thinking, because the solution for certain problems related to handling computers comes to them from the morphic field.

With adults, intellect and reason tend to predominate, and the intuitive information that speaks from the feeling is often overruled. For the intellect there is always a "yes, but." All sorts of arguments are allowed to overrule intuitive perceptions in this way, and the ability to learn spontaneously and intuitively diminishes as we grow more "sensible."

Everything Is Present Here, There, and Everywhere

Everything consists of energy, but everything also has a morphic field of its own, within which is found all the information about its past, present, and development toward the future. Morphic fields have no boundaries in space. This means that all the information about everything that was ever on this planet is present here, there, and everywhere. All that information is present at this moment, at the place you are right now. This thought is unimaginable and is the consequence of the theory of the morphic fields.

Resonators and Antennae

We now know that contact with morphic fields occurs via morphic resonance. A monkey resonates with the monkey morphic field, and an oak tree with the oak tree morphic field. Everything resonates with its own field. But is it possible for humans to contact other morphic fields?

According to Dr. Sheldrake, not only does the whole monkey resonate with the monkey morphic field, but each part of it, even a single hair, does as well. This is logical, because a hair is part of the same system. Thus a drop of a human's blood or saliva is in resonance with the morphic field of that person. According to Sheldrake, all three things—the person, blood, and saliva—are resonators, or antennae. The same applies to the leaf of a tree, or a soil sample taken from land under cultivation.

Today, in our ECOintention training and practice, we take the view that a photograph or a map is also a resonator. The concept of similarity plays a big part here. According to Sheldrake, similar structures are in resonance. A photograph of a house shows similarity to the real house (see Figure 4.5). The collection of

FIGURE 4.5. Morphic resonance and similarity
A house resonates with its own morphic field. The same is true for a representation of the house, whether it is a floor plan or just a concept in the imagination. All three are similar and are connected to the morphic field through morphic resonance.

black, grey, and white dots has been arranged in such a way that it forms a picture that is true to the nature of that particular house. Thus, in some sense, the two are similar. Because of this, an aerial photograph or a map also resonates with the morphic field of a house, a company, or a forest that it pictures.

Anyone can make contact with a morphic field by looking at a picture in a relaxed way or by putting their hand on it. This is my conclusion after twenty years of experience and working with over a thousand people. Making contact probably occurs via the right hemisphere of the brain, where our intuition and our imagination are based.

A resonator, or "attractor," is like an antenna; it makes contact easier, but contact will also take place if you have a clear picture of who or what you want to contact in your mind. By forming an image of your home in your mind, you connect to its morphic field through morphic resonance. A good inner picture is similar to the actual thing. Experience has shown us that the size of the entity doesn't matter in making or not making contact. You can make contact with whatever you can comprehend with your consciousness. For one person that may be a kitchen, a garden, or a shop; for another it might be a National Park or a multinational corporation.

Interpreting Intuitive Information

Making intuitive contact with the help of imagination works very well when your concentration is focused. A photograph, map, or blueprint makes contacting the morphic field much easier. It is even possible to make contact with a person's morphic field by just mentioning his or her name, though this takes skill and training. It usually only works if you know that person, or if there is someone present who does. Then the information from the field comes to you, with the help of your intuition, if the contact is good. In this way it is possible to get an impression of a person, an organization, a forest or park, and so on. You can evaluate this intuitive information by paying attention to how it makes you feel.

If the feeling is good, in most cases that is positive; if the feeling is bad, it is negative. It is not easy to receive intuitive information with 100 percent clarity. It takes practice, because we have to learn how to distinguish feelings that really have to do with the subject from feelings that are our own. We often tend to project all sorts of biases into this kind of work. Staying neutral and learning to listen to your inner voice are two conditions for a clearer perception.

It is important to ask in advance for permission to make contact with the morphic field of the person, organization, or entity you wish to connect to, for the field is an open book containing a lot of private information. Always ask the individual or the owner of the company (the guardian) if you can proceed before you do so. Clarity and ethical practices are preconditions for being able and being allowed to do this interpretive work.

Aura Awareness

Everyone resonates with his or her own morphic field but is also connected to the field of their family. In your work, you resonate with the organization's field. You "carry" these fields with you every moment of the day. In Chapter 8, "Natural Time and the Rhythm of Life," we will see that the morphic field gathers around us like a vortex. All of your personal information, as well as that of your family, your close contacts, and your workplace, is around you as a turning, radiating, subtle material field. You could call that radiation your aura (though that is not entirely true, because an aura is much more complex). But everything to which you are connected is present in your aura as information. Sensitive, intuitive people can pick up this information consciously or unconsciously. Are things going badly at work? If so, the tension and stress in the company field will be in the field around you all the time. Even if you don't think about it during a nice dinner, it is present and can influence the atmosphere.

In fact, the first thing you see in the morning when you open your eyes is not your partner, the bed sheets, or the alarm clock on the bedside table but rather the energy and patterns in your aura. This aura awareness is always with us and colors every perception. For instance, if you are feeling deeply troubled, your aura could be very murky. Your outlook on the world then is like looking through a dirty window, and you may tend to find fault with the world for looking gloomy.

Attention and Intention

It is possible to make intuitive contact with a morphic field to get information. Is it also possible to add information to the morphic field that will influence the formative force in a positive way and benefit the development of the whole? Morphic fields lead systems to final goals or destinations. The information in the morphic field therefore has a meaning. But how do you add a goal to this information? The answer is easy: "With your intention!"

I wrote about the power of intention in Chapter 2. We now know that focusing your intention only works on one aspect of the formative force, namely information. The formative force, however, consists of information and life energy. To "boost" the formative force, you also need to connect the information with energy from the zero-point energy field. And the easiest way to give energy to anything or anyone is by using or giving it your attention. The five exercises below are designed to assist you in developing this ability.

Exercises for Focusing Attention

Below are five basic exercises to help you reach the relaxed state of consciousness that is necessary for focusing attention. Sit down in an easy chair and do Exercises 1 to 4. If your thoughts have not come to a place of stillness, finish with Exercise 5, which uses the "analyzer," an imaginary "machine" described below.

EXERCISE 1: Getting to Yourself

There is nothing you can do or perceive of effectively if you don't feel good. We usually have our attention focused everywhere else except on ourselves. This exercise will help you get closer to yourself and become more centered.

Sit in a quiet place in an easy chair. Close your eyes, relax, and concentrate on your heart. Visualize breathing through your heart and exhaling through your solar plexus, the energy point between your breastbone and your belly button. Focus on a true feeling of appreciation, care, or love for something or someone in your life. Hold those feelings while you radiate them toward yourself and others.

If your thoughts stray, quietly concentrate again on breathing through your heart and your solar plexus, and bring to mind again the feelings of appreciation, care, or love. Hold these feelings in mind as long as you can.

Then focus your attention behind your eyes, in the center of your head. Greet yourself in your mind by saying, "Hello," and wish yourself all the best. Don't do this too quickly, and repeat it three times.

To end the exercise, bend over and touch the floor with your hands. Do this at the end of all the exercises.

EXERCISE 2: Grounding

Standing in a grounded position with both feet on the floor is easier said than done. Often, though our feet touch the floor, our energy often hovers at knee height. The result is cold feet, also a feeling of not being able to get things done. If you are a bit light-headed, you can take this as a sign that you are not grounded. This exercise will help you get grounded.

After having greeted yourself in Exercise 1, go on with this exercise. Imagine you are a tree. You can choose any kind of tree you like. Later you may want to look at what that tree means to you, but for now don't think about it. Greet the tree by saying "Hello."

Feel your feet growing roots into the soil. Feel them go deeply into the ground, giving you something to hold on to so that nothing can topple you over and you can cope with all sorts of weather. Through your roots, you also get nutrients and energy from the soil. Feel those flowing up through your feet, your ankles, your lower legs, your upper legs, and ending in your behind.

You not only take in energy this way, you can also release energy through your feet. The large body of the earth will absorb it without any problems. Feel all sorts of accumulated energy flow into the earth through your legs and feet.

After doing this for a few minutes, come back into the center of your head and say your name again, as well as the date and the place where you are. Bend over, touch the ground, and end the exercise.

EXERCISE 3: Cleaning Your Aura

It has taken humanity a few thousand years to become conscious of the benefits of bodily hygiene. Today we think of people of the Middle Ages as amazingly unhygienic, and we are astonished that they were able to stay alive, living as they did. Though it is normal for us to wash ourselves regularly and brush our teeth in the morning and before going to bed, most people still look puzzled if you mention "energetic hygiene." "Cleaning" the aura? Is that possible? And is it necessary?

Just as your hands get dirty after a day's work, so does your energetic body, your aura. All sorts of thoughts and emotions from your environment and yourself stick to it. A lot of "plaque" blocks the healthy energy stream, and that in turn influences your mood and your health. The exercise below will help clean your aura.

Do Exercises 1 and 2 first. If you feel that your tree is well grounded, you can then shift your attention from your roots to your trunk, branches, and leaves. Feel how they connect you to your surroundings. These surroundings have a lot to say to you, but there is also a lot of dust in the air that sticks to your leaves, branches, and trunk. It is time to clear away that dust.

The rain and the wind will help you. Imagine a warm rain that rinses all the dust off you, like a shower. It comes off easily and streams down your trunk into the earth. When completely clean, feel the soft, warm wind that dries you.

EXERCISE 4: Making Contact with Your Sun

Everyone has a higher self or a guardian angel. It is a loving source of wisdom and energy that constantly lends you a helping hand. The higher self can also be described as a sun. For all things on Earth, the Sun is the most important source of energy, especially for plants and trees. This exercise will help you get in contact with your Sun.

Do Exercises 1, 2, and 3 first. After the rain has washed you and the wind has dried you, imagine that the clouds in the sky drift away and that the Sun comes out. Greet the Sun by saying "Hello."

Ask your sun to come closer and to fill you up with light and energy. Feel the Sun's power radiating into you through your crown. With each breath you take, inhale golden sun-energy. Slowly feel it fill your whole body.

In the lower half of your body, Earth- and Sun-energy mix. Feel the two flows working inside you and become aware that you have created a bridge between heaven and Earth. This new "blended" energy flows upward along your spine and comes out at your crown.

Come back into the center of your head and repeat your name, the date, and the place where you are. Bend over and touch the ground to end the exercise.

EXERCISE 5: **The Analyzer**

You can continue with this exercise right after Exercise 4. Here you use the "analyzer." This is a small, imaginary instrument found inside your head, which you can use to measure the frequencies of your brainwaves. The analyzer has a round knob and a little wheel that produces sounds. The faster the brain waves, the faster the wheel turns, and the higher the pitch of the sound. If you are relaxed, the wheel will turn slowly and produce a beautiful low tone. You can turn the knob in your mind to make the analyzer run slower or faster.

Focus your attention in the center of your head and listen to the tone of your analyzer. Say "Hello" to it. Now turn the knob of the analyzer in your mind to make the tone lower, lowering it gradually until you feel that your state is relaxed.

Creating a balance between your brain hemispheres is the next step. You can use an imaginary old-fashioned weighing scale or balance to do this. Visualize the scale, and then see if it tips to one side or the other. Balance the scale by adding something to one side or by taking away something from the other. In this way, create a balance between the two hemispheres of your brain, between the left/intellectual and right/intuitive sides.

Come back to the center of your head and repeat your name, the date, and the place where you are. Bend over, touch the ground, and end the exercise.

The Language of the Heart— The Power of Attention

5 :

The formative force consists of information and life energy. To "boost" the formative force, you also need to connect the information with energy from the zero-point energy field. And the way to give energy to anything or anyone is by using or giving it your attention. How can we use the power of attention?

Two Minutes of Full Attention

Researchers at Wageningen University in The Netherlands did tests with cows about the effect of attention on their health and achievements. The cows were divided into three groups. One group was treated normally. The second group got positive attention such as a pat on the back or a few caring words every day, and some were even cuddled. The third group had to make do with negative attention: not a pat but a smack, some even got kicked, and the caring words were replaced by scornful words.

The results were shocking. The cows that were given positive attention were a lot healthier than the normal group and gave significantly more milk. Of course that might be expected, but you might be surprised to learn that the group given the negative attention came in second in terms of health and milking.

As it turns out, even negative attention is better than no attention at all (this was also discussed in Chapter 2 in the section on communicating with plants). Nothing is worse than not being seen, being ignored. You can give a child as many toys and presents as you like, but the thing they really want is attention.

From research we know that to keep a relationship healthy, it is enough if you give one another two minutes of your full attention daily. Being there for one another—even for two minutes a day—is sufficient. This attention must be given without distraction from your work, your children, or your cell phone, from a place where you are both at the center of your wheels, in loving connection with each other.

The opposite also happens within two minutes: If a mother sits down in front of her baby without saying anything or without moving, the baby will do everything it can to attract the mother's attention. If the mother stays aloof, her child will become completely upset after two minutes.

Confirmation Through Attention

Everything flourishes when it gets attention and withers when it is ignored or remains unnoticed. From quantum mechanics we know that through our perception energy "freezes" and things take their solid shape. By giving attention we therefore affirm something or someone. In doing so we say, "You can be as you are. It is a good thing you are here in this world. Feel free and make yourself at home. You are very welcome here." In other words, with attention we give everything in this material world the right to exist. Therefore, everything in this reality wants nothing more than to be seen by us, to be heard, felt, or smelled.

Positive attention comes from the heart. "Hearty" people are warm and are interested in their fellow human beings and their surroundings. With positive attention comes a listening, empathic attitude. By asking someone, "How are you?" you give attention and confirm someone without judging or giving an opinion about them.

I always tended to have scores of solutions at hand when somebody told me about his or her problems. I was surprised and irritated that people weren't grateful for them. It took a while and cost me a few relationships before I understood that listening in itself is enough; the important thing isn't to offer solutions but to offer attention. Many complicated problems develop toward their solutions by themselves after that attention has been offered. As the saying goes, "a sorrow shared is a sorrow halved."

Giving attention and asking, "How are you?" also has its limits. It is very nice when somebody shows sincere interest. It probably still is if the same person does it again that same afternoon. But it becomes oppressing if you are called every hour and asked whether things are getting any better. After four or five times, the interested person has probably put you in a bad mood, and on the sixth occasion you might want to throw the phone at them! Too much attention is suffocating, because it literally pins you down.

Giving attention is not only affirming, it also works in a constructive way. Everything is given a longer lifespan by means of attention, including mechanical things. By giving attention to your car and maintaining it well, you give it a longer life. I'm thinking of those beautiful classic cars from the fifties, which are driven around as showpieces on Cuba.

They are treated like kings—polished every day and literally pampered.

I was once waiting for a bus in the countryside in Cuba when, to my great surprise, a bus came along marked "Amsterdam Central Station." It was an old cast-off from the municipality of Amsterdam that had been bought and put back into service in Cuba. The bus driver told me that the bus had served them well for the past ten years. I asked, "Why didn't you ever change the sign?" The driver said with a smile, "Now we are heading for Amsterdam every day. That feeling of freedom keeps me going."

Attention and Life Energy

What exactly is it that we give with our attention?

In giving attention, life energy is exchanged. Life energy gives life force. More life force, providing you handle it well, leads to a longer life. Longevity, in turn, is durability. Durability means that something can withstand the ravages of time. At best, this can even be an almost eternal durability, like the pyramids of Egypt. An object with long durability has something special. Something that is durable has quality and radiates beauty. This evokes astonishment and curiosity. In both cases, it gets new attention so that the amount of life energy again increases.

Life energy is an essential part of the formative force and the fuel for all processes of life. By giving attention with your heart, you give life energy, so to speak, to something or someone and you add, "Here, this is for you. Do with it what you want." In essence, giving attention is therefore unconditional. Attention gets meaning if you connect it to intention.

The life energy we give comes from the zero-point energy field. But how do you consciously make contact with it? If you know how to do that, you can give even more attention and life energy. You are also able to guide the formative force to work in a better way.

Our heart plays an important role in opening the gate to morphic and zero-point energy fields. We know that we must be in a state of relaxed concentration to contact morphic fields. In this state you turn down the activity of your intellect and make room for your intuition. The next thing you need is a good antenna, a so-called resonator. As we discussed in the last chapter in the section titled "Resonators and Antennae," this can be an inner image, a photograph, or a map.

The Heart Knows the Future

In 1991 researchers at the Institute of HeartMath in the United States showed that the heart is connected to an information field beyond time and space. This phenomenon was discovered when they placed a test subject in front of a screen where a new image appeared every few seconds. Some images were nice and pretty—a waterfall, a forest, a cute animal—but at unexpected moments there was a picture of a violent car accident, a growling dog, or a bloody knife.

The middle finger of the test subject was connected to a sensor that registered their heartbeat and other sensors that measured their brain waves. Between the images, the screen turned black so that the researchers could see how the heart and the brain reacted to the images.

What did they find after a few minutes? Even before the horrible picture was shown, the heart reacted by registering a big response. So the heart "knew" before the image appeared what was going to happen. The brain reacted a few seconds later.

In the magazine *Ode*, Rollin McCraty, director of research at the Institute of HeartMath, says it is one of the most significant research results at the Institute: "This research proves that man is apparently intuitively conscious of future events. It proves that the heart has access to a field of information that surpasses time and space."

This field of information is the same as the morphic field. A condition, according to the Institute of HeartMath, for a good reception of this information is that the heart should be calm and open.

The Rhythm of the Heart

To find out how open and receptive someone's heart is, the institute developed several computer programs, in which so-called "heart rhythm variability" could be seen. The heart rhythm variability is the variation in the time between heartbeats. The heart doesn't beat at a constant rate but varies. If this variation follows a fluent pattern, we speak of the "coherence" of the heart rate. The Institute researchers found that with this data you can see for yourself what the effect of certain thoughts or feelings are.

By way of this rhythm, the heart turns out to be giving signals to the brain and to the hormonal system. It doesn't really matter what the heart rate—the beats per minute of the heart—is; it is the rhythm of the heartbeat that is the determining factor.

The Institute of HeartMath discovered that information that is passed on with every heartbeat influences our feelings, our physical health, and the quality of our life. On the other hand, they discovered that feelings of compassion, love, caring, and appreciation can lead to heart coherence, while feelings of anger, frustration, anxiety, and danger cause heart incoherence. These, in turn, lead to specific hormonal, chemical, and electric reactions in the body. So, our heart rhythm affects our physical health, which in turn affects our thoughts and emotions.

This is very practical, because whoever experiences love not only feels glad and happy but also produces more DHEA, the hormone that fights, among other things, aging, Alzheimer's disease, loss of memory, diabetes, depression, and fatigue. At the same time it diminishes the production of harmful stress hormones such as cortisol. A "loving" body absorbs less cholesterol, so the veins have less chance of becoming clogged with plaque, and it produces more immunoglobulin A, an important indicator of the state of the immune system. Furthermore, it lowers blood pressure.

Positive thoughts create health in this way. The opposite applies as well. Someone who is angry produces less DHEA and more cortisol, and so on. The slogan of the Institute of HeartMath is "A change of heart changes everything," which summarizes this interaction nicely.

Open Your Heart

But how do you change your heart? The research at HeartMath shows that it is simpler than it sounds. First you consciously shift your attention to the area around your heart, then you visualize breathing in through your heart and exhaling through your solar plexus (the point of energy under the breast bone, above the belly button). While doing this you evoke positive feelings like appreciation or acknowledgement, and possibly also bring to mind a good memory. This causes your heart rhythm to change immediately—a phenomenon that always amazes students of the Institute of HeartMath, some twenty-five thousand people a year who come from companies, hospitals, schools, and other organizations.

Research by HeartMath suggests that meditation has more effect when the heart is included. The exercises for focusing attention mentioned at the end of Chapter 4 are much more powerful when you add to them to the exercise below. The heart lock-in exercise below is meant as a buffer against stress.

Heart Lock-In

1. Concentrate on the heart.
2. Visualize breathing in through your heart and exhaling through your solar plexus, the point of energy between your breastbone and your belly button.
3. Evoke a sincere feeling of appreciation, care, or love for something or someone in your life.
4. Hold onto those feelings of appreciation, care, or love while you are radiating them to yourself or others.
5. If you find that your thoughts are wandering, concentrate again in peace on breathing through your heart and solar plexus and evoke feelings of appreciation, compassion, or love. Retain these feelings for as long as you can.

The Heart Heals the World

Researchers at HeartMath also found that not only can your heart assess in a better way what is going on in a given situation, it is also aware of this earlier than the head. Since 1991 the Institute of HeartMath has provided abundant scientific proof that feelings are much faster and more powerful than thoughts and that the heart is much more important than the brain for the purposes of healing. Positive thinking with the brain is helpful, but positive "thinking" from the heart gives a much bigger boost to your health. The heart, not the brain, controls our life processes.

HeartMath has also discovered that a coherent heart rhythm has a significant positive effect on our surroundings. Our heart has a strong electromagnetic field that stretches far beyond our bodies and is five thousand times stronger than the field of our brain. With the electromagnetic radiation of our heart, we can influence other electromagnetic radiation. Because almost everything has an electromagnetic field, our heart can have a great impact on our surroundings. So if your own heart rhythm is coherent, chances are that your surroundings will behave coherently as well. Your own health is therefore the start of the health of your surroundings. In short, if you want to change the world you should start with yourself.

In an article in *Ode* magazine, Lew Childre, founder of the Institute of Heart-Math, puts it this way:

> *Many people feel powerless. Climate change. Poverty. War. There are so many things that make you scared. Where do you start as individual? It is important to know that you can have a measurable positive effect on the world. We can change the world. Positive feelings of appreciation and compassion give a positive radiation. These in turn have a positive effect on the health and vitality of others.*

The Meaning of DNA

According to U.S. scientist Gregg Braden, although the heart plays an essential role in the process, it is not the heart but our DNA that gives us access to morphic fields and the zero-point energy field. Braden proved that the structure of the DNA in our cells changes when we hold positive feelings in our heart. The DNA relaxes and thereby opens up and can then contact both fields.

Human DNA is a molecule with a double helix structure (double spiral structure), consisting of twenty-three pairs of chromosomes, and about thirty thousand genes, built from over three billion pairs of polynucleotides The DNA in every human cell is about three meters long and is curled up inside a cell nucleus that has a size of 0.001 millimeter. About 5 percent of the DNA is a code for protein. The remaining 95 percent has a function that is yet unknown and is called junk DNA.

The more complex and stronger an organism is, the higher the percentage of junk DNA. Human DNA differs by only 1 percent from the DNA of a mouse. Mice, however, have 10 percent fewer base pairs and a lot less junk DNA. Some single-cell animals (amoebas) have about thirty times as much DNA as humans, but junk DNA is practically absent in these organisms.

DNA Emits Light

In his pioneering experiments done in the 1990s, the German scientist Fritz-Albert Popp proved that living cells emit "coherent light" in the form of bio-photons. Although this light is about one hundred million times weaker than daylight, it can be measured. Coherent light can be compared to a laser beam in which all the light waves are coherent. As it turns out, this light is involved in the communication between the cells and directs biological functions such as cell growth, cell differentiation, and cell division. This is called bio-information. The light source of this so called biological "laser beam" is the junk DNA.

Science hasn't a clue how the junk DNA can produce coherent light and how it transports information. Where do they both come from? The informed light influences the division, growth, and differentiation of cells. In this way it works in a formative way on the body.

All things considered, this is where we see the formative force at work. As we have often said, the formative force consists of life energy plus information. The life energy comes from the zero-point energy field, and the information comes from morphic fields. Gregg Braden is not the only one who sees the DNA as a gateway to both fields. In his book *Consciousness Beyond Life*, cardiologist Pim van

Lommel writes that DNA seems to be the coordinator of all information necessary for the optimal functioning of our body. According to van Lommel, DNA doesn't carry the hereditary material for this itself but receives the information from morphic fields. Every cell is connected to this field through the DNA in its nucleus.

The Emotional Language of the Heart

An open and coherent heart creates certain conditions. It opens and relaxes DNA, so that an optimal connection with morphic fields and the zero-point energy field can take place. According to Gregg Braden, our heart and the all-embracing energy field speak the same emotional language. Focusing your attention has an effect, but only if you do this with your heart and soul. Through an open, sensitive heart, you connect to the zero-point energy field. With your intention you give a meaning to this energy.

Focused, loving attention from the heart amplifies the power of our intention, because loving attention makes the thought waves we broadcast more coherent, more connected, unambiguous, and therefore more powerful. All thoughts and feelings have their own characteristic vibrations. Coherent vibrations are attuned to each other and amplify each other. A mix of negative thoughts and turbulent feelings is incoherent and chaotic. These vibrations weaken, or even extinguish, each other. Instead of a win-win situation, we get a lose-lose situation.

If, however, we can bring harmony into our thoughts and emotions, and focus on the same, what we broadcast will be coherent and powerful. That is the deeper meaning of doing or giving something your heart and soul. You are connected to it with all of your attention and consciousness. It comes "from the bottom of your heart."

Seek and You Will Find

We have seen before that our energy system doesn't make a distinction between a powerful image in our imagination and a powerful image of something that is really happening in physical reality. Our energy system simply reacts to where our attention is focused, and the degree to which we do that. If, therefore, you vividly imagine what you expect, then that is the message you broadcast. And because you attract exactly what you broadcast, you get what you expected.

Gregg Braden points out that it is important to take the position that your desired goal has *already* been attained, so to speak. Therefore, treasure feelings of compassion, gratefulness, and appreciation for what you have, and *what you are about to get*, in your heart. That language of emotion is what the Universe under-stands and what works best to make your dreams come true. In this way you speed up your personal vibration enormously, as well as the vibration you broadcast, and you attract similar energies with high frequencies.

This explains why some wisdom traditions recommend that you feel grateful before your wish is granted. Because in this way you will feel very much supported by the world around you when it comes to making your dreams come true, and you will find what you are looking for.

Braden emphasizes that the opposite applies as well. By thinking about things such as anger, accusation, judgment, sorrow, jealousy, or feeling unwell, and by giv-ing them additional attention (for instance, by discussing them often with others), you attract exactly that what you don't want. Also, when you resist something, you focus on something you don't want instead of focusing on what you do. The more you fight something you don't want, the more negativity you create.

A similar effect occurs when you focus your attention on a problem instead of on the solution by, for instance, worrying about it. By focusing on the problem, you will make it larger instead of smaller. And if your expectations are limited, what you attract will also be limited.

Attention Plus Intention Generates a Formative Force

By distinguishing between attention and intention, it now becomes clear how to work with the formative force. Attention is connected to life energy, and intention to information. We can substitute the line, "life energy plus information generates a formative force" with, "attention plus intention generates a formative force."

If you relax your mind and connect to your intuition, you can make contact with the morphic field of, for instance, your child, your pet, or your house with the help of an image or a photograph. Wherever you are, by taking that image into your heart, you connect to the zero-point energy field. With your intention you can give this energy a direction or purpose (see Figure 5.1).

I know farmers who, for a minute every morning, make contact with their cows in faraway meadows. They bring the pasture and the cows into their minds and ask them how things are going. If everything remains calm, they stay at home. If they get a bad feeling, they get into the car and drive out to them. Usually there is something wrong and they can set things right on the spot.

It is helpful for the farmer to do this every day, because even if there is nothing wrong, he or she gives the cows life energy by focusing his or her full attention on them, which is beneficial to their health. The same idea is applicable in many situations. I remember that Floris, the son of one of my relatives, had to go to daycare once a week soon after he was born. His parents both worked, and neither of them could get the day off. Baby Floris was brought to the center early in the morning and often cried in his cot all day. The staff at the daycare facility didn't know what to do. His father and mother didn't know either.

FIGURE 5.1. With the help of your intuition and an inner image, you make contact with the morphic field of, for instance, your home.

By taking that picture into your heart, you make contact with the zero-point energy field. From life energy plus information, or from attention plus intention, comes the formative force. In this way you can perceive from a distance what is happening somewhere and have an influence on it.

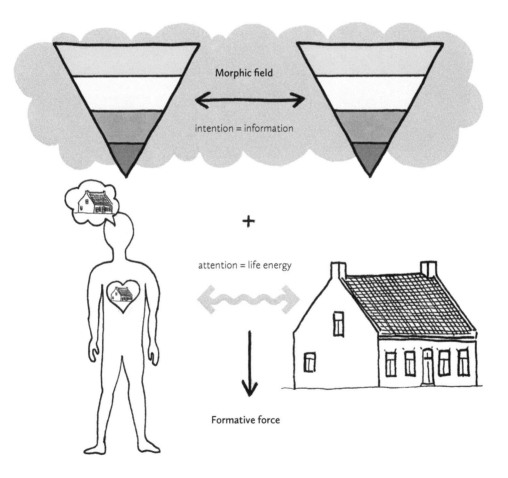

I suggested they take a quiet moment and make contact with their baby from a distance by thinking of him or by looking at his picture. I said, "Floris misses his father and mother. He wants your attention. Think of him, make contact from your heart, and say silently, 'I love you, I am with you.' That is your intention."

A few weeks later I got a phone call. "It really works! Floris is the sweetest and calmest baby of the whole daycare," an enthusiastic voice said on the other side of the receiver. It was my relative. He and his wife had taken the advice and had followed my suggestions. They hadn't found it at all difficult to make contact with Floris from a distance. They both felt clearly that there was a connection and that it was indeed much easier with a photograph. They enjoyed doing this so much, in fact, that they "visited" their baby several times a day. The only problem was finding a quiet spot in the busy office.

"How do you do that?" I asked out of curiosity. My relative said, "Well, the bathroom is the only option, so we go there more often now. Our colleagues must be convinced by now that we have a chronic bladder condition, but we think Floris is worth it."

Dream On

Can you also use the formative force to create good luck? We saw before that we can influence coincidence with our intention. Can you influence the future in this way—not only your own future but, for instance, also that of your organization? The future comes toward you, happens to you, and we call that luck or chance. But is everything chance? Chance can bring us good luck or bad luck. If the formative force affects the development of your whole, can you create good luck with your attention and your intention?

I found the answer to that question when I placed the wheel of life in time. The wheel moves through time: It comes from the past, is in the present, and goes to the future. On a piece of paper, you can depict the timeline from left to right. If you draw the two forces with spirals in the wheel, the left-turning, inward-bound spiral starts at the top at Mind, and the right-turning, outward-bound spiral ends below at Matter (see Figure 5.2).

You can now extend the red, right-turning spiral and you will see that it points to the past. In itself this is logical. This is the force that makes the wheel roll forward, the force that works the engines of all vehicles, for instance. Every action causes a reaction. The cause of what is happening now, of what you are now, lies in the past. You are a product of what you have done in the past and what you have experienced.

FIGURE 5.2. Push and pull
The right-turning, expansive force pushes
from the past; the left-turning, formative
force attracts the future. Life is push and pull.

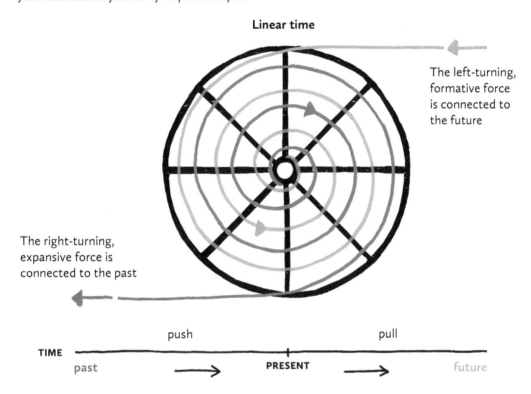

Life Is Push and Pull

But are you a product of your past? If you only look at the right-turning, expansive force, you are. You are pushed into the future from the past and your life is mainly determined by what happened yesterday. The future is uncertain and everything happens by chance. But it becomes a different matter when we take the left-turning, formative force into account. The arrow of this creative force points to the future, in fact it attracts the future. By making use of this formative force you can thus create your future yourself. In that moment, dreams come true.

Is there really a force that attracts the future and is affecting your present? It's difficult to imagine. And the idea that things that lie in the future influence events in the present, isn't that strange? But in fact, the future has a constant influence on your daily life: If I am going to take an important exam next week, I may be working on it now. It may not be something I am looking forward to, and I may get more and more nervous every day, which will influence my surroundings and my daily life. In the worst-case scenario, I may be so moody that everyone will avoid contact with me. The opposite could be true if I am going to go on vacation in two weeks' time: Now that future goal is both literally and figuratively attractive. Every day, as the vacation comes closer, I get happier—and a smiling face attracts happy people!

In short, we are not only pushed from the past but also pulled at from the future.

Creating Good Luck

How do you create good fortune? By attracting the right future. Therefore, know what you want. Put it in your mind. Focus your attention on it, connect to it from your heart, and affirm your goal for the future. This is called an affirmation.

If you have your goal clearly in mind and you affirm it, you are throwing a line with an anchor forward into the future, as it were. With every repetition of the affirmation, this line is strengthened and anchored more securely. Once the anchor is secured, the left-turning, feminine force can pull in the line. In this way, what you have affirmed for the future will happen. In this way you can pull your wheel toward the goal you have imagined.

You could also say that every affirmation is a new text in the morphic field of the wheel. At first the text is vague, but every affirmation prints it bolder and more powerfully, so that in the end you get a blueprint for reaching the new goal.

In this way, the past pushes and the future pulls you forward. It sounds simple, and in essence it is, but there are a few huge catches in this story.

A Burdened Past

What happens, for instance, if you have a past that is burdened with negative events and experiences that you have not yet come to terms with? You may have memories, maybe even vivid pictures, of shocking events that keep going through your mind. Every time you think about them you feel bad—this accident, that failed relationship, the unexpected dismissal from the company where you had worked for years, the sudden death of a friend, and so on.

You can have a past that is such a burden to carry around and that pulls you back in such a way that you can't move on.

Even worse, maybe you feel afraid of the future. Suppose you start a new relationship and that ends badly as well.…

In that case you will be afraid to look forward and will cling to the past. The two forces are then reversed: The past pulls and the future pushes. We don't advise affirmation of a new future in a situation like that, because on the one hand you confirm a pulling force in the future, but on the other hand the past is still pulling. This sort of energetic split doesn't create healing but rather division. You can affirm all you want, but as long as the past still pulls, it is like trying to drive a car with the hand brake still on.

Attracting the Future
with Affirmations

6

Once I understood how the formative force worked and how to boost it with attention and intention, I decided to find out more about how to affirm and how to release the influence of a burdened past. In this chapter we learn how to make the best affirmations.

Affirming

With an affirmation you confirm and reinforce something you would like to have or to be. Affirmations are positive thoughts. For instance, "I am healthy" or "I live in a beautiful house." Affirmations work in a more powerful way if you also visualize them. So, for example, instead of just thinking, "I am healthy," see yourself as completely healthy and above all *feel* completely healthy. The more true to life the image, the better and faster your goals will be realized.

Affirmations work best if they are kept in the present and are formulated positively. "I will get well," may not be effective because you could always be busy getting well but may never *be* well. The affirmation "I am not ill" is also best left out, because you will probably always be ill. The Universe has a positive attitude and "thinks ahead." Words like "no," "not," and "never" are not found in her script.

A good example of the effect of a negative affirmation can be seen in the director's cut of the documentary about the music festival at Woodstock. In the world-famous film from 1969, you mainly see and hear the bands on the stage. In his 1994 cut, film director Michael Wadleigh shows the people on the festival grounds with their varied but generally positive attitudes.

At a certain point dark clouds gather above the festival grounds, the wind gets stronger, and the spectators start looking desperate. Then two hippies climb onto the stage, grab a microphone, and start yelling, "No rain, no rain, no rain!" They keep at it until the whole crowd is chanting with them. Five minutes later it starts raining cats and dogs and Woodstock turns into the most famous mud puddle in history, where "love and peace" reign supreme. The song "Let the Sunshine In" would have made a better affirmation, but that song hadn't yet been written at the time.

Affirming Together

Affirming well is an art. We know, for instance, that focusing your intention alone doesn't work. You must also give attention; that is, loving life energy from your heart. Affirming is therefore not something that can be done off-handedly. On the other hand, affirming also has its limits; with repetition the text is imprinted more and more boldly in the morphic field, but if you go on for too long, it can become a smudge and feel not like an "attractive" goal but rather something to avoid.

Affirming once a day with full conviction is enough. You can usually feel when an affirmation is ready to bear fruit, and once that blueprint is firmly in the field, the work is done. If the ritual feels like it has become a routine, that is the moment to stop or to formulate the affirmation in another way. If you succeed and it feels good, you can keep on affirming. If not, you must wait to see if your wish comes true and if so, when. (In Chapter 9 we will see that a maximum of thirteen affirmations is enough.)

Ego or Higher Goal?

Are you allowed to wish for whatever you want for yourself? Can you create every possible future? In principle you can, but at the same time you are on your way to your destiny, you are on your path in life to reach your higher goal. On that path there are stations in between, and on the way you gain all sorts of experiences. Maybe you are meant to have financial difficulties during a certain period in your life and are meant to do without many things. You can affirm a goal of getting a million dollars or having a party every night, but chances are that these won't be given to you from "above." Then you will have to smile and bear it until, in time, you become aware of the deeper meaning of this experience.

So if you affirm a goal of getting the first prize in the lottery, you may be creating a pulling force contrary to the stream of your life. This will only tire you. Always check if your affirmation comes from a deep, real, longing and is attuned to the whole you are directing. You can do this by getting into a state of relaxed concentration and, while in contact with your higher self, asking if the fulfillment of this affirmation may be "given" to you.

If you find this hard to do, try starting your affirmations with, "I ask the Spiritual World to realize the following affirmations." It is a good idea to always end an affirmation with something like the following: "This, or something even better, will be done for me in a perfectly satisfactory and harmonic way, for the greater good of all who are involved." If you wish, you may add, "So be it" or "Amen." In this way you attune to the Universe and give more space to the natural flow of your life.

There are people who have great difficulty affirming and setting a goal. Of course you may totally surrender to the plan God has for us and affirm, "Thy will be done." But if you are the manager of a company or the captain of a ship, it is important that you have a course planned and that everyone knows where the ship is headed. Otherwise, there is a good chance you will land on a sand bank. Life is generous by nature and open-handed. Because of our free will, the Spiritual World can only react if we ask for what we want. So just ask away. The Universe will be glad to give many answers and huge gifts if those help us to reach our destiny.

The End Justifies the Means

Who wouldn't want to win first prize in the lottery? We all dream of it, and a lottery ticket is easily bought. I have never spent a lot of money on lottery tickets, but for a while I did try to use a pendulum to divine the winning numbers. I never did better than to break even. I couldn't get rid of the idea of getting rich quickly, so I saw myself rolling in money like Scrooge McDuck and tried all sorts of methods of prediction until one day I realized why it didn't work: Money is not the goal, it is a means!

The Universe wants to know what is on your wish list. If you want to buy a friend a birthday present, you want to know what is on their wish list, don't you? It will be a present you give wholeheartedly, and the cost is not important. If a person doesn't have a wish list and says, "Give me money," it's rather boring because it doesn't require imagination or creativity, and that is exactly what the Universe needs.

To give money is only nice if you know what it is for. In short, first think about what you want, then find out what it costs and send both your wish list and the bill to the Universe! If it is something that may, in the scheme of things, be given to you, the cost is of no importance. You might even win enough money to buy your dream palace!

Professional Skill and Knowledge

As we said in Chapter 4, the "what" and "how" of things are written down in the scripts of the morphic field. According to Rupert Sheldrake, morphic fields contain information: scenarios with step-by-step plans, comparable to the blueprint for a house, as well as instructions that say where to begin. "What" is the goal to which a development is leading, "how" is the way to get there. In other words, you may have a wish or a goal, affirm it, and visualize it, but it is also important to keep in mind when and how that wish can come true.

Take, for instance, the long-term goals of a company. Say there is a clear view on where a company wants to be in two years' time in terms of its turnover, number of employees, and location. The board of directors has all of these things clearly in mind, which is great because this in itself is a powerful affirmation. These long-term goals are also translated into shorter-term and middle-term goals, based on the number of steps that must be taken in order to attain them. Questions remain, such as how to go about doing that, what resources are needed, and when each step should be taken. In this way the "how" becomes clearer and the larger goal can be more easily realized.

For work with attention and intention to be a success, you cannot detach it from professional skill and knowledge. This knowledge is derived from the physical world, acquired with our intellect, and based on the expansive force that pulls our consciousness outward. With our intellect we give everything a place in the material world and we place it in the flow of time.

A professional knows how long a job will take. You can sow wheat tomorrow and affirm a good harvest every day, but you will have to wait for at least a few months to see the result. The time must be right for it. In the meanwhile you can affirm short-, middle-, and long-term goals that will enhance your chances of success, such as providing enough water and sunshine, and pulling weeds at the appropriate times.

The saying "time is money" also has to do with expertise. Because you know what is feasible and how long it will take to complete a certain job, you can make a good estimate of what something will cost in terms of money. Money is energy. It is very condensed life energy. Time and life energy are therefore connected. Our thoughts travel faster than light does, but in material reality it costs time, and therefore life energy, to fulfill a wish. A timetable stimulates the flow of life energy and through this activates the formative force.

Big Names Have Big Dreams

The book *Think and Grow Rich*, by American research journalist Napoleon Hill, was published in 1937, and around the turn of the century it was proclaimed one of the five most influential books of the century. Over a period of twenty years, Hill interviewed highly successful American entrepreneurs, among them Henry Ford, Thomas Edison, John D. Rockefeller, Alexander Graham Bell, and Woodrow Wilson. As it turned out, all these people were extremely serious about their dreams, their heart's desire. On top of that, they were able to transform these dreams into clear visions and plans of action that they focused upon daily. Hill saw from his interviews that as soon as a person starts radiating his or her dream or vision, it is only a matter of time before the vision becomes a reality.

Hill also found that the idea that toil and difficulty were needed to get to the top of one's field was obsolete. Their many hours of hard work did not determine the success of these people as much as their attitudes. Hill says, "Being rich starts with a state of mind, with determined focusing on your goal."

How much time realizing a wish takes doesn't depend solely on the magnitude of that wish but also—and especially—on whether the world is ready for it. Nelson Mandela had a great dream. He was in prison for twenty-five years because of his ideal of a free South Africa. When a journalist came to visit him once and asked him, "How are you?" He answered, "I am doing fine. I know exactly what I want, I have a clear image of it, and I am convinced that one day it will happen. I have been here for ten years now, and we are coming closer to success every day."

Mandela's heartfelt desire was a clear picture in his mind, but one could say that he had to wait for twenty million people to get ready for his dream to come true. Nelson Mandela was ready for it, but the world wasn't ready for him. So, perhaps that beautiful palace *is* intended for you, but as long as the previous inhabitants are still in it, there is no room for you. Everything has its own cycle.

The Spiral of Creation

In his book *The Spiral of Creation* Marinus Knoope describes the process of realizing goals in twelve steps (see Figure 6.1). It is easy to connect the spiral of creation to the wheel. Using this spiral, the best way to affirm your intentions will become even more clear, as will the reason why things are sometimes not (yet) successful. In the following summary of the spiral of creation, I let Marinus Knoope do the talking. His description is followed by the relationship of this spiral with the wheel.

FIGURE 6.1. The spiral of creation, with the twelve steps necessary to realize your goal

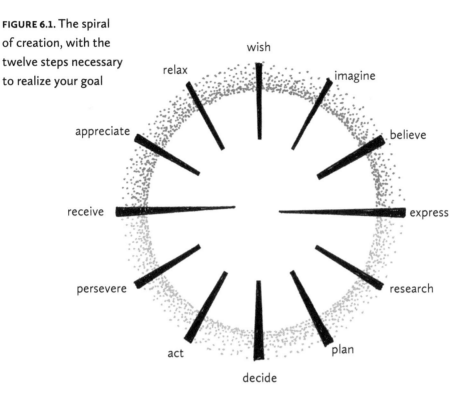

wish
relax
imagine
appreciate
believe
receive
express
persevere
research
act
plan
decide

Wishing and Imagining

According to Marinus Knoope, what is required for the realization of your dreams is to first find a wish within yourself that gives you a warm feeling, that you feel passionate about, and that you are really prepared to work on. In short, a wish that has your whole heart and that is a guiding principle on your path in life. Don't focus on the things you don't want. People who talk about all the things they don't want often linger in that same unwanted situation for a very long time.

To concern yourself with everything you don't want can also be perilous. Imagine being the passenger in a car and hearing the driver, while overtaking a truck, muttering about all the possible disasters that could happen during this maneuver. Wouldn't you get out of the car and find another driver? Having fantasies about a crash is asking for trouble.

Always formulate your wishes in a positive way. Give room to your imagination. Make the image as clear as possible, use all your senses—sight, smell, taste, touch. Feel the future you desire. Create, in your fantasy, a reality that is every bit the one that you want. Enjoy it and make it attractive. The more attractive you make it, the more it attracts.

Believe in It

At a certain moment your common sense will probably start telling you that what you have been imagining is all very nice but in reality isn't attainable because you are too old, too young, you haven't had the proper training, don't have the right experience, aren't business-minded enough, or lack something else. Or maybe you think, "Well, I could do it, but others don't recognize my qualities and will get in my way—my partner, my boss, the banks, the authorities." Or maybe you think that it isn't because of you or others but rather because the project is just not possible or practical, and that life itself is in the way.

Someone who wants to make their wishes come true needs to believe that they will. Belief is no guarantee, but it does help your plans along. It is one of the conditions you have to fulfill to be successful in the end.

Expressing and Researching

Knowing what you want, having a clear picture of it, and believing in it are the first three of the twelve conditions for making your wishes come true. The next condition is that you express your wishes, that you share your desires openly.

If you tell someone you have a new idea and they ask, "Do you really believe it's possible?" and your answer is, "Well, maybe it's not," then you might as well forget about it. In other words, belief is a necessary condition if you want your surroundings to take you and your wishes seriously. You must be firmly convinced of what you want.

Don't share your wishes with others until you have enough faith in your ability to cope with possible criticism in a positive way. You are bound to get tricky questions sooner or later, such as "Just how do you propose to do this?" Don't try to answer that question. Of course you don't know yet. Just say, "Good question, do you have any ideas?" And if the other person says, "Well, no, I haven't," then just say, "Let me know when you do."

The next stage in the process of creation is research, but not research into whether your wishes are feasible (because that is what you already believe). This research is on how, with what, and with whose help your wishes will come true. Go in search of ideas, people, information, and things that may help you. The trick is not to attempt to do everything in life on your own but to surround yourself with people who are better and stronger than you are in ways that serve your goals. Make sure you get the right qualities, knowledge, and information. When you have that, you can make the transformation from fantasy to reality.

Planning

So far there has been imagination, thinking, and talking, but nothing has really happened. You now need a process to take you from dream to reality, and this process is called planning. Planning is done right at the border between fantasy and reality. So let's say, based on what you know from your research (expertise), that your plan of action shows that there is a good chance of success and that you will realize your goal in two years' time. The next step is to fill in where you will be in the process a year and a half from now, a year from now, in four months, in four weeks.

If you take all these steps in the right sequence, it should be smooth sailing to realize your wishes. To recap: You have something you really want. You find a comfortable place to sit undisturbed and start fantasizing about a future in which you get that something, and then you decide to believe in it. When your belief is strong enough, you tell others about it. If they ask if you believe in it yourself, you say YES wholeheartedly. People take you seriously and you gather responses until you run into the right people and a number of good ideas. You make a plan, and before you know it, you decide to actually get going. You make the change from deciding to acting, and from thinking to doing—which are the next two steps in the process of creation.

Deciding, Acting, and Persevering

Making good decisions is difficult if you skip the imagining, believing, expressing, researching, and planning. But if you do take these steps, you grow toward deciding well. Decisions come to you seemingly by themselves. You decide, "I want to do it, I can do it, I will do it!" After that you act. You throw everything into the bargain. You discover, use, and develop your talents. The real work has started. Now it is a matter of practice and perseverance, of work and sweat, of starting up…and going on.

You may have prepared yourself well, but once the action starts there may be unexpected problems to be solved. It may take longer than you think. You might lack certain practical skills, or a big order is cancelled or some other unexpected financial blow might occur. In short, there may be setbacks, and you need to persevere.

This next step in the process of creation is persevering, which is placed opposite belief in the spiral. Belief is saying "yes" to your own wishes, while persevering is saying "yes" to the hard work that is required. You could say that persevering is the phase in which your belief is tested.

Just as perseverance is opposite of belief, acting is the opposite of imagining. Acting has to do with the work that has to be done with the material, whereas imagining is the work of the architect.

Receiving

After perseverance comes a difficult step—receiving. In fact, for most people receiving is the hardest step in the whole process of creation. We are usually better at wanting to succeed in something new than at enjoying the success once it comes. The art of receiving is to be able to enjoy when you get what you desired.

A cat will show you how to receive successfully. If you stroke it and he likes it, he will make a sound that lets you know he does. That stimulates you, the donor, to go on stroking. If you stroke your friend and she formally says, "thank you," you will probably stop doing so. In other words, if you like being stroked, practice purring. Those who want to get what they desire need to practice receiving. So try never to say, "Oh, but you shouldn't have done that." If you make these kinds of remarks when you get something, you discourage the other from giving you something, and in the end you get less and less. Someone radiating that they like to receive will generally get more than someone who insists that they don't need much. The Universe and Mother Earth are generous. There is nothing they like more than to give you pleasure. Open your arms and receive wholeheartedly.

If you want people to come to you when they are in a generous mood, radiate that you would like to receive something and show plainly that you are enjoying it. You will get more and more. This applies to compliments, love, or money. We prefer giving to someone who receives wholeheartedly and who enjoys what he or she gets. The same applies to life.

Appreciate and Relax

The next steps after receiving are appreciating and enjoying. Never ask yourself what you have done to deserve something. If you tell a rose how beautiful it is, she doesn't need to account for the trouble she took either. You deserve the compliments, love, and gifts because of who you are, exactly as you are. Make sure you get and get and get as much as you can. And if you have had enough, then give it away again, but don't give it back. Pass it on. Let the money and the love flow. You don't have to be afraid there will be a shortage. If you have faith that you will always get what you want, you can also give what you wish to give. Receive and enjoy. Be rich and give. Be royally rich and spread the wealth.

After appreciating and enjoying, the last step in the process of creation is re-laxing. Those who have harvested and enjoyed can slowly settle down into a time of reflection and introspection, appreciating and seeing things at their true value, feeling how it feels to be fulfilled. If you stay inside yourself long enough, new desires will come up and you will find, at a deeper level, what you really want in life.

Keep this wish a secret for a while. Develop an image in yourself first. Once you are familiar with that image, then you might decide to believe in it. Then you can say, "Amen, so be it." Only when you come out with it and find people and things that can help you realize your wish will the whole process of creation start afresh.

The Spiral of Creation and the Wheel

The spiral of creation is a helpful instrument. When taken together with the wheel and the formative force, we can apply it even more broadly. Marinus Knoope shows all sorts of surprising links and connections in the spiral of creation. One of these is that the upper half of the spiral can be found in our inner world (i.e., our thoughts) and the lower half can be found in the outer world (see Figure 6.2).

Here you immediately see the connection with the wheel and the formative force. The formative force has its origin in the upper half of the wheel, which is

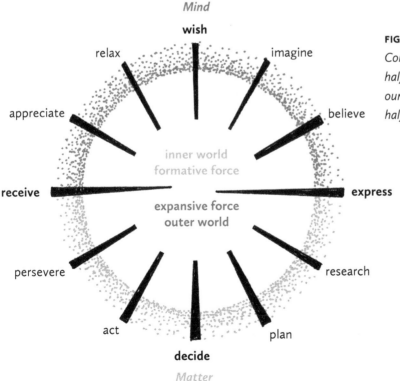

FIGURE 6.2. The spiral of creation. *Comparable to the wheel, the upper half of the spiral of creation is set in our inner world/Mind and the lower half is in the outer world/Matter.*

connected to the mind, the world of thoughts. Receiving, appreciating, relaxing, wishing, imagining, and believing are properties of the formative force. According to Marinus Knoope the spiral goes clockwise, step by step—first you wish, then you imagine, and these are followed by belief. Receiving, appreciating, and relaxing are found at the end.

We know, however, that the material appearance in the outer world is a consequence of the formative force. Therefore the upper half comes first, followed by the lower half, the physical reality.

The conditions Marinus Knoope mentions are correct, but I believe they will be more effective if we take them all together and if we change their sequence. The first step to boosting the formative force is not wishing but relaxing. You shift your attention inward first and go into a state of relaxed concentration.

Next you make contact with your wish and you check, in contact with your higher self, if realization may be given to you. This deepened wishing is followed by imagining. You visualize your wish and make it true to life. This focuses your intention, and what comes next is connecting to your attention by taking your wish, your affirmation, into your heart. By doing so, you open your heart to receive your heart's desire.

This is also what Gregg Braden says: "Take the view that your wish has come true and feel yourself at that moment. Receive that fulfillment and feel the gratitude and appreciation in your heart." In this way you evoke feelings of appreciation and compassion in your heart, and in doing so you radiate your wish and start attracting your future.

The last thing you need to bring the formative force to full strength is belief. As we shall soon see, this last step is the most difficult and is the reason why many wishes are not fulfilled.

To bring the formative force into practice, it helps to make a plan of action and to get going. This corresponds with what we said above about research then planning, then decision and action.

Belief, Perseverance, and Firm Conviction

So far, so good, but what remains is persevering. In the spiral of creation, this is the longest and most difficult period, in which you work until you drop and wait for what sometimes feels like forever. You can lose courage, and you can start getting desperate. Whatever were you thinking when you started on this project? In some ways it feels like the last part of the labyrinth, where you are on the perimeter for a long time.

Nevertheless, as Napoleon Hill writes, the idea that you should toil and have a hard time to get to the top is obsolete. The many hours of hard work did not determine the success of the top leaders and managers he interviewed. It was, above all, their state of mind, their determined focus on their goal. Nelson Mandela and those other people at the top were fully convinced that they would attain their goal. This conviction is similar to the religious conviction or belief system some people have. It has everything to do with believing, but belief in what? In yourself!

Belief and perseverance are opposite each other in the spiral of creation. Is it possible that the stronger your conviction is, the more strongly you believe in yourself, the shorter the period of perseverance will last.

If this is true, the opposite also applies: You can affirm that you are wealthy as much as you like, but if you are convinced deep down that you are worth nothing, life will not give you a penny. Your negative convictions and burdened past are then obstacles that will cause misfortune.

The Burden of the Past, the Mystery of Time

I felt that I had found insight into the way in which I could boost the formative force with my attention and intention and use that to create my future with affirmations. I successfully applied Knoope's spiral of creation until, at a certain moment, I noticed that I was not reaching my positive goals. In fact it was more and more often the opposite: Instead of positive results I had more and more negative results and bad luck.

This moved me to gain more insight into the possible effect a burdened past was having on my affirmations. If everything consists of energy, and equal vibrations resonate with each other, then perhaps part of my burdened past was in resonance with the goals that I wanted to attract and my goal would continue to be blocked by part of the past until this was transformed.

I began to feel that affirmations can not only attract your future but also parts of your burdened past that resonate with it. But is that really so? Why did my affirmations go well for a long time and then stop? Why did they even seem to fail more and more often, so that I was confronted by ever-larger disappointments with ever-increasing regularity? I began to look for a pattern in this.

The past and future both have to do with "time." That was another subject that kept me busy. Does time fly? Can you make time? I already knew how to create good luck, but is it also possible to create spare time?

These questions were the reason I became fascinated with the concept of "time" and the measuring of it.

Measuring Time
and Making Time

7

Sometimes when I meet old friends, it reminds me how quickly time passes. And it makes me wonder if we've utilized our time properly. Proper utilization of time is so important. While we have this body, and especially this amazing human brain, I think every minute is something precious. Our day-to-day existence is very much alive with hope, although there is no guarantee of our future. There is no guarantee that tomorrow at this time we will be here. But we are working for that purely on the basis of hope. So, we need to make the best use of our time. I believe that the proper utilization of time is this: if you can, serve other people, other sentient beings. If not, at least refrain from harming them. I think that is the whole basis of my philosophy.

— The Dalai Lama in *The Art of Happiness*

Questions About Time

We have now seen how to boost the formative force and how to attract the future. You have your goal clearly in mind, and at a certain moment your affirmation is securely anchored in the morphic field. But can something be said about when your goal will be reached, when your dream will come true? What is the time lapse between dream and reality?

With the help of the formative force you can create good luck, but good luck is of no use to you if it knocks at your door and you are not at home. Chances pass. So the moment when luck "drops in" is also important; you must be ready for it. The time must be right.

People often say that affirmations take time, and that's why they don't do them. But what if you could "earn back" the time you invest in affirmations? Suppose five minutes of meditation and affirmation every day could bring you two weeks of holidays—that is a return on your investment of over 450 percent! Five minutes every day is a little over half an hour in a week, which is two hours a month or twenty-four hours over a year—or three work days. If that could bring me fourteen

days of leisure, I wouldn't consider it a bad deal. I think it is possible—in fact I
know many cases in which this has happened.

Coherence and Resonance

To be able to give an answer to these questions about time, it is not only important
to look at the concept of "time," but also at the concept of "coherence." What
is that?

Everything consists of energy that vibrates. Everything has a unique vibration.
Equal vibrations amplify each other, and that is called resonance. If you resonate,
you are not only figuratively on the same wavelength but literally as well. Sometimes vibrations can dampen or cancel each other; for instance, if one wave is
going up at the same moment that the other is going down, then the net effect will
be zero. Therefore, for amplification you have to make sure that both objects are
not only vibrating at the same or related frequencies but also that the waveforms
of their vibrations are in the same phase; that is, at the same point in the cycle,
increasing or decreasing, at the same time. According to physics, they are *in phase*
(see Figure 7.1).

FIGURE 7.1. Equal vibrations can amplify or cancel each other, depending on their phase.

So it's about timing. If the sources causing the waves start moving independently, there is a good chance that disorder will set in. As an example, consider
what would happen if the singers in a choir didn't start at the same time. If they
do, however, a whole comes about, in which the components amplify each other.
We call such a whole coherent.

Resonance and coherence are two different things. For a long time I thought
that only resonance was important. Now it has become clear to me that both play
an equally important role in letting all life processes take a good course and in the
application of the formative force as well.

We all know that for music to be coherent, timing is very important. When a
group plays together, it is crucial that different instruments or sections come in on

time and keep to the rhythm. A musician not only needs a good ear, he or she must also be able to count as well. You need to be in the same key and also in the same rhythm, and only then is the music a connected, coherent whole—only then does it "swing." And in life, just as in music, you have to be there at the right moment. You may be attuned to your partner, but if you are an early bird and she is a night owl, you won't see each other very much. The sun and the moon are a beautiful couple, but they don't see each other a whole lot.

For a team to cooperate, it is important that they "click" with one another and that everybody knows their job. But even if they do, if one person is always late in doing his or her part of the job, the group will never "swing."

Entrainment

Someone who understands a situation can influence it with a single word, but only if that word is said at the right moment. Coherence can create good attunement in a team, which is good for cooperation and efficiency. Then, with the proper timing, you only need a little bit of energy to get the system going. You can send a swing really high by giving it just a little push at the right moment.

It is a well-known fact that objects and individuals can influence each other to move synchronously. In 1656 the Dutch astronomer and physicist Christiaan Huygens (1629–1695) observed that the pendulums of a number of clocks that hung from the same wall began to swing in the same rhythm after some time. They were "phased" or "coherent." He discovered that when the rhythm of one of the clocks was disturbed, it would soon return to the rhythm of the group. The larger the number of clocks, the more stable the system and the harder it was to disrupt the rhythm.

This phenomenon, where vibrating objects that are in proximity begin to vibrate on the same cycle, is called *entrainment*. Entrainment also occurs among groups of people. The menstrual cycles of women who have lived together for some time often start to happen at the same time. The same happens to the heart rhythm of a group of people who work together in an intensive way. Perhaps this was Michael Jackson's inspiration when, in his album "Thriller," he synced the tempo of the music to the heart rhythm of dancing people.

The Dalai Lama As an Attractor

You will be a better attractor if you are coherent. Everything you want to attract will then come to you more easily. I noticed this clearly when I went to a lecture by the Dalai Lama in Antwerp, Belgium. It was on a weekday, and the lecture was in a huge sports arena near the center of town. In spite of the traffic, the journey there went quite quickly. It took much less time than I had expected.

It seems that all the visitors had had a good journey, because all twenty thousand seats were taken when the lecture began. Nowadays usually at least one or two out of twenty participants in a course or workshop are late because of traffic jams. That is five to ten percent. With an audience of twenty thousand, that would mean one to two thousand people might have been late under "normal" circumstances, but not a single chair was empty. Everyone was on time!

Most visitors had come from far away, and I had only one explanation: The Dalai Lama was such a strong, coherent attractor that he had piloted everyone through the traffic. By attuning to him, consciously or unconsciously, all the visitors resonated with his field and energy. This led every traveler to have good luck, with the result that their travelling time was shortened.

At the Center for ECOintention we give many courses and—this may sound strange—if our students are late, I always wonder what I could do to improve our coherence as an attractor. One thing I can fully recommend is starting on time! This is the first condition for coherence. If you do so, everybody will be happy, even the people who are still on their way, because by doing this you can "pull" them through traffic more easily and it will be easier for them to find you. After a while you will see that the people who are always late come earlier, and after three or four times everyone will arrive on time.

From "Sun" Hours to Equal Hours

The morphic field consists of scripts, and every script has its own timetable, its own pace. Therefore it is important that there is mutual attunement not only about what is going to happen, but also about when, so that every script can develop at its own pace with its own natural rhythm. What determines that rhythm? Is there such thing as a natural rhythm? Is there a natural time?

Before we answer that question, let's look at time in general. Time, as such, is an abstract concept—you cannot "grab" time. We can only perceive and measure time because things change. When I studied the history of time measurement, I saw to my surprise that in early history time was connected to the cosmos and the course of the sun (sun hours), but over the ages it has been increasingly connected to matter. As this happened, time became fixed and standardized (equal hours). We went from a cosmic, dynamic understanding of time to a more material, static one.

In antiquity the measurement or counting of time was based on the movement of the sun in the sky. The shadow pointer, or sundial, was one of the first clocks and was in use by 3500 BCE. It was made of an upright staff or obelisk that cast a shadow on the ground. The first hemisphere sundial dates from the eighth century BCE. At the beginning of the fourteenth century, Richard van Wallingford built the first mechanical clockwork in the abbey of the Benedictines of Saint Albans near London. On it you could not only read time but also the position of the celestial bodies. St. Benedict emphasized that time had been given to man by God and was therefore precious.

Mechanical clocks, built using weights or a spring, were in use until the beginning of the twentieth century. This changed when the electrical clock was invented in the United States, followed by quartz crystal clockwork mechanisms in 1929. These had a quartz crystal that produced an electric current, and the frequency of the current served to measure time. For some decades, this was the most accurate clock in use, until the British invented the cesium-atom clock in 1955. To this day, this is the most accurate clock in the world. Since 1971 time is no longer based on solar time but on international atomic time, measured by these atomic clocks.

Static Time

From a world where at first every individual and then every individual city had its own time, we transformed into a planet with a standard time structured in twenty-four time zones. Over the centuries, time has been anchored to matter and standardized more and more. From a cosmic, dynamic time we went to a material static time, so to speak. Some connection to the Universe and the "whole world" got lost in the process.

A standard time has many advantages, because it makes trains run on time and enables us to make international appointments and start on time when doing a job. Starting at the same time is a condition for coherence. Modern life is unthinkable without standard time. It is interesting that this "freezing of time" coincided with the development of a worldview in which everything consists of particles that move in a predictable way, and in which man is present as an outsider.

Since the development of quantum mechanics, we know that this worldview is not correct. The whole Universe consists of energy, information, and consciousness. Everything is inseparably connected. Our consciousness and our perception have influence on our material reality. In that sense our perception can therefore also influence the pulsation of the cesium-atom. That means that standard time is actually not static but relative. This relative time is the subject of the relativity theory of Albert Einstein.

Relative Time

Albert Einstein formulated his theories of relativity at the same moment in time that quantum mechanics was being developed. According to these theories, space and time are connected, and movement and gravity have influence on the course of time. Based on his theories of relativity, in 1905 Einstein predicted certain effects of this influence, and his theories were confirmed by experiments in the 1960s and 1970s.

Einstein's theories say that time goes more slowly in the vicinity of massive objects, like the earth, because of the effect of their gravity. This means that for someone at a great height—a tower or the top of a mountain—where they are farther from the center of the earth, time goes faster than for someone at sea level. This prediction was tested in 1962, with the help of two very accurate clocks—one at the foot of a water tower and one on top. As it turned out, the clock that was closer to the earth did indeed go more slowly. This was in complete accordance with the general theory of relativity.

Practically speaking, this would mean that if you have twins, and one moves to a mountain top while the other stays at sea level, the one on the mountain will age faster. If they get together again later on, one of them will be ever so slightly older. In this case the age difference is very small and not noticeable. In space, however, these small time differences play a huge role in communication with satellites above the earth and an even greater role with space probes on the way to other planets in our solar system. Thanks to Einstein's theories we can explore space.

Letting the Clock Tick More Slowly

Returning to the metaphor of the wheel, Einstein's theories could mean that the closer you are to the center, the slower time moves, so you have more time to get a job done at the center than on the perimeter of the wheel.

The influence of the direction of movement on time was researched in 1971. Two very fast jet airplanes both had a very accurate atomic clock built into them. A third clock remained on the ground at the starting point. At the start of the experiment, all clocks were synchronized. Both airplanes flew around the world in opposite directions. One flew in the direction of the rotation of the earth, while the other flew in the opposite direction.

When the experiment was over, the clock on the airplane that had moved with the turning of the earth was slow in comparison to the clock that remained on the ground. The clock in the airplane that had gone against the earth's rotation was fast.

What this really means is that the subatomic processes in the atomic clock that flew against the turning of the earth went faster. We can safely think that this did not only happen in the clock; the movement had an influence on all the atoms in the plane. Everything went faster: the combustion, the rotation in the jet engine, and the life processes of the pilot as well. Biologically speaking, this means that the process of aging goes faster when an object—in this case a plane—moves against the rotation of the earth. The experiment proved Einstein's assumption that the direction of the movement influences time. The greater the ground speed, the faster time goes. Against the flow, time accelerates; with the flow, time slows down. In other words, time really "flies" at the periphery when compared to time at the center.

Making Time by Grounding

To summarize, we can say that time goes slowest at the center of the wheel. When you are there, you "have time." Time goes even slower if you go with the flow while remaining anchored in the center. But how do you stay anchored at the center and go with the flow in the wheel at the same time?

You do this by being well grounded energetically. Being well grounded means being connected to the center of the earth at any given time, which is the center of the largest wheel we are all turning in. The gravity is highest there, and time moves the slowest.

When you are well grounded you are also connected to your own, unique vibration or key note and you attract similar vibrations. If you are not grounded, or are unadjusted and false, you attract similar false vibrations. These false events and goals are usually not in agreement with your destiny.

With the help of relaxed concentration, inner peace, and meditation, you therefore literally make time. If you also go with the flow, you can give yourself even more time. Practically, this means that you ground yourself and surrender to the flow of life, and trustingly wait for the things that are about to happen. Don't put pressure on things—forget about all the "shoulds" or "musts." Nothing "has to" do anything in this world. Everything has the right to be there, and everything has its own pace. You can't make the grass grow faster by pulling it—though you can by thinking about it.

Natural Time and
the Rhythm of Life

To everything (Turn, turn, turn)
There is a season (Turn, turn, turn)
And a time to every purpose, under heaven
A time to be born, a time to die
A time to plant, a time to reap
A time to kill, a time to heal
A time to laugh, a time to weep.

— adapted by Pete Seeger from Ecclesiastes 3:1–8

Looking for Natural Time

Over the centuries we have created a standardized clock time that is the same for everyone. We know now that time is a relative concept. Motion, gravity, and our consciousness have influence on the course it takes. On top of that, we are able to lengthen or shorten our experience of time with good grounding and inner tranquility. The better you ground yourself and the more your inner rhythm synchronizes with the natural rhythms in the outer world, the more coherent you are and the more energy and time you have. Now I decided to search for a natural time. I had read about the calendar of the Maya, in which all sorts of cycles of time were described and in which there was talk of a natural time. Did this calendar give indications we could use for a coherent attuning between the outer and the inner world, and a life with more spare time?

Also, the relationship between a burdened past and my affirmations for the future was still not clear to me. If a relationship exists between the past and future, it means that time is not linear but cyclic. This is not a new or strange concept: Life is full of cycles—think of the course of a day or a year. The Maya calendar, too, is nothing but cycles.

I decided to study natural rhythms and the Maya calendar to unravel the riddle of time even more. By doing this I discovered an important connection between the Maya calendar and the formative force.

Turn, Turn, Turn

In 1952 the American folk singer Pete Seeger wrote the song "Turn, Turn, Turn (To Everything There Is a Season)," adapting text from the Bible. In 1962 he sang it in public for the first time. Many people were touched immediately by the lyrics and the melody. Many artists took the song into their repertoire and in 1965 the popular group The Byrds recorded a version of their own. Their beautiful vocal harmonies and the twelve-string electric guitar of David Crosby led to the song being a worldwide hit.

Few fans probably realized back then that they were singing verses taken from the Bible. "Turn, Turn, Turn" is a song about the cycles in time. There is a time to plant, a time to reap. There is a time to be born, a time to die. The song, therefore, is about the rhythm of life—a pattern that keeps repeating. All of life is rhythm, it is constantly moving, up and down, in one complex flow: your heartbeat and your breath, night and day, the surge of the seasons, the tides in human life. Without rhythm, life would be dull. You would only hear the ticking of the clock that beats time like a rigid metronome, and in between would be silence.

Music swings because of rhythm. A mambo has its own rhythm, just like a foxtrot or a waltz. The same applies to life, but while there are countless natural rhythms in life, the good and unique part is that all those cycles and patterns are in tune. In all its complexity, life is wonderfully coherent. Nature can do both the swing and the shuffle without losing its balance. Try to copy that!

By nature, life swings. We live in a cosmic dance and our partners—the stars and the planets, the seasons and the tides, the trade winds and monsoons, the shoals of fish and the migratory birds—all invite us to join in. All we have to do is to get aboard. Life is moving, and movement is best done in the flow. Movement in a natural rhythm takes the least energy. Better still, it gives you energy. Dancing in harmony with the spheres you can go on for hours, days, months, or years.

Biorhythms

Repeating cycles and patterns make up a rhythm. In the life of a human being, we can discern several cycles or phases. For instance, there is a phase of building in the first 21 years, a phase of strong vitality until the 42nd year, and diminishing vitality after that. In another model it is sometimes said that you start doing what you came to do on Earth at 33 years of age, you do your life's work until you are 66, and then you start reaping the fruits of your work in the third and last phase of your life.

There are big and small cycles, and long and short rhythms. Our body temperature has a rhythm of its own. In the morning your temperature is lower, and in the evening it is higher. You also need to take care of your heart rhythm. We saw before that a healthy heart rhythm helps us achieve inner balance and a better relationship with our surroundings. Disturbances in heart rhythm are more and more common nowadays.

According to many researchers, the so-called biorhythms have the most influence on us. They not only influence our body, they influence our feelings and mental abilities as well. According to Chinese medical science, at certain moments of the day some energies are extra active and others are more passive. In the West, in the late nineteenth and early twentieth century, physician Wilhelm Fliess and psychologist Herman Swoboda—and later, Alfred Teltscher—identified three dominant rhythms in our body. These biorhythms are:

1. The physical, masculine cycle (desire) of twenty-three days. It regulates physical strength, energy, perseverance, libido, trust, ambition, resistance, and the recovery from illness. In the building phase—as the energy in this cycle increases—you feel great. You are in prime condition, you are enthusiastic, and you can cope with the whole world. As the energy decreases, it is as if nothing works—you feel weak, and the workload seems heavy.

2. The feminine, emotional cycle (feeling) of twenty-eight days. This cycle is connected with emotional ups and downs, susceptibility, sensitivity, creativity, affection, and depressions. This cycle especially determines your emotional life, your sensitivity and how you deal with other people. In the ascending phase you have self-confidence and are accessible and optimistic; in the descending phase you are pessimistic and curt. In women, this cycle is sometimes synchronized with the menstrual cycle.

3. The intellectual cycle (thinking) of thirty-three days. This dominates the intellect, the memory, mental alertness, and logical thinking. In the build-up phase you are highly concentrated and can study effectively. In the let-down phase things don't go well; you are easily distracted and have difficulty concentrating.

Days to Take Care

The biorhythms in men and women are equally strong. All cycles start at the same time, when you are born. From that time they start ascending and after that go from a high to a low and a low to high rhythmically, in a fixed period.

As we mentioned earlier, when a cycle is ascending, the characteristics that are connected to it will increase positively. The opposite happens when the cycle descends. You are at your best when two or three cycles are at their apex, especially if they don't coincide exactly. When there are lows in two or three cycles at or around the same time, this can point to a period of listlessness or restlessness, and it may be better to take things easy at that time (see Figure 8.1).

FIGURE 8.1. Biorhythms
Reproduction of three biorhythms. There is a so-called critical or caution day when a wave goes through the middle horizontal line. In an ascending line there is one critical day, in a descending line there are two.

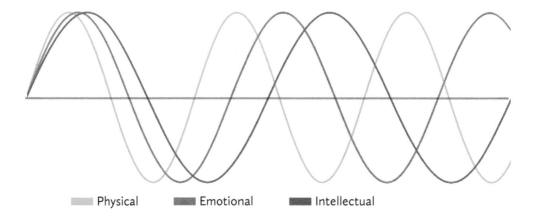

▬ Physical   ▬ Emotional   ▬ Intellectual

The day when a wave goes through the central, horizontal line is a so-called critical day, a time to be careful, a time when you are extremely vulnerable. In an ascending cycle there is one such day, in a descending cycle there are two of these days. Statistically speaking, you have a five times higher risk of disappointments and accidents. If two or three cycles cross the horizontal caution line at the same time, you really need to be on your guard.

Before the Internet was developed it was not very easy to figure out your biorhythms. Nowadays it is a piece of cake. Google "biorhythms," and you will get access to several sites that show you, within seconds, your future biorhythms.

Biorhythms cannot predict anything. All they do is show you what state you are in: when you are at a high or a low, when it is a day for caution. This gives you more insight into how you will be doing in days to come. By being aware of your caution days, you can diminish stress, accidents, and disappointments.

In Japan, biorhythms are an accepted part of life. Large insurance, aviation, and transport companies, as well as other industries and even the police, teach their employees to be conscious of their caution days. Some insurance companies even give their clients free biorhythm charts, hoping to reduce accidents. Several aircraft companies use extensive biorhythm programs for the work planning for their staff.

The Influence of the Full Moon

In the previous chapter we discussed how you have more time and possibilities to "make things work" if you are in the flow of life. Biorhythms are an example of this: Starting a risky enterprise during your caution days is not a very wise decision. But are there larger and perhaps even stronger natural rhythms?

The sun and the moon offer good examples. Both have great influence on our daily life. Not only do they influence the cycles of day and night, and the tides, but they also influence all life processes on earth. This is the reason our sense of time was directly connected to sunrise and sunset for centuries. In many cultures the cycles of the moon also play an important role in determining what happens during the year and the way human activities are attuned to the seasons.

By moving with the rhythm of the sun and moon you connect better to the natural flow of life. While everyone is aware of the rhythm of the sun, the moon is often forgotten. In his book *Bij heldere Hemel* (In a clear sky), Dutch biologist Willem Beekman provides numerous results from scientific research on the influence of the moon on plants, animals, and mankind.

He describes how researchers at Bradford University in England asked twelve hundred prisoners in Leeds to keep a diary. The conclusion of the study was that during a full moon there was a sharp rise in violence between the prisoners, and that the prisoners wrote that they felt miserable and aggressive considerably more often. American researchers studied 1887 murders in Dade County in the period 1956 to 1970. They concluded that psychologically "colored" crimes like murder, arson, and kleptomania occur more often during a full moon, even when it is cloudy and there is no moon to be seen. According to Beekman, similar results were found in Florida and Ohio.

For centuries now there have been stories about werewolves who appear when the moon is full. Whether the stories are true or not, those nights are definitely more turbulent and exciting. Research has established that we have more stress hormones in our blood when the moon is full or new.

The Maya Calendar

You can read the sun time from the cyclic movement of the sun and moon across the heavens. In our solar system, however, several planets orbit the sun. Sometimes they are close to earth, and at other times they are quite distant. In addition to that, we all travel through the Milky Way along the different signs of the zodiac. There are cycles within cycles and influences on influences. Everything is energy, and everything is connected. The flow of life is influenced by everything in the Universe.

All those cycles can make your head spin, and, all things considered, it is complicated to find your way through this. A good way of not only tuning yourself in to the flow of life but to cosmic time as well is the calendar of the ancient Maya. They lived, as they do today, on the Yucatán peninsula in Mexico, and their calendar, which dates from the period from 2000 BCE to 250 CE, connects the sun and cosmic time to our daily life. In this calendar all natural cycles revolve like wheels within wheels through and within each other, which is called natural time.

The early Maya did something that seems next to impossible: They developed a calendar system that is the most advanced in the world, and with it they calculated, without the help of computers and software, the movement of the Earth and of our whole solar system in relation to the center of our own Milky Way system. The ancient Maya knew the duration of the average solar year with a precision of several decimal points. Their Venus calendar was accurate to within two hours in five hundred years. Every cycle in the Maya calendar has a fixed length, and because the lengths of the cycles vary, it takes 18,900 days, or 52 years, to run through all the combinations. Every day has a unique character with its own unique energy. Using the Internet and your date of birth, it is quite easy to determine your "Maya-seal," much as you might get a horoscope. After that you can see how the cosmic wind will blow for you in the time to come.

The Maya were not only able to predict the character of the seasons and the course the year would take, they also had great insight into the beginning and ending of long, cosmic cycles. According to them, such moments are accompanied by special events on Earth. I give extra attention to the Maya calendar, not only because of the cyclic and predicting character but also because it gives us more insight into the structure of time.

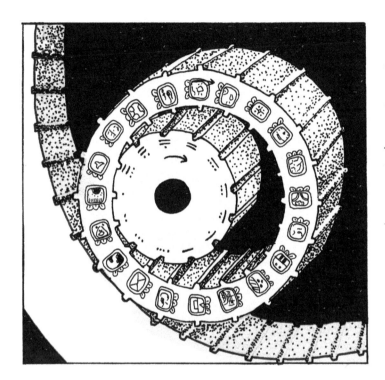

FIGURE 8.2. The Maya calendar consists of wheels within wheels. *The innermost wheel has the shortest cycle of 13 days. This turns in a wheel with 20 days. Both wheels together form the Tzolkin, the holy year, with 260 days. The Tzolkin wheels turn around in the big wheel of the Tun, the year of the sun/solar year, with 360 days.*

The Cycles in the Maya Calendar

The shortest cycle and the smallest wheel in the Maya calendar is a period of 13 days. This wheel turns inside a larger wheel of 20 days, and this is the origin of the *Tzolkin*, a Holy year of 13 × 20 = 260 days. This spiritual calendar was used for the planning of rituals and religious festivals. For "outdoor" life, like the sowing and reaping of crops, the Maya used a second calendar, the *Tun*. This had 18 months of 20 days; that is, 18 × 20 = 360 days.

As Figure 8.2 shows, the wheel of the Tzolkin year turns inside the wheel of the greater Tun year, and these wheels are actually like gears. When both these wheels run together, you get a complex "clockwork" that returns to its starting position after a very long orbit/revolution. In fact, it takes 18,980 days for the spiritual calendar of 260 days and the sun calendar of 360 days to return to this starting position. That is precisely 52 terrestrial years. If you divide 18,980 by 260, you get 73. A Maya cycle, therefore, lasts 52 terrestrial or 73 holy years. At that age, you have lived through all of the possible combinations of the different energies. According to the Maya, you are then an elder or sage.

Life, however, doesn't stop at 52, and the Maya calendar looks further into the future as well. There is an even longer cycle, with an even larger wheel, along which the Tzolkin and Tun run. That is the so-called Long Count. At the end of this cycle of 26,000 years, our solar system, our sun, and our planet will be in alignment with the heart of the Milky Way or, more accurately, with the equator of our Milky Way.

The Maya had knowledge of the precession of the equinoxes. They calculated it with the help of the Tun of 360 days. In their calculations it will need 26,000 × 360 = 9,360,000 days. The Maya divided the precession of 26,000 Tun into five large parts that are called the Long Counts. A Long Count lasts for 5,200 Tun, or 5,125 of our calendar years. The Long Count at hand is the fifth and last of a Great Cycle of almost 26,000 years, and it started on the 11th of August, 3114 BCE, and ended on the 20th of December, 2012 CE.

The winter solstice of 2012 therefore not only marked the end of a cycle of 5,125 years but also the end of an even larger cycle: the year of precession that started 26,000 years ago. Earth then started her journey along the twelve signs of the zodiac. When we crossed the threshold of the galactic equator in 2012, we not only started a new era of 5,125 years, but we also completed a year of precession along all the constellations of the zodiac.

In 2000 the world celebrated the birth of a new millennium with huge parties and fireworks. The extremely rare phenomenon that both large cycles in the Maya calendar ended simultaneously in 2012 was in a way more significant than the start of the new millennium. These are truly remarkable times.

The Wave of Time

The Aztecs of Central Mexico shared the Maya belief that the Universe consists of huge waves of energy that manifest as cycles of time. Every cycle has a unique character based on the wave that carries it. As the wave ripples through creation, its movement synchronizes nature, life, and time. Universal consciousness and human consciousness evolve step-by-step over these long periods of time. This development of consciousness has a cyclic character. Wheels of time turn within wheels of time. These cycles are depicted in the Maya calendar.

According to the Maya, every new cycle gives us an opportunity to rise above the way in which we think, which may have limited us in the past. Thanks to their insight into these great energy waves and cycles, the old Aztec and Maya timekeepers knew that this period in our history marks the end of a great cosmic era but is also the new beginning we have all been waiting for for so long.

If time is a wave, then what does that wave look like? In 1913 mathematician Eli-Joseph Cartan (1869–1953) came up with a new form of mathematics that could clarify some of the mysteries of space-time that were left open by Einstein's relativity theory. The result was the "Einstein-Cartan Theory," which describes space-time as something moving in a special way, following a special path, and then creating a special effect. The path is a spiral, and the effect is what is called a torsion field.

Torsion Fields

What is a torsion field? During the past few decades, several Russian physicists, among them Anatoly Akimov, have proven that every life form and every substance has a subtle energy field. They call this a "torsion field." According to them, this revolving energy field, which has the form of a vortex, is the result of all the miniature vortexes that all matter is made of. These torsion fields provide the information with which physical matter is formed.

According to Russian researchers, the torsion field consists of information, but there is also a subtle, bioscalar energy that amplifies the way in which the information works. In her article "Bioscalar Energy: The Healing Power," Valerie Hunt describes that this bioscalar energy is the same as *ch'i*, *prana*, or life energy. Bioscalar energy is static, has no frequency, and can therefore not be measured with the devices we commonly use today.

From the connection of information with the bioscalar energy, bioscalar waves originate and form the torsion field. These scalar waves exist in physical reality and beyond space and time. As such, they are conveyers of information between the various levels of reality.

From the Russians' research we know that torsion fields interact with other torsion fields, and in doing so exchange information. Also, torsion fields are dynamic systems that are permanently subject to interaction, influences, and changes that are conveyed through resonance. Physical changes in substances or life forms are said to be the result of changes in the torsion field. The human energy field is also a torsion field that can interact with other torsion fields and thus exchange information.

The Relationship Between
the Formative Force and the Torsion Field

From the above, it would appear that the formative force and the torsion field are probably the same. Both use life energy and information, shape matter, and are the basis of all forms.

The torsion field is generally depicted as a vortex, while the formative force has been imagined, so far, as a flat spiral. A vortex is a three-dimensional spiral. Could it be connected to the Wheel of Life?

I then remembered the depiction of the morphic field as a triangle (see Figure 8.3). Information revolves, evolves in the morphic field. If the triangle is another representation of the morphic field, then the information revolves in that too. This revolving causes an eddy, or vortex, and this vortex is the torsion field!

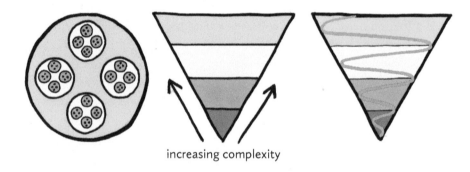

increasing complexity

FIGURE 8.3. The morphic field contains scripts with information.
It can be depicted as an upturned triangle. The complexity of the scripts increases toward the top. The morphic field revolves. This is the torsion field with the formative force.

The only—and a big—difference is that the morphic field can be found everywhere—we call that nonlocal—whereas the torsion field is connected locally to an organism or organization. You could say that the torsion field and the formative force are local manifestations of the morphic field in connection to life energy.

Linear and Cyclical Time

Therefore the formative force is, in reality, not a flat spiral but a torsion field consisting of a vortex with information from the morphic field and bioscalar, or life, energy from the zero-point energy field.

The torsion field, and with it the formative force, is also associated with time.

The ancient Maya and Aztec saw time as a wave of energy that condenses as a spiral. It still baffles us where they got their knowledge, but recent research shows that it is not without foundation. Scientists like Cartan and Akimov confirm that the ancients were right. Russian scientist Dr. Nikolai A. Kozyrev also says that there is a relationship between torsion fields and the phenomenon of time. He calls the torsion field the "time wave."

Meanwhile, I kept thinking: How can I connect this with the Wheel? I stared blankly at the Wheel until I was dizzy, hoping to discover the connection. It didn't get any easier when I looked at the two forces again: the blue, center-seeking formative force comes from the future and the red, centrifugal expansive force points to the past (see Figure 8.4). Perhaps this is the way in which the wheel connects the past, present, and future?

I thought that it was a nice image, but I suddenly realized that I had another problem: This image suggests time is linear. You come from the past, are in the present, and go to the future. As mentioned earlier, life is a push and pull. The past pushes if it is unburdened, and the future pulls, provided it is well anchored. When time is linear, that is the only connection between the past, present, and future.

The Maya calendar, however, is based on the idea that natural time passes in rhythmic cycles that are like wheels turning within wheels. In a wheel or circle, the

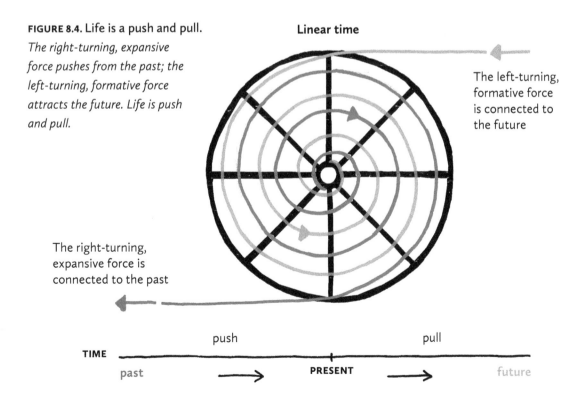

FIGURE 8.4. Life is a push and pull. *The right-turning, expansive force pushes from the past; the left-turning, formative force attracts the future. Life is push and pull.*

Linear time

The left-turning, formative force is connected to the future

The right-turning, expansive force is connected to the past

push   pull

TIME

past   →   PRESENT   →   future

beginning and end are connected. That means that there is a connection between the past and future in a time cycle—they are in contact with each other. What you have done or not done in the past not only has influence on the present but, according to cyclic time, will also have influence on your future. The French say, "*L'histoire se répète*": History repeats itself. A burdened past is not only a hindrance to your current development, it also casts its shadow onto your future.

You can imagine the Maya calendar, like the morphic field, as wheels within wheels. The cycles in the Maya calendar are connected with the scripts in the morphic field. If you didn't understand the story the first time, or if you haven't executed what the blueprint said, then it will come around a second and, if necessary, a third, fourth, or fifth time, until you understand how things work. Everyone on earth has a job to do and a lesson to learn.

A Donut, a Torus, and a Side View

There is a saying that the darkest hour is the one before the dawn. I woke up one morning and the solution to the problem was staring me in the face. It was so simple that I didn't understand why I had overlooked it for so long. All I had to do was put the wheel on its side. When you look at it from the side instead of from the top (see Figure 8.5), you see two vortices! I took a pen, and the next thing I did was to connect the past to the future. And *violà*, we had a time wave!

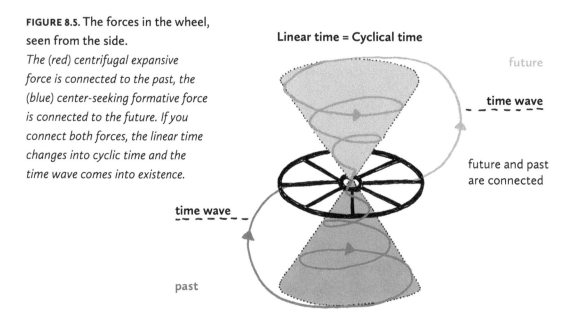

FIGURE 8.5. The forces in the wheel, seen from the side.
The (red) centrifugal expansive force is connected to the past, the (blue) center-seeking formative force is connected to the future. If you connect both forces, the linear time changes into cyclic time and the time wave comes into existence.

Linear time = Cyclical time

future

time wave

future and past
are connected

time wave

past

But there was more. In a flash I understood the meaning of what I had just drawn. The quest with the wheel had taken me to a point I had never dreamt of reaching: This was not just a drawing, this was a torus and a reproduction of space-time!

Quantum physicists have discovered that the quantum waves of which matter consists turn around in circles and move like vortices. These vortices are composed of two opposed spirals that amplify one other. The result is a complex combination of sphere-shaped spiral movements that is constantly turning itself inside out (see Figure 8.6). Physicists and mathematicians call this a torus. Such a revolving torus has a "donutlike shape"; that is, it is a sphere with a hole in the middle.

This donut behaves like a mini-magnet with an axis in the middle and a negative and a positive pole at the ends. The donut, in turn, is part of a larger system of vortex movements. In fact, it is an interdimensional vortex consisting of many layers. In the way an onion has layers, there are tori within tori. You can compare it to a set of Russian nesting dolls.

A torus stores energy and information and transforms these into a (life) form. The form and the properties of this donut-shaped field that both devours itself

FIGURE 8.6. The torus
From two opposed vortex movements a rotating torus originates that returns to itself and amplifies itself. This is the basic structure of space-time and of all energy systems in the micro- and macrocosm.

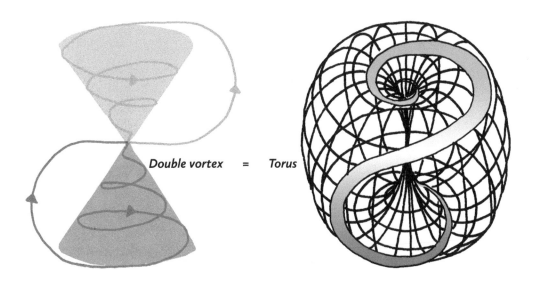

Double vortex   =   Torus

and then spits itself out are quite similar to what the Russian researchers describe as a torsion field. Meanwhile science had discovered that a torus is seen not only at sub-atomic level but also in the Universe; for instance, in the form of a galaxy. Some scientists even regard the torus as the basic structure of all energy systems in the micro- and macrocosm. We could, in fact, consider the world as built from tori that are nested in each other.

A torus consists of energy that has been brought to vibration by information. So every torus has its own unique vibration. Tori that are nested in each other all have the same vibrational frequency or a harmonic of it. Therefore they are in resonance and amplify each other. All things in the Universe are connected by this resonance. In that way tori connect the infinitely small to the infinitely large.

Space-Time and the Circle of Life

My quest had begun with the discovery of the formative force and the wheel as metaphor for creation. The Wheel of Life not only depicts your own life, in which you, as the driver, are on your way to your destiny, but it also represents the Universe and the whole world. It describes the balance between yin and yang in the smallest particle and the largest whole. And it turns out to be more than an ancient symbol: It consists of two vortices that create a donutlike shape together. This form, the torus, is, according to the latest scientific discoveries, the proto-form of the Universe and Endless Space or, in the words of Einstein, space-time.

What is space-time? We know that you cannot perceive time directly. The only way we can describe time is through the events that happen inside it. Also, time, space, and the events that happen in time are closely knit—you cannot separate time from the events themselves; in essence they are the same. It is, therefore, even scientifically acceptable to consider time as a material substance.

Newton saw time as an absolute. Time is what it is and is not influenced by the Universe or by events. This perspective was changed by Einstein's work (see Figure 8.7). To put it simply: Time is part of the Universe and cannot be separated from the space in which it travels. Space and time are connected; they cannot be separated and are two sides of the same coin. And together they form space-time.

The torus creates matter and everything in the Universe that has taken shape and space. At the same time, the spirals of the torsion fields are the waves of time. The torus is therefore the perfect image of space-time. The time wave of the future condenses like a spiral from the outside inward, from time-matter to subtle matter, in order to manifest in the center of the torus, in the center of the wheel, in the here and now, as a gross matter (life) form. This condensing process is also known as implosion.

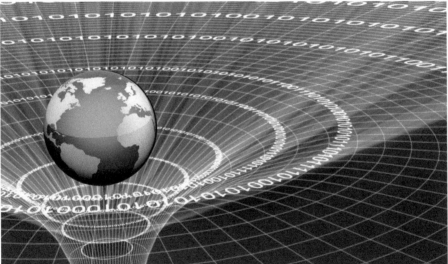

FIGURE 8.7. Newton and Einstein

Newton saw time as an absolute quantity. According to him, space and time have no influence on each other. According to Einstein, time and space are connected; the stronger the gravity, the more space condenses and the slower time moves.

After that, the two forces change poles; the material form decays and becomes the past. Gross matter is broken down step-by-step by the rotations of the lower spiral to very small subtle matter particles that flow back to the future on the outside of the torus as time-matter. That is the endless cycle of life, or "the circle of life."

Spirals and Paths in Time

9

I had found the connection between the formative force and the torsion field before this, but now the formative force was also connected to a time wave. This wave condenses step by step in the shape of a spiral. Matter transforms from time-matter to subtle matter to gross matter. The future therefore gets more and more concrete when it comes closer. If time and the formative force condense like a spiral, are those condensed, material spirals visible in our gross matter reality?

Yes, you can see spirals everywhere in nature. In fact, they are the proto-pattern for a large part of the Universe. If we start with large things, like galaxies, and work toward the smallest things, which are invisible to the naked eye, it becomes clear that the spirals of space-time are crucial to the code of nature: spiral-shaped weather systems, water that runs down the sink, tornados, hurricanes and whirlwinds, sunflowers, seashells, and so on.

The presence of these gross matter spiral shapes in nature suggests that the time waves do, indeed, follow the paths of spirals. In our 4-D world we experience those paths as cycles in time. The things that happen in your life and in the world can now be seen as places that manifest themselves along these expanding spirals of time. It doesn't make a difference if you speak about this time in terms of seconds, years, or ages; you can measure, calculate, and even predict those places with the Maya calendar.

We have discussed before that the past pushes and the future pulls. However, we now know that time is cyclic and the past and future are inseparably connected. The Maya studied these short and long cycles, worked out the length of some of them, and showed that the cycles are based on a spiral. They believed that if you know where you are in that spiral and know the moment of the origination event that set a cycle into movement, you would be able to predict when the conditions of the past will repeat themselves in the future.

The theory of morphic fields says that if an event took place once, chances are that it will take place a second time. This is especially true if the event was intense and charged or burdened. Every repetition makes the imprint bolder in the script of the morphic field and makes the attractor stronger. Chances that such an event will repeat itself in the future will therefore increase. So far, however, it is unknown when it will happen. Sheldrake's theory doesn't mention it, nor will you find anything about it in the literature about zero-point energy or life energy.

As described on pages 98–100, the scripts in the morphic field rotate like the wheels of the Maya Calendar, so it will take a while before the script returns to its point of origin. This venue is the moment the event happened in the past. However, because of the turning of the wheel, some time has passed, and you have arrived in the future.

The questions are therefore: What does such a spiral look like? And what kinds of spirals are there in nature? Natural spirals can teach us more about the spirals in time, and with this knowledge, you will be able to say more about the cycles that connect you to the past and also about the moment when you start a new cycle—with an affirmation, for example—and about the moment it will probably become reality in the future.

Spirals

A coiled rope, the spring of a clock, a carton of toilet paper. Wherever you look—in the air or in the water—and whatever you do—whether you cut a cabbage or count the seeds of a sunflower—you will find spirals. Spirals are everywhere, from your fingerprints to galaxies. Some are obvious, others are obscure, but they are there, hidden in the tiniest detail or radiant in the largest whole.

There are many kinds of spirals. The two most common are the Archimedean spiral and the logarithmic spiral. In the first, named after Greek mathematician Archimedes, the distance between any two points on the spiral curve, as measured on any ray from the center, is always the same. Examples are the coils in a watch spring and the grooves in very early gramophone records. Spiral staircases, screws and bolts, and stripes on a stick of candy are 3-D versions of this spiral. Most human-made spirals are of the Archimedean kind.

The logarithmic spiral (see Figure 9.1) is different. In this spiral, the radial distance

FIGURE 9.1. The Nautilus squid shell is one of the best known examples of a Fibonacci spiral.

FIGURE 9.2. The little flowers in a sunflower grow in Fibonacci spirals. *The number of left-turning and right-turning spirals are always Fibonacci numbers: 21 and 34, 34 and 55, 55 and 89, 89 and 144.*

(as measured on any ray from the center) between the curves increases by a constant factor. A special case of this is the Fibonacci spiral. Here the constant factor of increase is the infinite number *phi* (1.618033988749895…). This number is found in the Fibonacci sequence, which I discuss more in the next section. The Fibonacci spiral can be seen everywhere in nature, in the shape of galaxies, in whirlwinds, vortices, shells, pinecones, sunflowers (see Figure 9.2), the horns of animals, and our body.

The Fibonacci Sequence and the Number *Phi*

The Fibonacci sequence, or series, consists of the following numbers:

0, 1, 1, 2, 3, 5, 8, 13, 21, 34, 55, 89, 144, 233, 377 …

This series is derived by adding any two sequential numbers to get the next number. So:

0 + 1 = 1, 1 + 1 = 2, 2 + 3 = 5, 5 + 8 = 13, and so on

Using the formula above, the series would continue after 377 as follows:

233+377=610, 377+610=987, 610+987= 1597, and so on

As the numbers get larger, sequential numbers move toward being in the same proportion, for example:

610/377 = 1.618, 987/610 = 1.618, 1597/987 = 1.618, etc.

Mathematicians express this by saying that the ratios of successive numbers in the Fibonacci series converge on the value 1.618, which is what you get when you round down the special infinite number called *phi* (1.618033988749895…), also often called the golden ratio or the golden mean.

As I looked for the shape of the time spiral, I thought the Fibonacci spiral may be suited for this, because the golden ratio and the Fibonacci sequence are found in many places in nature and in human art and design.

Seen in three dimensions, this spiral is a vortex. As we discussed in the previous chapter, a torus consists of two identical vortices that rotate in opposite directions. The lower vortex, the material one that manifests itself in space, is most likely based on the Fibonacci spiral, because we see its shape all around us in nature. As the lower and the upper vortex are identical, one can presume that the upper is also a Fibonacci spiral. The upper vortex is the formative force, which is connected to the future. This would mean that events in the future happen according to the Fibonacci series.

As the table below shows, you will not find the exact number *phi* in the small steps in the beginning. The ratios are less constant there, in fact in the first six there is no agreement. From step ten (from 89/55) onward, however, the sequence follows *phi* very closely, approaching 1.618 more and more.

1	1/1	= 1
2	2/1	= 2
3	3/2	= 1.5
4	5/3	= 1.667
5	8/5	= 1.600
6	13/8	= 1.625
7	21/13	= 1.615
8	34/21	= 1.619
9	55/34	= 1.617
10	89/55	= 1.618
11	144/89	= 1.618
12	233/144	= 1.618
13	377/233	= 1.618
14	610/377	= 1.618
15	987/610	= 1.618

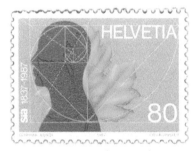

FIGURE 9.3. A modern application of the golden mean appears on a Swiss stamp.

The Fibonacci series is a good example of the sayings "all beginnings are difficult" and "perseverance pays." If you start something new, it often seems that you are getting nowhere in the beginning. During the first six steps the wheel sways and goes forward in fits and starts. From the tenth step onward, the ratio becomes a constant: The wheel turns with regularity and development takes its course. From step 12 (from 144 to 233) onward, the wheel runs at full throttle and moves forward with great leaps.

A derivative of *phi* is the so-called reciprocal value of *phi*, 0.618. This is the number you get when you divide 1 by 1.618. Both numbers (1.618 and 0.618) can be found not only in spirals but in all kinds of other shapes in nature and in our culture.

The Universal Measure for Space and Time

Since Einstein, we have known that space and time are connected. They are two sides of the same coin; if space condenses, time will go more slowly, if space expands, time will go faster. The things that surround us are, as it were, congealed time. If *phi* is the universal constant for all spatial forms, then perhaps *phi* is also the key to understanding the "shape" or "structure" of time, with events occurring or recurring at regular intervals of 1.618 or 0.618 units of time. Once again, it is unimportant whether these units are seconds, hours, weeks, months, or years. Time is a cycle, and *phi* keeps the rhythm.

In that case, *phi* not only determines the measurements or ratio of a shape, it also governs *when* an event takes place or repeats itself. However, *phi* doesn't determine *what* happens at that moment, just as it doesn't determine whether a dolphin becomes a dolphin or a tiger becomes a tiger.

That information for the shape of dolphins is laid down in the script of the morphic field. *Phi* sees to it that this script rotates with regularity and manifests itself in congruency with other wheels at the right moment and in the right proportions in the material world. *Phi* lets the wheels go around with regularity, no matter what is in the scripts. *Phi* is therefore not a measure of information but of energy, of zero-point energy and life energy.

Time Is Money Is Energy Is Time

Time ticks by with the regularity of *phi* and coagulates in *phi*-determined shapes. The saying "time is money" is based on experience, because experience tells you how long a job will take and what you can put on the bill, but it is more than that: It is a universal truth. *Phi* is a template for time and for the "inflow" of life energy in material reality.

Time and life energy are therefore connected. This life energy condenses into material shapes. Money, which in days of old usually meant gold and silver, is a precious material. You can do a lot with it in this world, but it is basically nothing but condensed energy. Time, money, and life energy are the same. Time is money is energy is time is money is energy and so on.

The Time Code Calculator

But what about good luck and bad luck? I wanted to know if anything can be said about the moment these kinds of events take place. In any event, I now knew that there was a connection to the Fibonacci sequence and with *phi*.

In the book *Fractal Time* by Gregg Braden, I found an answer to my question. Braden also comes to the conclusion that time moves according to a Fibonacci spiral, and that the lengths of the cycles are connected with the number *phi*. In his book he describes a so-called "time code calculator" that enables you, with the help of *phi*, to calculate when an important event from the past will repeat itself in the future. The cycles of his time code calculator apply to both positive experiences of love and success, and to painful life lessons.

It is not the event per se that repeats itself, but, after a certain period of time, circumstances may be similar to what they were at the moment you had an important life experience. With the help of the time code calculator, you can prepare for things that are going to happen. Just as biorhythms predict days to be careful, Braden's calculator predicts, for example, when you should not get into a car if you had a car accident a certain number of years before, based on a factor of *phi*.

How does it work? Braden speaks of "seed events." These are the moments in life when you had a drastic positive or negative experience. These events usually occurred in your childhood or youth. In those years, many "seeds" are sown for circumstances that will affect the rest of your life. Your memories of your very first seed experiences usually fade away by the time you are mature, so just go back as far as you can in your memory to a moment of success or pain. Taking your age at the moment of the event as the basis, calculate the length of the cycle or recurrence by multiplying that age by 0.618 (the reciprocal of *phi*) and there you are—you have the length of your cycle. It is simple arithmetic.

You can calculate the cycle even more accurately if you know the month in which the event occurred. In order to make the calculation, you first need to convert months, which each represent 1/12 (8.333 percent) of a year into a decimal format. For example, three months are 3/12 = 0.25 of a year; six months = 6/12 = 0.50 of a year, etc.

If something drastic happened in your life when you were 11 years and 6 months old, you were 11.5 years old at the time. After how many years will the same circumstances recur?

11.5 × 0.618 = 7.1 years…add your original age, and you get 11.5 + 7.1 = 18.6 years.

So when you are about 18 years and 6 to 7 months old, circumstances will be such that you may experience something similar to what happened at the seed event. This cycle of 7.1 years will keep repeating, so look for recurrences when you are 25.7 (18.6 + 7.1), 32.8 (25.7 + 7.1), and so on.

While circumstances *may* lead to a repetition of the seed experience, there is no guarantee that it will happen, and it is rare that there is an exact repetition of the original situation. The important thing is to pay attention at the end of a cycle and try to uncover the pattern that is underlying the event. The wheel of life keeps turning and the conditions keep recurring until you recognize the underlying pattern of the seed experience and consciously break it. Ask yourself why you give yourself this experience over and over again? What lesson is life trying to teach you?

When you become conscious of this, the spell will break and the cycle will come to an end. Braden adds that if we don't recognize the underlying pattern and consciously break it, the pattern will repeat itself with greater intensity at later dates. According to the theory of morphic fields, this is right: The pattern gets stronger if it is imprinted and confirmed through repetition.

Gregg Braden gives several varieties of the time code calculator in *Fractal Time*. You can also find information about it on his website, www.greggbraden.com, including a software program that allows you to input your data and find out the length of the time cycle for your critical or "seed" event.

Open-Ended or a Dead End?

The time code calculator tells you when the circumstances or conditions of your seed event are going to be repeated. Your date of birth is your zero point and, as we said, your age at the moment of the event determines the length of the cycle, which repeats with a *"phi"* regularity if the cycle is open-ended. Everything comes to an end, however—life on Earth is not open ended, everything has an end.

As a cycle passes through time and nears the end, the end becomes more important than the beginning. At the age of eighty you are more concerned about death and not so much about your childhood. That doesn't only apply to someone's personal life but also to worldwide cycles, like those calculated with the Maya calendar. The cycles in time are a consequence of an underlying spiral. As a spiral goes into its center, the coils get shorter. As far as that is concerned, it may be taken for granted that certain cycles in time get shorter as the end gets closer. That will certainly be true in a cycle that is based on an important pattern for/in your personal development or the worldwide development of humankind. An important cycle like that shortens by 0.618 every time.

In the example I provided, there was a seed event at 11.5 years. The cycle that came from it lasts 7.1 years. As the end of the cycle draws near, this cycle shortens by 7.1 × 0.618 = 4.4 years, and after that by 4.4 × 0.618 = 2.7 years, then by a period of 2.7 × 0.681 = 1.7 years, and so on.

Life will point out the facts stronger and more often until in the message is received. You cannot sit out the cosmic dance if it concerns the development of consciousness—you will get a push in the right direction again and again.

The Elliott Wave Principle

Gregg Braden based his time code calculator on the work of R.N. Elliott, an American scientist and philosopher. Between 1938 and 1946 Elliot wrote a number of impressive essays and scientific articles on the way in which a few special laws of nature rule many aspects of daily life, including the cycles of nature. The highlights of his work were re-published in 1994 with the title *R.N. Elliott's Masterworks*.

In the 1970s two stock-market forecasters, Robert R. Prechter Jr. and A.J. Frost, discovered Elliott's work. Using Elliot's principles that the world economy and the stock exchange are indicators of optimism or pessimism within the world of investors, and that natural cycles are also involved, Prechter and Frost elaborated on Elliott's ideas and designed a highly successful instrument for predicting developments in the market based on the history of the New York Stock Exchange.

Their book, *The Elliott Wave Principle*, was published in 1978 and is still widely in use. You can find a lot of information and workshops on this subject on the Internet. The success of the Elliott Wave Principle is based on two assumptions:
  1. The market will always rise and fall in exact intervals. These are the waves of the Elliott Wave Principle.
  2. If you know where the rise starts, you can calculate when and how often the falls will occur.

I knew about the Elliott Wave Principle before reading Gregg Braden's book, but I had always regarded it as an instrument for people who wanted to get rich quickly. I had never looked at it as being applicable to the development of other parts of our big whole. Gregg Braden's work aroused my interest in the Elliott Wave Principle, and I am grateful to him because that led to a number of important discoveries about the relation between time and the realization of affirmations as described in Chapter 6.

The Up-and-Down Waves According to Fibonacci

What exactly are the waves of the Elliott Wave Principle? Elliott discovered that the price of a share of stock rises and declines according to a specific basic pattern. This is illustrated in Figure 9.4 on the next page. Every development starts with a pattern consisting of 8 segments, waves, according to Elliot: first a rise of 5 waves, followed by a decline of 3 waves. Inside these 5 and 3 waves, there are further rising and declining waves, with a rise always followed by a decline.

After these 8 waves, development goes on. The first "eight wave" is followed by a second, but then something new happens: The third step in development starts as usual with 5 steps up, but then it doesn't decline in 3 but in 5 steps. A fourth "eight wave" follows, but this goes backward: There is a rise of 3 waves, followed by a decline of 5. The result is a rising tendency of 21 waves, and after that, a decline of 13 waves. This second important basic pattern consists of 21 + 13 = 34 waves, and is illustrated in Figure 9.5 on the next page.

According to Elliott, the second basic pattern is the most important, but there is also a third pattern, which is the largest and longest pattern. It starts with a rising tendency of 89 waves followed by a decline of 55 waves, for a total of 89 + 55 = 144 waves (see Figure 9.6 on page 118). There are no more waves after that.

Elliott's work showed that the golden number *phi* turns up everywhere. He also found it in the basic patterns of market development, where *phi* is hidden in the sequence of the number of rising and declining waves, which follows the Fibonacci sequence perfectly. A rise of 5 is followed by a decline of 3 waves. That makes 8 waves together. These are three consecutive numbers in the Fibonacci sequence. The next three numbers are 13, 21, and 34, and they are found in the second basic pattern. The third basic pattern consists of 89 + 55 = 144 waves. And there you are, if you put everything in line, you have an important part of the series of Fibonacci: 3, 5, 8, 13, 21, 34, 55, 89, and 144 (see Figure 9.7 on page 118).

Of course there are all sorts of variations on Elliott's basic patterns, and Prechter and Frost describe them at length in their book. Nowadays we have software, which makes it is even easier to recognize the Elliott Wave Principle and to predict the fluctuations of the stock market. I wasn't looking for money, however, but for more insight into cycles of time. I wanted to know when a wish that I desired with all my heart, and which I had projected into the future, would be granted.

FIGURE 9.4. The first Elliott Wave Principle, with 8 waves. A rise of 5 waves is followed by a decline of 3.

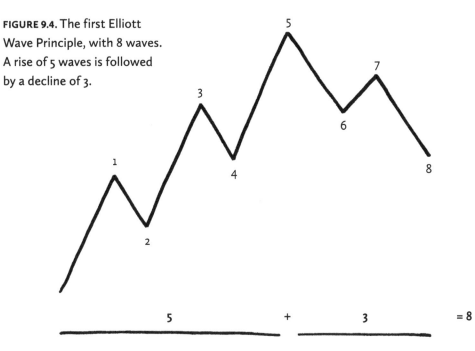

FIGURE 9.5. The second and most important Elliott Wave Principle consisting of 34 waves—a rise of 21 waves followed by a decline of 13 waves.

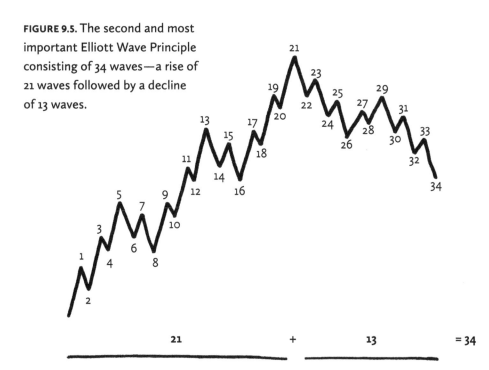

FIGURE 9.6. The third and longest Elliott Wave Principle consisting of 144 waves—a rise of 89 waves is followed by a decline of 55 waves.

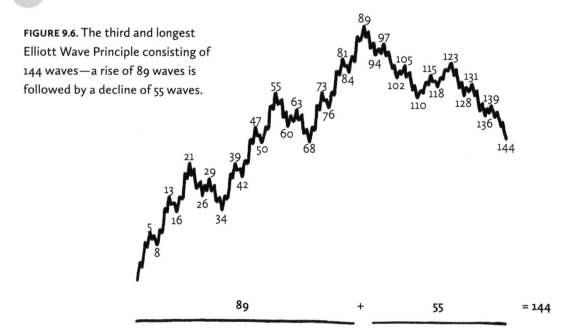

89   +   55   = 144

FIGURE 9.7. The first Elliott Wave Principle, which has eight waves.

Here the inward-focused formative force (blue) works strongest during the first five waves. The outward-focused expansive force (red), is strongest during the last three waves. In the end, there is more capital or life energy than at the beginning.

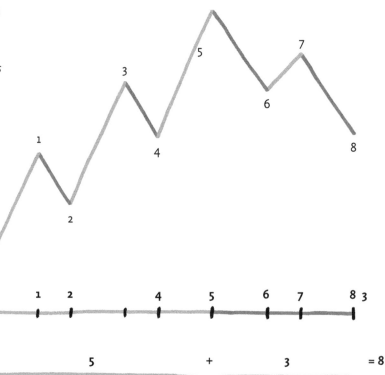

5   +   3   = 8

The Harmonic Factor: 34.560

According to Elliott, the basic pattern with 21 + 13 = 34 waves is the most powerful. He found this in practice, but he didn't have an explanation for it. I found the answer in the work of scientist Ray Tomes, who developed a theory that he calls "Harmonics Theory." Tomes worked for years on all sorts of economic models to be able to predict price fluctuations in trade goods. He discovered a cyclic behavior in the prices, which, as remarkable as it is, were related to the orbit time of planets. According to Tomes, the relation between these totally different phenomena is the harmonic factor 34.560. This connects everything in the Universe to everything else, from the quantum world to the huge Universe itself. For instance, if you take the average distance of all moons to their planets and multiply this by 34.560, you get the average distance between the planets. If you multiply this value by 34.560 again, you get the average distance between the stars and so on.

The factor 34.560 turns out to connect the proportion of the following objects from small to large: elementary particles, atoms, cells, moons, planets, stars, and galaxies. According to Ray Tomes, many cycles of time in the Universe are based on the number 34.560. Tomes' work confirms the importance of the second Elliott Wave Principle with its 21 + 13 = 34 waves.

The Buildup of Capital

The Elliott Wave Principle may be a successful instrument for making money in the stock exchange, but are the basic patterns described by the Principle also applicable to the development of other systems?

It is difficult to connect the rise and decline of share prices to the development of an organism, or the power of an affirmation, unless you think in terms of energy. As you know, everything is energy, even—as we said earlier in Chapter 6 and also in this chapter—money is condensed life energy.

The value of a share tells you something about the value of a company in hard currency. The stock exchange therefore determines the financial worth of a company, the capital it holds. With this capital a company can invest, produce, trade, communicate, and so on. In other words, it can conduct its business in the world and hopefully make a profit. If the company executes a new plan or project, the risk taken and the necessary investments will temporarily decrease the exchange rate of the shares and the capital. However, if the plan is a good one, the action will be rewarded and the capital will increase again.

So there is a perpetual alternation between internal planning and building up of capital, and external action and spending money. For a company, the financial capacity or capital it has determines its ability to act. For an organism, the ability to act is governed by the amount of life energy it has. If you connect this with the Elliott Wave Principle, it means that in a rising wave, the capital or amount of life energy of a system increases. Attention is focused inward at that time. This is followed by a declining wave. During this phase there is active work in the outer world. The attention is focused outward, and the life energy diminishes.

The Two Forces Related to the Elliott Wave Principle

It looks as though the rise and fall of Elliott Waves reflects the perpetual play of the two proto-forces: the constructive, feminine formative force and the destructive, masculine expansive force, which are present everywhere and in everything. According to the Elliott Wave Principle, the formative force, focused on the inner, is strongest in the rising waves, and the outward-focused expansive force is strongest during the declining waves (see Figure 9.8).

FIGURE 9.8. The second basic pattern of Elliott, which has 34 waves. *The working of the formative force is strongest during the first 21 waves. This is the time for inner work. This is followed by 13 waves, or time units, for outer work. During this time, the expansive force works best.*

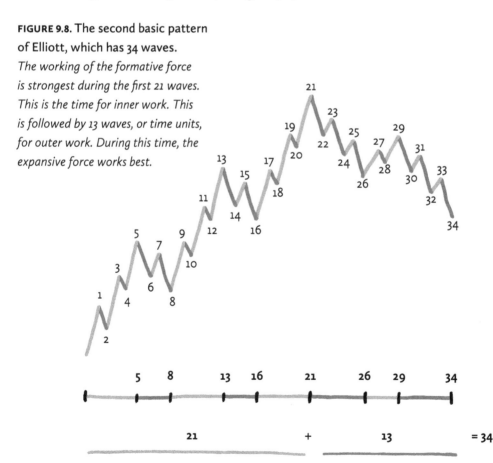

This made me think of the law of dynamic balance formulated by Marja de Vries. This law says that the two forces are present in everything but that there will be development only if the feminine formative force is stronger than the masculine force. To me this appears to be true. Whatever basic pattern of Elliott Waves you look at, the capital—the amount of energy at the end of the development—is greater than that at the beginning. This shows that after a phase of development, at the end of a cycle, the feminine formative force is still the stronger force.

Inner and Outer Work

The Elliott Wave Principle sheds a new light on the dynamics between these two proto-forces. His graphs not only show the rise and decline of stock prices and the amount of life energy but also how this development happens in time.

On the vertical axis is the value of the stock or the amount of life energy, and on the horizontal axis is the time. The length of a wave in Elliott's graph takes a certain amount or unit of time. In Elliott's day the time unit related to the exchange of stocks was one day, but now it is significantly less, because stocks can now be traded in a matter of milliseconds. In other, larger systems it could be a week, a month, or a year.

Regardless of the length of the unit of time, the rule in all cases, according to the second basic pattern, is that there is an increase of 21 and a decrease of 13 time units. This means that, if, for instance, the unit is a day, the formative force works strongest during the first 21 days, and the attention is focused mostly inward. This is followed by a period of 13 days, with action in the outer world.

Within the periods of 21 and 13 days, there are also days with a more outward or inward character. Look again at the second basic pattern (see Figure 9.8). During the first 21 days the attention is focused as follows: 5 days inward (rising waves), 3 days outward (declining waves), 5 days inward (rising), 3 days outward (falling), 5 days inward (rising). Then comes a period of 13 days with the accent on the outer world. The attention is focused outward (declining waves) for 5 days, inward (rising waves) for 3 days, and outward (declining) for 5 days.

In this way we have inner and outer work. During inner work the attention is focused inward and the feminine formative force works strongest. During inner work you will mainly be occupied with your inner development, with internal processes and the upper half of your spiral of creation. During outer work the attention is focused outward and the masculine expansive force is working full throttle. You suit the action to the word and execute your plans. During this phase you are active in the lower part of the spiral of creation.

Surfing on the Waves of Time

What does the Elliot Wave Principle mean for the affirmation of your future? Recalling the text from Ecclesiastes, there is a time for everything: There is a time for inner work and a time for outer work. The first period lasts 21 time units, and the second 13. To attract your future, you need to boost the formative force. It has now become clear that you get the best results during the first period with inner work. If everything gets on track energetically during that time, it is possible that your dream will come true during the second period of 13 time units.

If that does not happen, you go on to the third basic pattern, which has 144 waves (see Figure 9.9). According to that pattern there is a new period of 21 time units of inner work after the first 34 waves. After that, the second period of 13 time units of "harvesting time" starts. If by then your dream still has not come true, the phrase "the third time's the charm" applies: The last period of 21 units of inner work dawns, followed by the last and longest period of harvesting of 55 time units.

This is a time frame in which things can happen. It indicates the periods in which your heart's desire may come true. During the periods of outer work, you

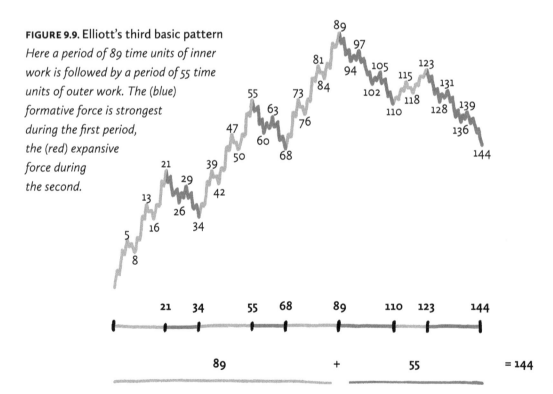

FIGURE 9.9. Elliott's third basic pattern
Here a period of 89 time units of inner work is followed by a period of 55 time units of outer work. The (blue) formative force is strongest during the first period, the (red) expansive force during the second.

must therefore pay extra attention to the signs the world gives you and the messages it sends.

The Time Is Right If You Are Ready

To realize your heart's desire, you also need expertise. You must be able to assess, in a realistic way, how much clock time is necessary to make your wish come true. The time is only right when you and the world are ready for it. Your castles in the sky will only manifest on earth when you have learned and done what you were supposed to.

Let's take an affirmation for getting a new house as an example. If you take a day as the time unit, that will mean, in practice, that after the first 21-day period of affirmation, the chances are good that your new home will come to you in the following period of 13 days. That would be great, of course, but you could have a problem if you haven't sold your old house yet or if other things need to be taken care of that are necessary for the move.

In that case it may be better to use a week as the time unit. Generally speaking, this is a good period for the affirmation of middle- and long-term goals. You have more time and space to prepare everything well. The first period of 21 weeks, which is roughly 5 months, can be mainly spent on inside work. You are at work in the upper half, and in the quadrant at the bottom right of the spiral of creation (see Figure 9.10 on the next page).

In the 13 weeks that follow, roughly 3 months, you look out for and seize any opportunities that come toward you from the outer world. In that period you are working in the bottom half, and in the quadrant at the top left of the spiral of creation.

If nothing has happened by then, it is important to take another look at your goals and affirmations. Give your efforts a fresh charge and start in on the second round of 5 months of inner work. Again this is followed by three months of harvesting. Once that period starts, you will have been looking for a new home for 5 + 3 + 5 = 13 months. That is not very pleasant, but it happens often.

In a "worst case scenario" you may have to wait for a new home for 13 + 3 + 5 = 21 months, almost 2 years, working at your affirmations all that time. You may begin to think, what have I gotten myself into? That is understandable, but have faith that there are natural cycles that will allow your dream to come true and it will, sooner or later. Better late than never, right?

On the other hand, the timeframe mentioned does not work like a tight schedule that only allows good luck to happen after five months. Life is always dynamic

FIGURE 9.10. Inner work

The (blue) formative force works strongest during inner work. During inner work, your attention is focused on the upper half of the spiral of creation. During that phase there are two short periods when the attention shifts outward. You are active in the bottom-right quadrant of the spiral of creation.

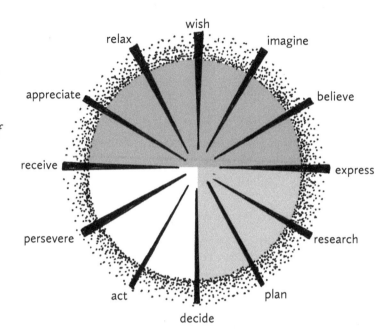

and surprising. The second basic pattern with 34 waves is the most powerful. In this cycle, 5 and 13 days of inner work are always followed by 3 days of outer work (see Figure 9.11). So stay on the lookout for signs of opportunity for action. Also, in every cycle an inner day is followed by an outer day. A miracle may therefore happen tomorrow.

FIGURE 9.11. Outdoor work

The (red) expansive force works strongest during outer work. During outer work your attention is focused on the lower half of the spiral of creation. During that phase there are two short periods when your attention goes out again. You are then active in the upper-left quadrant of the spiral of creation.

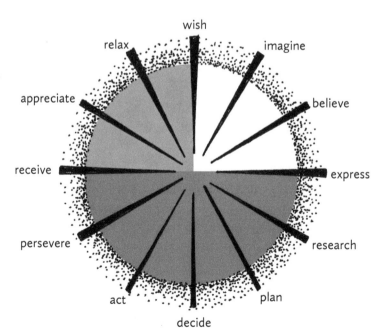

A Maximum of Thirteen Affirmations

Should you do affirmations every day? Does the Elliott Wave Principle say anything about the necessity for, and frequency of, affirmations?

At the beginning of this chapter we saw that according to the Fibonacci sequence, you have to do something at least 10 times before regularity sets in. During the first six steps the wheel jerks and goes forward in fits and starts. From the tenth step onward, the ratio becomes a constant: The wheel turns smoothly. From step 12 onward (from 144 to 233), the wheel runs at full throttle and goes forward with great leaps. The *phi* spiral and the wheel are turning at a regular pace. We also know that you must not exaggerate an affirmation, try to affirm the impossible. The idea is to try to create a blueprint for what *can* happen. If you push it too far, you may get something that will have a contrary effect.

From step 12 onward, the spiral has larger and more powerful coils. The wheel is then at full speed. Affirming and visualizing something twelve to thirteen times, with your heart and soul, is probably enough. The spiral and the wheel rotate at such a speed and are so powerful that they might go into overdrive if you affirm more than thirteen times.

So let us say you have twenty-one days or weeks to get your wheel up to full speed. During that time, you can only affirm your heart's desire a total of thirteen times. Affirmation once a day is generally enough to give the energetic push that is needed and to anchor your goal. The Fibonacci series shows us that the first six times are crucial to getting the wheel turning. Because the first five coils of the spiral don't approach *phi*, the wheel is unsteady as it goes forward and might even topple over.

This means that in the first five days or weeks you make the affirmations once a day, or once a week. A fixed time of day or a fixed day of the week is best. After that, only do your affirmations on the uneven days or weeks (7, 9, 11, 13, 15, 17, 19, and 21), as the formative force works best then. Together that makes 5 + 8 = 13 affirmations. And how long do these affirmations take? How many minutes? If one minute is your time unit, it is quite simple: Take no longer than 21 minutes, because after that time the formative force will diminish for 13 minutes. If you have less time—and are good at affirming your heart and soul, even 13 and 5 minutes are enough. The lower limit should be about 2 minutes of affirmation. This is also known as a short prayer.

Life Is a Meaningful Whole

To review: The Maya described time as a wave. Through study and reflection, I found this time wave, and many things fell into place because of that. I got even more insight into the functioning of the formative force and now also knew how it worked in time. I understood that I can do all the affirmations I want, but if that affirmation is not in agreement with my destiny, if the time isn't right and/or if a burdened past is still in the way, then nothing will happen.

Even in our darkest hour, life will let you finish this part of your road to your destiny before you can start the next cycle. Life has all the time in the world; it can wait. It is therefore not about finishing your job or saying what you have to say, but about becoming conscious of who you are and that you are reaching toward your destiny. In doing this, the road is your destiny, because along that road you get life experience and your consciousness will grow. In this way, becoming conscious will lead to higher consciousness.

Everything Has Consciousness

10 ⋮

"Becoming conscious leads to higher consciousness." This conclusion from Chapter 9 brought me back to where I started my quest. I had started with:

Life energy plus information plus consciousness generates a conscious formative force.
A conscious formative force plus matter generates a conscious life form.

The question that remained was: "What is consciousness and who am I?" That is what we will look at in the following chapters.

Consciousness

Every second about 500,000 cells in our body die. That makes over 43 billion cells a day. Luckily new ones are formed every moment, but everything in our body changes constantly. It is a good thing we don't really notice it and that we find great continuity in our life. That is the essence of consciousness. It is always there, while all else originates and decays.

What really is consciousness? Without consciousness there is no perception, no thinking, no feeling, no knowledge, no memory. We know there are different kinds of consciousness. We have, for instance, a subconsciousness, a self-consciousness, and a higher consciousness. Somebody who is in a deep and dreamless sleep usually doesn't experience consciousness, and somebody who is awake usually does. The latter is called everyday consciousness.

Since the beginning of the seventeenth century, this everyday consciousness has been increasingly linked to the intellect. In the year 1637 René Descartes wrote his famous line, "cogito, ergo sum" (I think, therefore I am). It marked an important moment in the development of human consciousness because, from that moment on, the separation of mind and matter became more commonly accepted, and people in the West began to see the surrounding material world as something separate. We no longer saw ourselves as part of a vast cosmic whole but as observers looking at a reality beyond ourselves from which we were disconnected.

This world invited us to think about it and to look for explanations for the many phenomena and processes we saw. This wonder and curiosity was, in many ways, the beginning of modern science, from which we still profit.

The Brain As a Receiver

Since the theories of quantum mechanics were formulated at the beginning of the twentieth century, the view that mind and matter are separate has been shaken to its foundations. We now know that our consciousness plays a crucial role in the perception and shaping of reality. Quantum mechanics has proven beyond a doubt that our consciousness creates our perceptions, and with them our reality. Perception is not an objective, passive account of reality but an active creation of our consciousness. This consciousness is all embracing, and reality as we experience it only exists in our consciousness and is at the same time influenced and eventually determined by it.

Until recently, consciousness was seen as an effect of processes in the brain. In his excellent book on near-death experiences, *Consciousness Beyond Life*, cardiologist Pim van Lommel proves beyond a shadow of doubt that the opposite is true: Consciousness is infinite. Based on his research into near-death experiences, recent results of neurophysiological research, and concepts from quantum physics he shows that consciousness is not restricted to a certain time and place. He calls this non-locality.

Non-locality suggests that consciousness is infinite; it is everywhere and is not bound by time and space. Past, present, and future are simultaneously present and accessible. This infinite consciousness is continuously in us and around us. The brain and the body are reception centers that receive a part of our total consciousness and part of our memory, leading to our awareness.

This non-local consciousness contains much more than our awareness. The brain actually limits our consciousness of ourselves and of reality. Rather than producing consciousness, the brain can be seen as a receiver–transmitter that facilitates consciousness, that makes it possible to experience consciousness.

There are also more and more indications that consciousness has a direct influence on the function and anatomy of the brain and the body. Our DNA probably plays an important role in this.

Van Lommel comes to the conclusion that this consciousness has always existed and will always exist, independent of our body. He sees consciousness as a prime characteristic of the Universe, always present everywhere, outside of space and time. The brain is a link between material reality and non-local space—where the morphic field and zero-point energy are also present.

Consciousness Beyond Life

This consciousness is all embracing, and all aspects of it are linked. Our awareness is an aspect of the all-embracing consciousness, as are the notions that we exist, that we can perceive something, or that we have memories. The fact that we can think about what we think or that we can realize that we are dreaming are yet other aspects of our personal consciousness.

Apart from the "ego," which has awareness, psychiatrist and psychologist Carl Jung distinguishes the "self," a broader aspect of personal consciousness around the ego that includes both the conscious and the unconscious part of the personality.

According to Van Lommel, there is also a universal or collective human consciousness that links every individual to everything that exists and to everything that has ever existed or will exist. This collective human consciousness can be compared to Jung's concept of the collective unconscious.

In his book *No Boundary*, Ken Wilber describes the infinite consciousness, also called unity consciousness or eternal consciousness. He describes this as the transpersonal self, or "the witness," which regards itself as being one with everything it perceives.

"But what you witness and what you experience is not you…" Wilber writes. "I have a body, but I am not my body. I have desires, but I am not my desires. I have feelings, but I am not my feelings. I have thoughts, but I am not my thoughts. Everything that remains is a pure nucleus of consciousness. I am. This consciousness rises above the individual and connects man to a world outside of time and space. This eternal consciousness differs from all other levels of consciousness because it embraces all levels of part-consciousness."

Wilber calls this borderless, infinite consciousness the "spiritual aspect of every human being." This consciousness is present at every moment. In the here and now there is no past and no future. The here and now has no beginning and no end, in it there is no border between self and non-self, everything is connected to everything else. The "perpetual now" or the "timeless moment" is consciousness. This consciousness is without boundaries and endless, and therefore every part of consciousness is also endless.

According to the philosopher Peter Russell, everything develops, and so does the Universe and with it consciousness. It is all in the mind. Everything we know, perceive, and feel is a shape that appears in the mind. It is all about informing the consciousness.

Full Circle

When I read this, I realized that my thinking had come full circle. Consciousness is the initiator of a formative force that connects to matter and manifests itself as a conscious life form. This consciousness gains experiences during its life in a material form. In human life, experiencing the outer world and interpreting this experience is a process of becoming conscious. If you do this well, you learn something from it. The process of experiencing or learning, in other words of becoming conscious, leads to a higher state of consciousness in the end.

If the way is the goal, it means that the goal in life is the development of consciousness to ever higher levels of consciousness. This would mean that not only is everything made of energy and information but also that everything has consciousness and that the development of this consciousness to a higher level is the aim of the Universe.

To summarize:

- Consciousness + life energy + information generates a conscious formative force.
- Conscious formative force + matter generates a conscious life form.
- The perceptions and firm convictions of this conscious life form generate reality.
- Living in this reality provides experiences.
- Experiences inform the consciousness and lead to becoming more conscious.
- Becoming conscious leads to attaining a higher consciousness.

Everything Has Consciousness

This means that everything has consciousness and that the development of consciousness in all life forms and everything else that appears as form contributes to the development of the infinite consciousness of the Universe.

Many animal lovers support the idea that dogs and cats have consciousness. A flock of birds doesn't act as if it is comprised of separate individuals but as a coherent unity with a group consciousness. As I mentioned previously, in an experiment by the French researcher René Peoc'h, a group of chickens was able to make a robot come toward them with their intention.

Cleve Backster became world famous in 1968 for his experiments with plants that he connected to a lie detector. As it turned out, the plants had a measurable response to the thoughts of people intending to harm or burn them. According to this experiment, trees might also have consciousness. For most of us this is taking it a bit far. Still, there are people like myself and many of my students who say that they can communicate with trees.

And if we go a bit further still, can we say that a company also has a consciousness or behaves as if it were an entity, a being? Is this really so? We know that many sailors talk about their ships as if they have a personality, and musicians sometimes name their instruments.

Renowned physicists like Freeman Dyson and philosophers like Alfred North Whitehead argue that even elementary particles are provided with a certain form of consciousness. Dyson says, "in quantum mechanics, matter is not a passive substance, but an active agent that makes choices between several alternatives all the time. It looks as though the mind, the way it shows in the ability to make choices, is to a certain measure inherent to every electron."

In his book *Science and the Akashic Field*, author Erwin Laszlo comes to the conclusion that certain forms of consciousness are present in all things in nature, and that there is no proof that consciousness is limited to our brain. According to him, there are no boundaries in the grand architecture of nature that would allow us to say, "beyond this there is consciousness, and before this there are only physical and chemical reactions." Everything has consciousness. The measure or complexity of the consciousness depends on the level of organization of the organism or system. The consciousness of matter at a lower level culminates in a more complex consciousness at a higher level.

Wheels Within Wheels

Let us take the position that everything has consciousness. Can we link that to our understanding of the Wheel of Life and the theory of morphic fields? The wheel symbolizes the Universe and every entity in it. It is a whole, a holon. As we saw in Chapter 4, a morphic field is organized in the same way as a holarchy. What do we see when we connect the picture of a holarchy to that of the wheel? A holarchy is comprised of "wheels within wheels." Every part, every holon in the morphic field, can be interpreted as a wheel. Each wheel has the script with information to organize itself.

As we learned in Chapter 3, the wheel has consciousness by way of a conductor: you, whether as the creating force of your life, the CEO of a company, or the manager or leader of a project. In our terms, the guardian.

As we will see, the center is the best place from which the guardian can steer the wheel: There you find consciousness of the whole, there you pull the strings, there the movement is zero and time has come to a standstill.

We now see in this holarchy of "wheels within wheels" that the guardian of the largest wheel is connected to the guardians of the smaller wheels (see Figure 10.1). The spokes of the wheel are therefore the lines of communication between the principal guardian and all other guardians. We can take a company as an example. A company, and each part of it, has a morphic field of its own. The small, red circles represent the employees. These are organized into several sections with a section head. The yellow circles are branches in various cities, with the manager at the center. The green circle is the umbrella organization with the general manager.

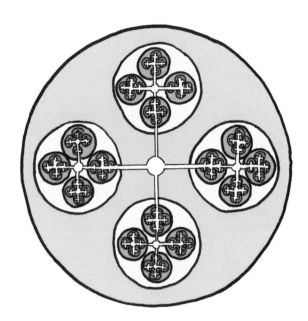

FIGURE 10.1. Wheels within wheels
The image of "wheels within wheels" originates when we connect the image of the morphic field to the wheel. The guardian has his seat in the center. This is the place where consciousness is concentrated. The spokes of the wheel are the channels of communication between the various parts, or their guardians.

If communication is the condition for good cooperation, then according to this image, communication will only be optimal if every manager is at the center of his or her wheel. If one of the managers is on the outside of their wheel, this will result in misunderstandings.

The Higher Consciousness and Spirit of a Company

Every guardian represents the consciousness in his or her wheel. According to the holarchy of wheels within wheels, a certain level of consciousness is linked to every morphic field. Every life form thus has consciousness. Sheldrake confirms this. He, too, takes the stand that everything has a spirit.

This consciousness develops into higher consciousness. We understand this when we connect the holarchy of the wheels within wheels to the triangle of the morphic field (see Figure 10.2). The centers of the various wheels now form a central axis through the middle of the triangle. In this axis is the seat of the consciousness. Every level has its own consciousness. You could say that all levels of consciousness collectively form the consciousness of a company or the spirit of an organism or organization.

Figuratively speaking, you could say that at the bottom of the triangle there is a lower and at the top there is a higher level of consciousness. From all the layers of consciousness together comes a "higher" level of consciousness, because the whole is more than the sum of the parts. In short, the consciousness of the whole company is more, or "higher," than the consciousness of all employees combined. According to this image, all life forms have a "higher" consciousness, which most probably informs their "higher" goal.

When I found this connection, I thought it was an interesting model: a triangle with several levels, a consciousness axis in the middle, and a higher consciousness on top. I had discovered previously (see Chapter 9) that the triangle was an expression of the Fibonacci spiral, which is described as a torsion field by science. Now, all of a sudden, there is a sphere of consciousness above it. Immediately the question arose: Does that higher consciousness really exist? Can you perceive it? And if there is a development of consciousness, how does that work in nature? I decided to explore this using energetic perceptions and knowledge related to theosophy and anthroposophy.

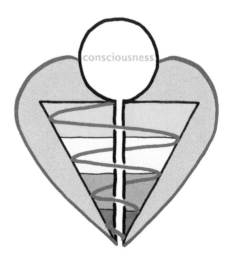

FIGURE 10.2. The consciousness of the various wheels, or holons, is in the center. *All the centers together form a central "axis of consciousness" that produces the higher consciousness of the entirety.*

The formative force in the wheel, focused inward, is depicted here as a vortex, which condenses from the top down. This vortex has the form of a Fibonacci spiral and is described by science as a torsion field.

Realms of Nature

The esoteric teachings of theosophy and anthroposophy speak of four realms in nature: minerals, plants, animals, and man. Every realm has different morphic fields. There is a distinction between the physical-chemical, etheric, astral, mental, and causal fields. The physical-chemical field has the lowest frequency, and the causal field the highest. They are connected to several realms of nature that, one after the other, take a gross materialistic, solid shape (see Table 10.1).

The physical-chemical morphic field condenses into minerals and metals. Living nature originates when the etheric field connects to matter. From this comes the realm of plants. A plant has a physical body and an etheric body. This etheric, or life, body, guards the life processes and sees to it that the plant can recover from injuries, reproduce, and adapt itself to the weather. A stone cannot do that. Time wears it down, and eventually all there is left is rubble. In plants you can find vessels that moisture and food can pass through. The etheric energy flows through the meridians, which are known from acupuncture.

An animal has a physical, ether, and astral body. The astral body houses emotions. Animals, therefore, have emotions. The astral body forms the senses and the nervous and muscular systems. Astral energy flows through the chakras.

Humans have a brain that is more developed than the brains of animals, and it contains special glands, like the pituitary and the pineal. Humans have the three bodies mentioned above, and a mental or thought body that enables us to think about ourselves and the world. We also have self-consciousness. An animal does not have this but is rather connected to the spirit of the group, or what we call the

TABLE 10.1. Realms of Nature and Their Morphic Fields

Morphic field → ↓ Realm	Physical-chemical	Etheric	Astral	Mental	Causal
Mineral	✘	○			
Plant	✘	✘	○		
Animal	✘	✘	✘	○	
Man	✘	✘	✘	✘	○
God-man (saint)	✘	✘	✘	✘	✘

✘ = field connected to the organism
○ = next step in development

"herd instinct." Plants and trees are connected to the collective morphic field of their genus; for example, the morphic field (or, as it may be called in India, the *deva*, the "god" or "spirit") of oak or birch trees.

According to anthroposophy, every natural realm is developing into the next. The higher goal of stones and metals is to become a plant with a life body and with life processes. The plant strives to become an animal with an astral body and emotions. And self-conscious humans, with their mental body and thoughts, is the example the animal wants to copy. The goal of humans is to develop into a loving god–person with an all-embracing consciousness and a causal body, which, according to Helena Blavatsky, the founder of Theosophy, is considered the highest subtle body, beyond even the mental body.

Perceiving Yourself

The higher consciousness that I had drawn as a sphere above the triangle of the morphic field (see Figure 10.2) could therefore be in connection with the next step in development of the organism. This step—the higher goal or destiny—is a script in a higher, more complex level of the morphic field. This means that the consciousness connects to this script and thus leads the organism to its destiny at a higher level.

Are we able to perceive this sphere? Does it really exist? My students and I have researched this using energetic perception, energy sensing through the hands. I described this process of energy sensing extensively in my book *In Resonance with Nature*. We start out with a small rod magnet (according to anthroposophy, a magnet is the mineral that has come the furthest in the development of a life body). Indeed, most of our students perceive a small sphere just above the magnet, which has the character of life energy or ether (see Figure 10.3 on the next page). Around the magnet a strong layer of radiation can also be perceived with the hands. This feels less vital. These are the magnetic field lines, which become visible in experiments with iron filings. Then we sense a layer of more airy energy, which is connected to the small sphere above the magnet. This airy layer and the sphere form the life body of the magnet.

We can perceive the same things in a plant. Around it are several layers of radiation, and above it is a beautiful, radiant sphere filled with astral energy (see Figure 10.4 on the next page). In my book *In Resonance with Nature*, I described the radiation surrounding plants and trees in detail.

In humans, the higher self, as will be explained in Chapter 11, or our sun, as is mentioned in the fourth exercise in Chapter 4, is about three feet above our heads.

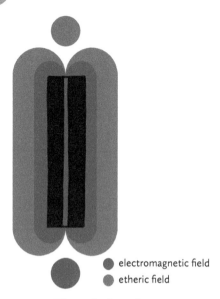

electromagnetic field
etheric field

FIGURE 10.3. The radiation of a magnet
This consists of an electromagnetic field followed by an outer field filled with life energy. Above the magnet a sphere filled with life energy can be perceived.

You can perceive your sun well if you stretch out your arms with your palms facing up. It is a beautiful energy—in fact it is your highest essence.

These different sorts of energy cannot as yet be reliably measured with scientific devices. They can, however, be perceived by humans who are sensitive to them or are trained to recognize them. This indicates their subtle nature. Science is based on observations that can be repeated, controlled, and communicated. From my experience in our courses and training, I have come to the conclusion that energetic perceptions meet these conditions.

A Column with Spheres

The central part of the body of a magnet, a tree, an animal, or a human being consists of a column or torso. In plants and trees you will find roots at the bottom of that torso or trunk and branches with leaves at the top. On the torso of an animal you will find legs; sometimes there is a tail at the back end, but at the front you will always find the head, usually on a neck. The world of plants is upright. Most animals move horizontally, but humans are upright. On our torso we have two legs that enable us to walk and two arms with hands with which we work.

FIGURE 10.4. The radiation of a plant and a tree
This consists of an electromagnetic, an etheric, and an astral field. Above it is a consciousness sphere filled with astral energy.

electromagnetic field
etheric field
astral field

FIGURE 10.5. The radiation of an animal
This consists, from inside outward, of an electromagnetic, etheric, astral, and mental field. Above the head is a sphere filled with mental energy.

● electromagnetic field
● etheric field
● astral field
● mental field

The energetic perceptions or sensing of over a thousand students, as well as my own, show that the next step in development, or the higher goal of an organism, manifests itself as a sphere above or in front of it.

As shown in Figures 10.5 and 10.6, at the positive pole of a magnet is a sphere with life energy. Above a plant is a sphere with astral energy, and above or in front of an animal there is a sphere with mental energy. The "sun" above our heads consists of causal energy. The

FIGURE 10.6. The radiation of a human being
Above our head is our "sun"; it consists of causal energy, has consciousness, and is connected to our destiny. The radiation of man consists, from inside to outside, of electromagnetic, etheric, astral, mental, and causal fields.

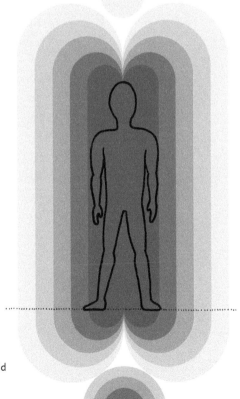

● electromagnetic field
● etheric field
● astral field
● mental field
● causal field

"higher" energy or the "higher" goal to which the organism is developing is always at the top or the front. Someone making intuitive contact with these spheres can perceive a higher consciousness that is more complex than the level of consciousness of the organism in material reality. This higher consciousness induces the life processes and the development of the organism.

This higher or front pole is the attractor that pulls the organism up or forward. In an onion one can sense this very well; long before there is a stem, the "flower" is there like a radiant sphere of energy. Students who perceive this often get spontaneous images of the flower or smell the specific odor. You can also do this exercise with fruits such as apples and pears or pumpkins. On the side where the flower was, a sphere with astral energy is always present. The lower pole connects the organism to earth. There is an energetic cord from the organism to this sphere, and from there it goes into the earth.

Energetic perceptions show that this "column with spheres" can be found in all organisms and organizations. You can also perceive this in the map or a graphic representation of a forest, house, or organization. Above the map you can feel a radiant sun with the higher goal of the organization "inside" it. This sun will be absent if the organization has no higher goal or mission. If the goal is too far off from reality, the sun will be very high. Under the map, under the table, a grounding cord goes to the floor. With your imagination, you can help the sun shine more brightly and direct the grounding cord down into the earth. This works for the whole organization, and many people now apply this technique successfully.

Many farmers use this knowledge. They ground their fields or their stables mentally by imagining a grounding cord that goes into the earth. It stimulates the growth of the roots of plants, among other things. Animals are more at ease in a stable that has been grounded. Above the field or the stable, the farmers imagine a radiant sun that stands for the spirit with the "higher goal"; for instance, healthy plants and animals. Many have good results with this.

Projective Geometry

One day I came across the book *The Plant Between Sun and Earth*, by mathematician George Adams and illustrated by Olive Whicher. To my surprise, Whicher had drawn the exact same energies and spheres we had perceived (see Figure 10.7), and Adams supplied the mathematical support for it. I have great faith in energetic perceptions, especially if others can repeat them. This had proven to be the case for the perception of the various energetic spheres, but I hadn't expected that there was also mathematical support confirming these "fuzzy" phenomena.

Adams and Whicher use projective geometry. It is possible to describe shapes and life processes in nature with this separate branch of geometry, which is over two hundred years old. Projective geometry has a number of starting points that differ from the Euclidean geometry we have all learned at school. One of these starting points is that there is a counter-space. The Universe is an infinitely large orb, and outside of it is the counter-space.

Does it help us in any way to know or understand that? Perhaps, because Adams takes the view that light and life have their origin on the border of space and counter-space. That is interesting, but you would have to go right to infinity to find out if that is true.

However, according to projective geometry there is another way, a shortcut: You can also get into the counter-space if you open the time-space you are in now. Everything around you consists of intersections, and these can be open or closed. These intersections are the gates to counter-space, and an intersection is formed by lines that come together at one point. The intersection will open when the

FIGURE 10.7. Radiation and projective geometry
In this drawing by Olive Whicher, the layers in the radiation of a broadleaf plantain can be seen quite well. Just above the leaves she has drawn the sphere with astral energy.

lines open up like a diaphragm. At that moment there is contact with counter-space and light and life originate (see Figure 10.8 on the next page).

It is a difficult story, but then, all math and geometry is. Let's not make things too difficult and simply take the view that there is something outside of space and time, and that light and life can originate from this source if we make contact with it. You can read about it in Adams' work, but other sources also support these ideas. For instance, the wheel symbolizes the world, the Universe, and space-time. According to ancient Chinese knowledge, the spiritual world can be found at the periphery of the wheel. This world is timeless and eternal. In quantum physics we take it that there is a nonlocal space.

The morphic field and zero-point energy also exist outside of space and time. The junk DNA emits light. That is probably zero-point energy that comes from the counter-space, according to projective geometry.

The Gate of Appearance and the Gate of Disappearance

I was interested in the two energetic spheres above and below the organism. According to projective geometry both are open intersections (see Figure 10.8 and its caption), and therefore gates to counter-space. Things appear through the upper gate and disappear through the lower one.

According to Adams, two fundamental forces are at work in reality: a contracting, center-seeking force and a radiating centrifugal force (see Figure 10.9). We recognize these from our discussion of the Wheel of Life. They can be compared to the formative and expansive forces. The contracting, formative force sucks/pulls as if it were a plant, out of the soil from above. The centrifugal, expansive force pushes and stimulates from below.

As explained in the caption to Figure 10.8, when these opposite forces overlay or run through each other a force emerges that Adams symbolizes by a lemniscate curve. This force works in all organisms and organizations, in our living and working areas, and in fact in humankind as well. It is responsible for the ongoing processes of breathing in and out, contraction and expansion, building and destroying, growth and decay. Adams never made the comparison, but I think his lemniscate force is the same as the torus.

The upper sphere induces the formative force. In Figure 10.9 on the next page you can see this sphere as a blue fan of lines that is opening. In the center of it you find the open intersection with the gate to counter-space. Higher consciousness and the formative force

FIGURE 10.8. Intersections

An intersection is formed by lines that come together at one point. The intersection opens when those lines open, like a sort of diaphragm. You can see this (blue) open intersection at the top right the drawing. At the top left of the drawing the intersection closes.

According to Adams, there are two opposing forces in reality: a radiating force and a contracting force. If these forces run through each other, a force arises for which Adams uses the symbol of a lemniscates, or a figure-eight curve. This is shown in the fourth drawing.

This force is responsible for the ongoing process of breathing in and out, contraction and expansion, building and destroying, origin and decay.

At the top of the lemniscate curve the intersection opens. This is the gate of appearance. At the bottom it closes; this is the gate of disappearance.

here are connected to destiny. This is the "higher goal" of the organism that "reveals" itself from the nonlocal space, or counter-space, into material reality. Therefore this open intersection has a radiant character.

During its path in life, the organism tries to attain its "higher goal" and gains experience in doing so. This is how consciousness develops. The enriched consciousness disappears again through the lower sphere into counter-space. The gate of disappearance is depicted in the figure by a red sphere in which everything is sucked to the center.

Putting It Together

I had researched consciousness, done energetic perceptions, and found connections. Once again it was time to review what I knew:

1. Consciousness is infinite and all embracing. It is the prime characteristic of the Universe.
2. Everything has consciousness. Life experience is the path, higher consciousness is the goal.
3. Higher consciousness is in touch with the next step of development in evolution. This next step is the destination, also known as the "higher goal."
4. Higher consciousness and the destination reveal themselves in space-time through a gate of appearance. This open intersection can be perceived above an organism as an energetic sphere.
5. Below the organism you can perceive a second energetic sphere. This is connected to the body, the memory, and experiences in life.
6. The material protoshape of an organism is a torus with an energetic sphere above it and below it.
7. Around this torus, an aura with energetic layers of radiation can be perceived. The lowest frequency is found in the innermost, and the highest in the outermost layer.

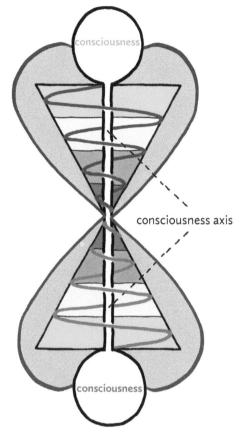

FIGURE 10.9. The morphic field manifests itself locally as a torsion field.

The morphic field has the shape of a phi vortex. The torus consists of two of these vortices, with a consciousness sphere at the top and bottom. These are in contact with each other through a consciousness axis.

8. According to projective geometry, the energetic spheres are in contact with counter-space, also known as nonlocal space, through open intersections.
9. Through these open intersections, consciousness appears and disappears.
10. In this way the developing consciousness of all life forms contributes to the development of the all-embracing consciousness of the Universe.
11. This consciousness is infinite and nonlocal.

If everything has consciousness and the prime goal of the Universe is the development of consciousness, then consciousness is the engine of the Universe. After having come to this conclusion, I decided to summarize my new findings in a couple of illustrations (see Figure 10.10 below and Figure 10.11 on the next page).

The morphic field with consciousness can be symbolized as a triangle with a sphere above it. This triangle is a rotating torsion field, with the shape of a *phi* spiral or vortex. A torus consists of two such vortices (see Figure 10.10). For this reason I designed Figure 10.10. This figure was in accordance with my energetic perceptions of magnets, plants, animals, and humans. This picture contains the column with the two consciousness spheres. The "consciousness axis" in the middle is the heartwood in trees and the spine and nervous system in animals and man.

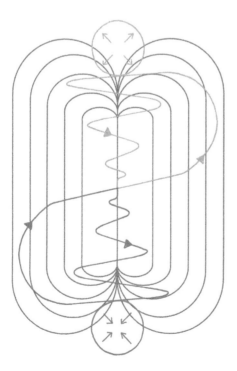

FIGURE 10.10. The two vortices together form a torus.
The flow of energy condenses in the torus and flows back up along the outside. This movement is the time wave. The torus is driven by the consciousness.

The next things I drew in Figure 10.10 were the layers of radiation and the time wave. This gave rise to Figure 10.10, with the torus. In this picture I saw that layers of radiation rotate around the coils of the vortices. The aura rotates in vertical circles, while the vortices flow through them horizontally. They create a donut. These circles of this donut can be seen when, for instance, you cut through the middle of a fruit. You can then see how the round layers of radiation have condensed into matter.

In Figure 10.10 you can also see that the torus and the donut are two different shapes. The layers of radiation form the donut. The two vortices of the torus flow through these layers. When all said and done, the subtle material layers of radiation and the gross material shape are a consequence of the torus that, in its turn, is driven by consciousness. The consciousness comes first. It is the "engine" of the "whole event." This consciousness comes and goes through the gate of appearance and the gate of disappearance. According to the latest scientific knowledge, the

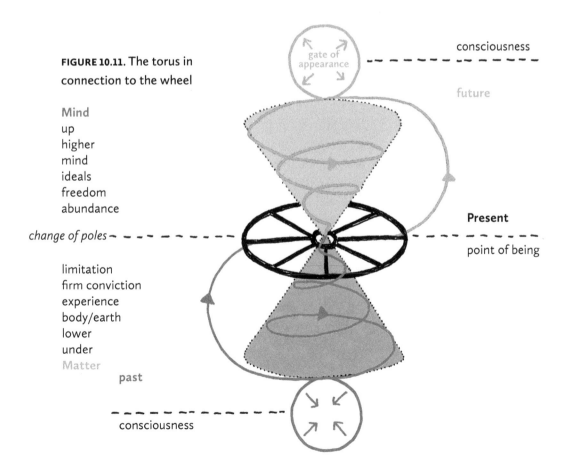

FIGURE 10.11. The torus in connection to the wheel

torus is the protoshape of the micro- and macro-cosmos, from the smallest particle to the largest entirety. The torus that science describes is not complete, however; at the top and at the bottom two open intersections are missing through which consciousness, the morphic field, and zero-point energy appear and disappear in time-space.

Back to the Wheel of Life

Eventually I wanted to reconnect everything to the wheel. In Figure 10.11 you can see it from the side. The two vortices come together in the center. Here you also more or less see the same picture as the one George Adams gave for the lemniscate-shaped force. At the top is an energetic sphere that is connected to the gate of appearance, and at the bottom is a sphere connected to the gate of disappearance. The upper blue spiral is the center-seeking formative force, which is directed toward the future. The red spiral is the outward-seeking expansive force that is directed towards the past; the two spirals are connected by the time wave. Both forces meet in the axis. That is where the present is, now. In accordance with the gates of appearance and disappearance, you could call this the "point of being."

By looking at the wheel in this way, and by again placing everything in the context of "mind–matter," as described in Chapter 3, I discovered new connections. The upper consciousness sphere is connected to spirit, freedom, ideals, thoughts, and higher consciousness. You could speak of an "upper world" with spiritual consciousness. Here you find the morphic field with the blueprint and the route to the destiny of the organism or organization. Other "plans for the future," like goals you have affirmed, can be found here as well.

The lower sphere is connected to matter, or the "lower world," and to everything you have done in your life. Here, successes and failures are linked to emotions and memories. They have led to life experience and firm convictions. You could speak of a "lower" consciousness in this sphere with its gate of disappearance, though I think "deeper consciousness" is a better term. You will not find plans of destiny in the morphic field that are connected to it, but you will find information about the past and about how certain developments unfolded.

Huna and the Whole Human Being

11 ⦂

I discovered that there was a higher consciousness to be found in the mind and connected to ideals, freedom, and abundance—a so-called spiritual consciousness. I could live with that. The mind is free, and in my thoughts I meet my ideals.

But Figure 10.11 on page 143 was also showing me that there is not only a higher, upper or spiritual consciousness but also a lower consciousness that we find in matter and in the body. This lower consciousness or deeper self is connected to memories and experiences. Therefore, you cannot find memory in your mind and brain but rather in the earth and in your body. Also, it is this lower consciousness—and that is probably the most important discovery—that guards your strong convictions.

Your firm convictions make the world what it is. Through these, boundaries and restrictions originate. If you can change those convictions, you can create freedom and new possibilities. This idea was not new; what was new to me, though, was the insight that these convictions are connected to the earth, the body, and the lower consciousness. I had always thought that memories are stored in the morphic field. Maybe they still are, but now, all of a sudden, there was a "high" morphic field with ideals, a higher goal, and a destiny, as well as a "low" morphic field with memories and a knowledge of life.

A question came to mind, and it was in fact the most important one: Where was I in this equation? Me, with my self-consciousness? There is a higher consciousness and a lower consciousness: This was something I could connect to. The lower consciousness could be compared to Jung's subconscious and the higher consciousness to the "Self," but where was "I," my ego with its awareness? I felt a strong need to clarify this.

The solution for letting go of a burdened past and for transforming my firm convictions was in my body rather than in my mind. To get access to it, it would be better to knock on the door of my subconscious rather than on the door of my higher consciousness. I felt I could do something with that, I could research it. But

ME—I—researching something? How could I do that now, when my "I," with my "middle consciousness," no longer fit into the picture?

I was nearly at the end of my voyage of discovery regarding the formative force, but just before reaching the finish I had lost myself in all the connections I had found along the way. Who was it that would reach the finish line? How could I "find myself" without losing sight of all the other connections?

I discovered that Huna, a philosophy based on the ancient wisdom of the Kahuna, the shamans of Hawaii, had the answer to that question.

The Knowledge of Huna

Huna means "secret." The word was used by Max Freedom Long, an American philosopher and linguist, as the name for a philosophical and esoteric system he created in the 1930s that was based, he said, on his study and understanding of the ancient spiritual and esoteric traditions of the Kahuna shamans of Hawai'i. Long wrote twelve books on Huna, the best known of which is *The Secret Science Behind Miracles*, in which the most important principles of his system are explained.

According to Long, the knowledge about Huna was guarded by Kahuna shamans and priests. Kahuna literally means "keeper of the secret," and some Kahunas were powerful shamans with great respect for nature. Every part of life was sacred to them and was treated with respect. They believed that the source of creation not only lived in them but in everything on this earth. They believed that *Mana*, or life energy, flows everywhere and manifests itself in a masculine force and a feminine force. Everything in life is a combination of these two forces. Humans have a physical body and a shadow body. The shadow body contains all memories, the chakras, and the blueprint for the physical body. Mana flows without restriction between these centers, provided that all obstacles, especially feelings of guilt, have been removed.

The Three Conscious Selves

According to Huna, human consciousness is threefold. There are three levels: a lower, a middle, and a higher self (see Figure 11.1). The lower self can be compared to the subconscious, the middle self to the ego, and the higher self to the super-consciousness, which is the guardian angel or the "sun" above our head. The three selves all have different tasks and characteristics and complement each other. The lower self guards life energy and the body. It regulates the processes of life and is the seat of memory and feelings. Your memories are not in your brain but in your

FIGURE 11.1. The Huna vision of man, with the higher, middle, and lower selves

In the body, the seven chakras are drawn with the colors that were assigned to them in the days of old. Above the head is the so-called sky channel, and underneath the body is the grounding cord.

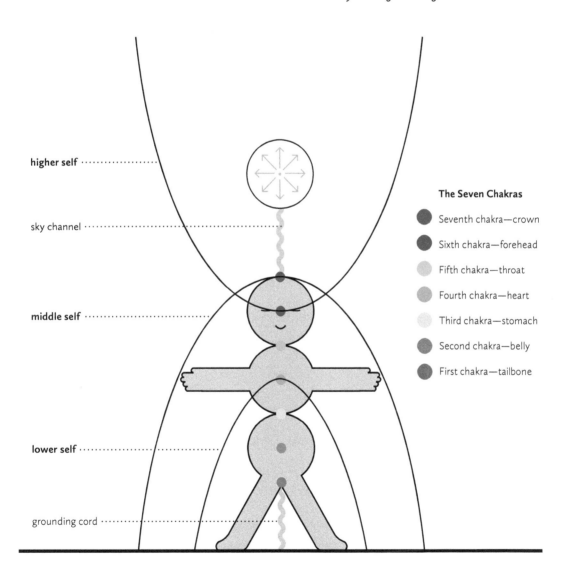

higher self

sky channel

middle self

lower self

grounding cord

The Seven Chakras

Seventh chakra—crown

Sixth chakra—forehead

Fifth chakra—throat

Fourth chakra—heart

Third chakra—stomach

Second chakra—belly

First chakra—tailbone

shadow body. The lower self has no notion of time. It has a sort of animal consciousness and lives only in the present. According to Huna, it is a separate entity that lives inside your body. Many cultures symbolize the lower self as a totem animal. This totem animal accompanies and protects you throughout your entire life. It can be compared to Jung's subconscious.

The middle self is you, as you see yourself. For its memories, the middle self has to depend on the lower self, but it has reason and intellect. In that way, the middle self can come to a correct interpretation of reality through its intellect and with the information of the lower self, which, as we said, is sometimes compared to an animal. The middle self rides on that animal and takes care of it. To be able to get farther along the path of life, one needs the other. The lower self, the subconscious, has power, and the middle self, the ego, has the ability to give it direction.

By nature, the lower self is restless and has difficulty determining which direction to go. It therefore seeks guidance and takes orders from the middle self. If you make a deliberate decision, all the lower self can do is follow. The greater part of humanity still lives unconsciously according to Huna, and it makes no deliberate decisions. Because of this, the lower self does not get any instructions and only does what it knows best, which is to follow the old ways of thinking, maintain rusty patterns of behavior, and make routine actions.

In Huna, the starting point is a spiritual world, but our middle selves cannot get to it using reason. That world is a bridge too far. However, our higher self, our sun, can make this contact with the spiritual world. Your guardian angel is always present but stays in the background, because he/she may only help if we ask for it. Humans have, as you know, a free will.

If the lower self is the animal and the middle self the jockey, then the higher self is the guide who points the way to your destiny. The higher self organizes encounters with other people and events in your life. The higher self supports your deliberate choices if these are in agreement with your destiny. If your lower self executes these choices, you are on a path of deliberate creation.

The Huna Image of Man and the Chakras

In Figure 11.1 on the previous page I provided a schematic reproduction of the Huna image of man. Our body consists of three circles. They symbolize the head, the heart, and the belly. The seven chakras are included in the illustration. These make the contact between our bodies and the astral and other higher energies. The middle self has its seat in the head and is concentrated in the sixth chakra. The lower self has its home in the belly and is concentrated in the second chakra.

The lower and middle selves both have three chakras at their disposal. The lower self uses the first, second, and third chakras, and the middle self uses the fifth, sixth, and seventh chakras. The two meet in the fourth, or heart, chakra.

Through these chakras, the middle and lower selves are connected to the other parts of the being and to its surroundings. The lower self is connected to the earth through the basic chakra (first), and through the stomach chakra (third), it is connected to the heart (fourth). The middle self is connected to the higher self through the crown chakra (seventh), and through the throat chakra (fifth), it is connected to the heart.

The higher self has been depicted separately with an extra circle. The connection of the middle self to the higher self goes through the crown chakra and—as I call it—the "sky channel." From the basic chakra there is a grounding cord to the earth.

Becoming a Whole Human Being

According to Huna, the goal of your life on earth is to become a whole human being. You attain that through complete integration of the three selves in your heart. This requires liberation from (guilt) complexes, consciousness of your middle self, and insight into the other two selves. Most important is a harmonic, respectful, and loving cooperation between the three selves. Once you have reached that harmony, you radiate the light of God. In the true meaning of the word you are "enlightened."

Listening and trust are essential to being able to attain this wholeness. The lower self has a lot of important information for you, but we often ignore our "gut feelings." It is therefore important that you learn to listen to the signals of your body, especially your belly. The lower self also needs guidance from you, the middle self. You attain that by using plain language and by taking charge. The lower self functions best when you give it structure, boundaries, and direction. Take the lead. Without guidance your horse doesn't know where to go.

You must also realize that your lower self always lives in the present but stores every impression and every feeling you have had in the past. If you were afraid of spiders long ago or of certain events, your lower self will still be afraid. You can heal this pain by talking to your lower self. This takes patience and understanding.

The lower self guards your life energy and, with it, your life power and high spirits. Whatever animal your totem is, it needs healthy food, fresh air, and sufficient activity. Of course there are some sloths that hang about in a tree all day, but they are the exceptions to the rule. Every now and then the animal in you has to come out and play. In our culture we invented carnivals and festivals for that purpose. At such event things may get out of hand for a few days!

Prayer and Contact with the Higher Self

In Huna, prayer is an important process. Prayer means asking—I think of the German *bitte*, *bitten*, and *beten*, which mean "please," "ask," and "pray," respectively. Your higher self, your guardian angel, knows your destiny. By praying you can ask him or her for advice or healing on your path in life. Kahunas don't direct prayers directly to God but to their higher self, who, if necessary, passes the prayer on to other (even) higher selves.

According to Huna, you pray from your heart. You think up the prayer in your head and take it into your heart. The lower self plays an important role in contacting the higher self. You can ask your guardian angel for help, but that prayer can only be heard if the lower self makes the contact from the heart with a so-called mana cord consisting of life energy. Along this cord, the question, the prayer, flows up. A good relationship with the lower self—and thus with your body—is necessary for clear contact with the spiritual world.

It takes life energy for the prayer to be heard by the spiritual world. Huna confirms what we already knew; that life energy plus information (the prayer) generates a formative force. Also, prayer only works when you do it with your heart and soul in connection with your belly and life energy.

So that is why so little has come of all our prayers. We have sent mail to heaven for ages, but most of it probably never arrived because we didn't put a stamp on it!

Clearing the Way

If you do stick on a stamp on your prayer in the form of life energy, your higher self answers through your crown chakra. The middle and lower selves meet in the forehead. So the answer literally falls in there, at which point you become conscious of it. You can call that inspiration or intuition. However, the contact between the higher and the lower/middle selves may be disturbed by blockages in the crown chakra. Entity-like "ether pirates" that give wrong, misleading information can lock on if the connecting channel between the seventh chakra and the higher self—the sky channel—is disturbed.

You can become conscious of an answer that occurred to you or that was *given* to you in several ways. Depending on your nature and your abilities, it may come to your mind as a clear image, but it may also come as a good feeling or an inner understanding. Sometimes Huna practitioners use a pendulum to translate the answer through the involuntary movements of muscles.

All three selves play an important role in prayer. For a good transfer, not only your sky channel must be clean but also the shadow cord. Bad memories or psychic complexes in the lower self can block this. In Huna, solving these complexes is called "clearing the way." The more harmonious and whole someone is, the more effective their prayers will be.

Ask All You Like

Prayer is also used for healing. It makes no difference whether you want to heal yourself or others or if you want to heal from a distance or on the spot. Either way, the method is the same: The middle self asks the lower self to make contact with the higher self from the heart and to "hand over" the prayer. The more mana that is sent up in doing so, the more help in the form of answers or healing power you may receive and the more your higher self can give.

And then you can ask all you like. In fact, asking is even necessary, because the spiritual world cannot do anything that goes against our free will. It is therefore good to know exactly what you want. The opposite applies as well: The less we want specifically, the more the spiritual world can do for us in general. In short, the more selfless your prayer is, the more freedom and possibilities the Gods have to fulfill your prayer.

You are least selfish if you surrender disinterestedly and with full trust when praying for something or someone else. Huna says that if you want to be successful and happy, become a whole person and live according to the principles of "Thy will be done" and "One should treat others as one would like others to treat oneself."

In business life, this distills down to wishing your biggest rival great success and high profits. If that is not "loving thy neighbor," then I don't know what is! You could, of course, arrange with them to wish the same for you, and then you would both benefit. That would be a good deal, but keep it to yourself—your higher self doesn't need to know.

The Belly–Brain

Numerous scientific discoveries confirm that Huna is full of deep insights. The idea of the shadow body in which the memories and the blueprint of the body are stored, for instance, shows great similarity to the concept of a torsion field.

Everything consists of intersections. Through your open intersections, you are connected to counter-space, which consists of all information and zero-point energy. Your power, therefore, really does come from within, as Huna suggests. By going into your heart and meeting there with your lower self, you can command it to open up to the perpetual source of mana. This is the same as life energy and zero-point energy.

As we mentioned earlier, Carl Jung also speaks of a threefold self in man. The lower self can be compared with his description of the subconscious. This lower self is seen in Huna as a being with a consciousness of its own. Jung didn't take that stand, but recent discoveries confirm that the Huna view is right.

Scientific research shows that our intestinal tissue has over one hundred million nerve cells, which is roughly equivalent to the number in our spinal cord. After the brain, it is the largest collection of nerve cells in our body. In addition, these cells have the same structure, receptors, and neurotransmitters as the brain. So in a sense, we can speak of a "belly–brain." It has been discovered that this "belly–brain" has a consciousness of its own and makes autonomous decisions. It also sends more information to the brain than the other way around.

Our belly, therefore, literally and figuratively has more to say than we think it does. Much of this information, however, we don't believe. Our neck is our "bottle-neck"; it is where our reasoning stops the flow of information. One consequence is what the Germans call a "thick neck"; another is tight shoulders because of all the piled-up information and feelings.

I Am the Middle Self

I had found myself once again sharing the Huna view that I am a middle self that is in connection with my higher and my lower selves. The knowledge I had received regarding the formative force and affirmations was confirmed by Huna. However, an important new insight was added. From what I had learned previously, I knew that an affirmation only worked if it was formulated clearly in one's mind after attentively connecting it to life energy in one's heart. Huna says that it works in exactly the same way, but the prayer and the affirmation are not confirmed just anywhere in the morphic field but rather "arrive" at the higher self first. Our higher self determines what happens to them after that.

The answer and the granting of our wish may be given when the prayer and the affirmation are in agreement with our destiny. If, however, the question is a selfish one that comes from our ego and is not attuned to the greater good, then we will probably have to wait forever. We also have to be energetically clean and free from any burdens from our past to be able to get the prayer across and to receive a response.

Huna also speaks of two fundamental forces. Mana, or life energy, manifests in a positive, masculine force and a negative, feminine one. All of life is a combination of those two forces. Projective geometry also describes these forces and connects them to counter-space. Consciousness is the engine behind these forces. It comes and goes through open intersections, the gate of appearance and the gate of disappearance. The higher self guards the connection with the gate of appearance. For the middle self—and that is "I"—this higher self is a sort of browser with which one can surf the spiritual Internet: You ask your higher self a question and it Googles the answer in the spiritual world.

Gaia and the Underworld

As we said earlier, according to Huna, the lower self guards our life energy and our body. It is seated, with our middle self, in our body; the middle self concentrates in the forehead at the sixth chakra, and the lower self has its seat in the belly at the second chakra.

It became clear to me, however, that something was missing in the Huna view of humanity. Next to the lower self there had to be another consciousness that guards the gate of disappearance. This "earth consciousness," or "deeper self," probably relates to the lower self in the same way the higher self relates to the middle self: It guards the connection to the gate of disappearance and the spiritual world behind it. The gate of appearance is the gate to the "upper world." The gate of disappearance leads to the "lower world." Is that where the consciousness of Gaia, Mother Earth, resides? I did not yet have an answer to that question.

The Huna goal of becoming a whole human being is attained by integrating our higher, lower, and middle selves in the heart. Our heart is the central point, the point of being. I was really taken by this idea, but once again I noticed that a deeper self that I felt was connected to the consciousness of Gaia had no place in this wholeness and integration.

If everything has consciousness, then so does Gaia. Mother Earth is often linked to unconditional love. I am on my way to my destiny, but does my path in life go past her without notice? Is she indifferent to my conduct, or does Gaia have warm feelings for me with every step I take? And what is the effect of our collective conscious on the consciousness of the earth?

The gate of disappearance is in the earth. Our enriched consciousness goes through the earth and through matter before it disappears. Do we enrich the earth in this way? Does Mother Earth become more conscious because of our conduct? That would mean that I am not only on my way to my destiny and higher consciousness but that my walk of life also contributes to the growing awareness of our planet.

I felt I had received answers to several questions from my study of Huna, but at the same time new questions now loomed on the horizon. In this way, life leads us from one mystery to the next. It is never boring—if you like puzzles.

Whole and Holy

Before going on, I summarized my thoughts about the wheel, the Huna view of humanity, and my new insights in the images shown in Figures 11.2 and 11.3. The goal in life, according to Huna, is to become a "whole" person; you do that by making your three selves into a threefold union in your heart. Our heart is the center of our wheel. In Figure 10.12 the two vortices come together in the center of the wheel, but I then realized that it doesn't depict wholeness. In that drawing, the heart is "shut." From days of old, we understand "wholeness" as a harmonious

FIGURE 11.2. The star
The triangle pointing downward is perhaps the oldest symbol for mind, spirit, heaven, and cosmic powers. The triangle pointing upward represents matter and earthly powers. Healing means the connection of heaven and earth, of mind and matter. This leads to wholeness. After a transformation, enlightenment can be attained, this is the stage of "holiness."

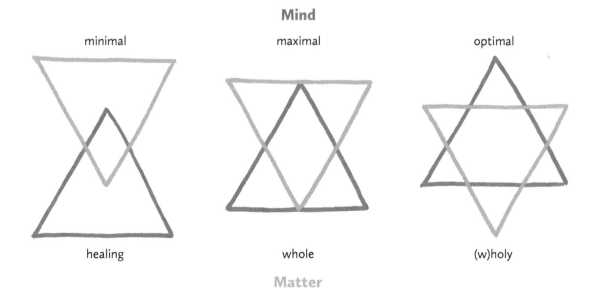

connection between mind and matter, heaven and earth—between cosmic and earthly forces. Life originates when the light of Father Sun and the love of Mother Earth meet in a point (the fertilized ovum). They connect and then permeate each other, and life takes its course.

The triangle pointing downward is perhaps the oldest symbol for mind, spirit, heaven, and cosmic forces; the triangle pointing upward is the symbol for matter and earthly forces. Wholeness results when the two forces are in harmony, and this is depicted by the overlapping triangles. "Healing" literally means "making something whole." A healer connects cosmic and earthly forces. He or she brings both these forces, which are fundamental for life, back into harmony, so that a healed person can continue life healthy and full of vitality.

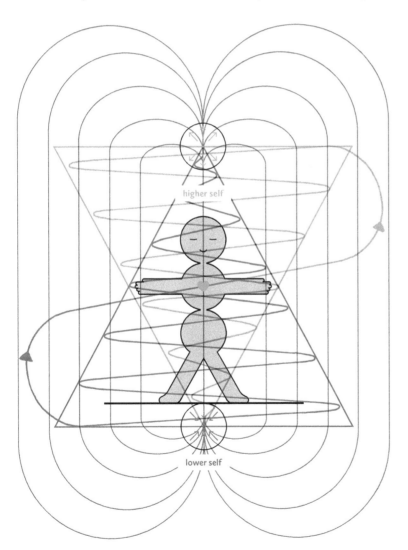

FIGURE 11.3. The whole of man with an open heart
The higher self is above the head and the deeper self is below the feet.
This picture shows the connection of the (blue) formative force and the (red) expansive force, the torus with the two vortices, the layers of radiation, and the time wave.

There can be a minimal overlap of the two triangles (see Figure 11.2 on page 154), where one's life is hanging by a thread, and a maximal overlap, where one is completely whole, full of strength, and healthy. The ideal is the balance shown in the star, where you have risen above everyday life, as it were. This is the stage of holiness where we speak of a holy person, a saint, or an enlightened human being.

In this way the open heart of a "whole" human being can be represented by two overlapping triangles, which is shown in Figure 11.3 on the previous page. The two overlapping triangles are, in reality, the vortices of the formative force and the expansive force. Together with the time wave that connects the past and future they form the torus, which moves above the head with the higher self and under the feet of the deeper self. Around the body is the aura with its layers of radiation.

Following Your Destiny

I hadn't yet solved the mystery of the deeper self and the growing awareness of Mother Earth, but little by little everything was falling into place: life energy, information, time, and consciousness. Consciousness comes first. It comes and goes in order to gain experiences during our stay on earth, to learn from them, and to develop to a higher consciousness. Consciousness, therefore, is the engine of the circle of life and the key player of events on the world stage. Consciousness comes from counter-space, the nonlocal space or the spiritual world—whatever you wish to call it—and connects to the zero-point energy field and a script from the morphic field. This script contains the "information" of your destiny and the meaning of your life.

The way is the goal. Your life path leads you, step by step, to your destiny. On the way you get life experience. If that experience is joyful and loving, you radiate, you light up. So destiny plus love becomes light—a light you literally and figuratively radiate out of joy and happiness but that also leads to a lighter and enriched consciousness with a higher frequency.

It is very possible that this consciousness feeds the consciousness of Mother Earth through the gate of disappearance and increases her awareness in that way.

If, however, it is a painful, nasty experience, destiny plus pain becomes sorrow. Sorrow, over time, becomes a burden and evolves into a burdened past. From that moment on there is great danger of you not getting any further on your path in life. What you have experienced keeps pulling at you. It drags you down every day until you are finally depressed. Instead of your consciousness developing, you become stuck, and life gets complicated. You don't radiate light but rather fall into a melancholic black hole.

FIGURE 11.4. Destiny

Destiny plus love generates light. Destiny plus pain generates sorrow. Sorrow that has been passed through changes to the past. This burdened past pulls at us, inhibits development, and, as a counter-force, is the cause of disappointments.

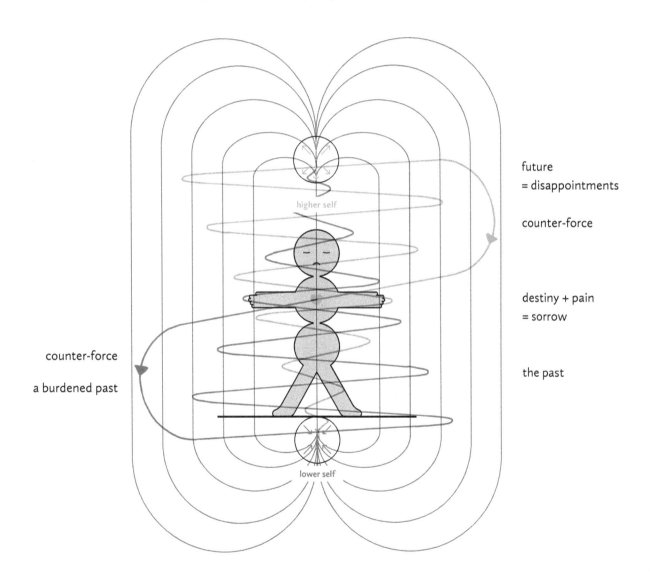

future
= disappointments

counter-force

destiny + pain
= sorrow

the past

higher self

lower self

counter-force

a burdened past

Repetition of a Burdened Past

All of a sudden I saw, in Figure 11.4 (on the previous page), what happens in daily life. The picture clearly shows how past and future are connected. We experience time as linear, but in essence it is cyclic. That means that I attract not only my future but at the same time my past, especially my burdened past. All experiences that have become sorrow and burden come by again and again. Using Gregg Braden's formula (see Chapter 9), I can even calculate when.

A burdened past will recur with the regularity of *phi* until I see, recognize, accept, and transform it to light with my full consciousness. At that moment the burden will fall from my shoulders, and it will become clear why I took it on my shoulders in the first place. This becoming conscious of the deeper meaning of the events in my life will then clear the way so I may continue my journey more consciously.

So a burdened past will manifest itself as an obstacle on the way to my destiny until the moment of awareness, and it therefore works as a counter-force in life. This counter-force is the cause of disappointments. It is very possible that every disappointment is directly connected to my affirmations and the good fortune I try to obtain. Remember that equal vibrations resonate with each other. This means that with every affirmation I not only attract the good luck I want but also the burdened past that resonates with it. So there is a direct link between the goals I want to attain and the things in my life that go against me or are disappointing.

So should I leave out affirmations and let my future come as it will? No, because on the one hand you cannot be sure, in advance, if an affirmation will be thwarted by a burdened past, and on the other hand, if that is the case, there is a good possibility I might become conscious of it more quickly and process it.

Is the awareness of a painful experience from the past nice? No, it usually isn't, but having disappointments all the time isn't nice either, in the long run. Awareness is the most important goal in life, so it is better to start working toward it today rather than tomorrow. Whether you like it or not, whichever way you look at it, you cannot deny or walk away from a burdened past. It is present everywhere in your aura or your torsion field. Sooner or later it will surface and be seen. Rescue the drowning person and save yourself.

Live with Compassion 12 ⦙

When I looked some more at Figure 12.1 on the next page and saw how the two vortices and the time wave come together in the heart, the following words came to mind:

pain	peace
passed	present
past	promise
forgive	love
forgo	live
forget	light

Is the heart able to heal the pain from the past? Is forgiveness the key to opening the gate? Love heals all wounds, doesn't it?

The Negative Spiral of Creation

As we saw in the section titled "The Burden of the Past, the Mystery of Time" in Chapter 6, Marinus Knoope, author of *The Spiral of Creation*, also distinguishes a negative spiral next to the positive one. The positive spiral describes how you can realize your heart's desires, how you can be successful, and how you can develop. With every step of development your consciousness grows and your goal draws nearer. The negative spiral describes how you can get more and more frustrated, how you can get yourself deeper and deeper into misery, and how you can get further and further away from achieving your destiny.

According to Knoope, the realization of success in your life doesn't start with applying the positive spiral of creation but rather with recognizing and ending the negative spiral. The negative spiral is practically identical to the positive one, but whereas a positive spiral starts with wishes, a negative one starts with worries, or rather the things you don't wish for. Knoope provides a good example of a "successful" negative spiral (see Figure 12.2 on page 161): Suppose you are afraid of something that might happen, something that you really don't want. For instance, if you are afraid of burglars, at first you might keep this to yourself, but at a certain moment you find someone to talk to about your fears. He says, "Stop whining, just think positively."

FIGURE 12.1. Destiny and forgiveness
By forgiving a burdened past we may forget,
and then we can live on "enlightened."

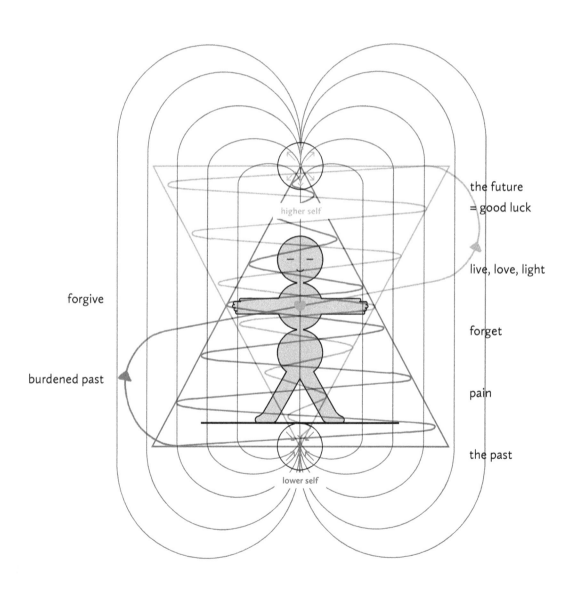

the future
= good luck

higher self

live, love, light

forgive

forget

burdened past

pain

the past

lower self

FIGURE 12.2. The negative spiral of creation

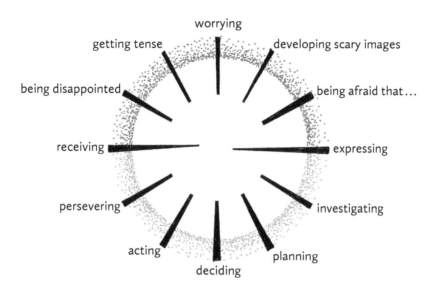

You think, "Well, that's easy for him to say, but I'm really scared." So you keep talking to people about it until you finally meet somebody who understands you and who says, "Yes, crime is increasing lately. They robbed a house around the corner just last week!"

This statement makes you instantly feel more at ease. As a human being, you are always on the lookout for people who think like you do; you look for a friend, coach, therapist, or literature that corroborates what you already think. That is comforting, and it doesn't require you to change.

By now you have surrounded yourself with people who share your fears and worries. At some point someone says, "You know what you should do?" and the first bit of advice comes at you: "You should buy rolldown shutters." You collect some more ideas, like a dog in the house, an alarm, or new locks. Shortly thereafter, you make inquiries about the quality and the price, and make a decision: Rolldown shutters it is!

The rest is a matter of action and perseverance, because once those rolldown shutters are installed, they must be opened and closed at least once a day. Then come the holidays, and before you go out of town to relax, you forget to ask a friend or relative to open and close the shutters on a daily basis. When you come back from your vacation you find out that it worked! You have been burgled!

Emotions Off and On

Most people are disappointed if their fears come true. If you look at it logically, that is strange. If you are worried, and your worries become reality, then something was a success, and the process of creation has worked. Yet, instead of appreciation there is disappointment, and someone who is disappointed doesn't become relaxed but stressed. Someone who is stressed starts to worry, gets more images of problems, and starts believing in them even more. Before you know it, you are in a negative spiral of creation.

According to Goethe, our wishes are premonitions of the things we are able to realize. Likewise, our worries are premonitions. The process of creation works in both positive and negative ways. But how do you break the negative spiral? To come back to our example, start by becoming aware of the fact that you are afraid of burglars, and then accept that fact.

According to Knoope, you shouldn't run away from your emotions, rather you should get on top of them. Emotions only become a problem if they are not allowed to be there, if you are not allowed to have them. Take fear, for example: There are people who will pay twenty dollars to experience fear on a roller-coaster. Fear can be exciting. Think about the millions of people who enjoy getting scared by a horror movie. Knoope thinks that people who have been taught not to be afraid when they were children are the ones who end up being scared for the rests of their lives. Fear is not the problem: Not wanting to be scared is the problem.

Welcoming Emotions

According to Knoope, the pain most people experience related to emotions they haven't come to terms with yet is not so much the pain of the emotion but the pain of resisting the emotion. He writes, "Pain is nothing more than resistance against what is. When you give up your resistance, enormous forces come free and you get back your original energy. Your vitality and life force awaken, which will make you flow, bubble, pop, and glow again."

Every so-called unwanted emotion has positive qualities, provided the emotion is adopted wholeheartedly. In fact, it seems that you get exactly what you need to be able to deal with specific pressures in a dynamic way. For example, anger can elicit feelings of power, action, and authority; fear can engender awareness and caution; and stress can bring with it energy for action. You might get angry if someone invades your boundaries, and then by establishing your authority you may well receive a desired result. You get scared when danger is imminent, which makes caution and awareness important. You get stressed when you are busy, and that stress can make you lively and energetic.

Wishes

Every positive spiral of creation starts with wishing. Knowing what you wish for means knowing what you want to be to the world or to someone else, but it also means knowing what you want for yourself. It is all about finding the balance that is right for you and that fits your mission in life; it is a balance between taking good care of yourself and meaning something to someone else, and finding the balance between focusing on the realization of your own wishes and being of service to others.

If that balance is not there, the creator in you will not feel well. The process of creation will stagnate, and you will encounter disappointment. Your body may react by giving you a warning signal; disagreeable emotions may come up, showing you that the balance has been disturbed. The discomfort that you feel prompts you to take action.

An emotion warns you and evokes certain actions. The warning given and action evoked are different for every emotion. If you let emotions into the equation, the effect is a movement toward balance, and things shift in the right direction. Because you experience them as disagreeable, you may at first want to "turn them off," to suppress them, but they can bring about the balance that is right for you.

The Difference Between Feeling and Emotion

There was a time when you were afraid of something. You suppressed that, and now you have replaced that fear with a fear of burglars. The way to start coping with that is by looking that fear in the eye and accepting it. If you are open to that emotion, it turns out that there is a hidden force in it: awareness. This makes you more alert, but it doesn't make you less afraid of burglars.

In dealing with suppressed emotions, it helps to make a distinction between them and feelings. In daily life, emotions and feelings are usually thrown in together. Nevertheless, according to Diana and Michael Richardson, authors of *Tantric Love: Feeling vs Emotion: Golden Rules to Make Love Easy*, there is an essential difference: Emotions are connected to the past, whereas feelings are connected to the present.

Emotions are all the feelings we haven't expressed in the present: angry feelings but also loving ones that were felt at a certain moment but that you, for whatever reason, did not express. These feelings change to emotions that are stored in our subconscious and pop up time and again to check on us in all sorts of ways. Emotions are an example of a burdened past.

The Richardsons asked a large number of people taking their workshops and classes to describe how they felt if they had emotions in their relationship. It turned out that everybody could do so quite easily, and the answers were unambiguous:

1. You feel estranged from the other. Like walking into a brick wall.
2. There is no contact. Even eye contact is difficult.
3. You blame your partner for the situation.
4. You blame the other. "You always do this…" or "You never do that…"
5. You withdraw and shut yourself off.
6. Your body is tense and cramped up, sometimes even painfully so.
7. Your field of vision is blurred and gets smaller.
8. You are tired or exhausted. You would really like to sleep.
9. You are on your guard and defensive.
10. You feel alone and deserted.
11. You feel misunderstood.
12. You are stubborn and insist on being right.
13. You want to pick a fight and provoke the other.
14. Your thoughts go in circles. You are negative and doubt yourself.
15. You feel helpless and the victim of the situation.
16. You see the future as hopeless and depressing.
17. Your partner can do nothing right in your mind.
18. You want your partner to change.
19. You react from your ego; at the same time, you don't know why you react in this way.
20. You think about events from the past all the time.

If there is anything you recognize in all this, then we are talking about emotions. Therefore, the cause of your bad feeling is not your partner but rather is hidden somewhere in your past. Somewhere, at a certain time, something happened that you didn't immediately talk about and put to rest, so it comes up again and again for the rest of your life until you become aware of it.

All emotions are waiting to be triggered. An extra problem is that most emotions are heavily charged; one small spark can lead to a massive explosion. An emotional outburst of anger is often excessively vehement, sometimes even destructive. Your partner gets the full impact of the blow and at the same time functions as the buffer that may receive it (lovingly).

Emotions Poison the Body

Feelings happen to you in the here and now. You are in contact with yourself and your surroundings. With an emotion you have lost that connection, that contact. The future gets darker and the present more gloomy. A downward, negative spiral takes you deeper and deeper into a bottomless pit. Your burdened past not only lingers in your aura but also in your body. It turns out that emotions accumulate most in the connective tissue. From there, they acidify our body and our temper.

"If anger and hatred are not dealt with, you are constantly poisoning your body," writes Renny de Bruyn, osteopath and author of the book *Pijn als positieve boodschap* (Pain as a positive message). He goes on to say:

> The brain is constantly stimulated, and it, in turn, stimulates the body to produce cortisol, a substance that causes stress. This overproduction makes your body bitter and causes cramping, acidification, and inflammation. Grudges and remorse often come out by way of the liver and the bile. There is some truth in the saying, "Don't let it embitter you." One person quickly reacts in a physical way, the next in a psychological way. The last category often also shows cynical and bitter behavior.

It turns out that the simplest and at the same time most powerful method for starting the transformation of your emotions is to drink a lot of water and get some fresh air and physical exercise.

Happiness Is the Meaning of Life

> I am convinced that the quest for happiness is the goal of our life. Whether someone believes or no, whatever religion a person confesses, everyone is in search of something better in life. So happiness is the motive of our existence. In other words, happiness is the meaning of life.

These words were spoken by the fourteenth Dalai Lama, spiritual leader of Tibet, Nobel Peace Prize winner, and champion of nonviolent resistance. He is a happy man who is always smiling, no matter how much injustice is done to him and his people. He bases his words on 2,500 years of Buddhist knowledge and a lot of life experience. Everyone can be happy, according to the Dalai Lama; your attitude is the key. Is the bottle half full or half empty? That's the question! If, for instance, you carry thoughts of hatred or intense anger deep down, it will ruin your health. Also, if you are mentally unhappy or frustrated, physical comfort will be of no use. If, however, you can maintain a tranquil, peaceful state of mind, you can be a very happy person, even if you have bad health.

The prerequisite for happiness is a state of inner tranquility, of inner satisfaction, and of inner value. The quest for happiness then leads inward. It is an inner voyage to our deepest being.

Accepting Pain and Sorrow

According to the Dalai Lama, harm that is done to us or the suffering of other people can disrupt the happiness we experience on our path in life. Therefore, denying our feelings of sorrow is generally the first thing we do, whether it be consciously or unconsciously. We just pretend the pain isn't there, keep walking, and stick our heads in the sand. These are normal human reactions, but they don't help us along; in fact, they help us out of the frying pan…and into the fire.

All pain—every form of suffering we don't accept—will repeat itself time after time with ever-increasing force. All emotions want attention, want to be seen, and want to be embraced with love and taken into the heart. If that doesn't happen, they will get in front of you, be obstructive, thwart you, bully you, and keep doing that until you cannot ignore them any more—until you see and accept them.

The ego denies sorrow out of self-interest. The soul accepts sorrow because it is connected to the whole world. The soul has its seat in the heart. Sorrow and pain should therefore be received with an open heart. The love in our heart can ease and transform all of the sorrow in the world. The heart is the gate, and compassion is the key.

Compassion

To some people compassion is a form of love. To others it is a virtue. In psychology, compassion is the ability to recognize the suffering of someone else and to feel connected to it. As the saying goes, "A sorrow shared is a sorrow halved." Compassion is based on sympathy and is often compared to charity and mercy; however, it should not be confused with sentimentality or "pity."

In Buddhism, compassion is what touches the heart when we see the pain of others. It is the antidote for anger and hatred. It is said that Buddha was once asked by his companion Ananda if it was true that the development of compassion and friendliness was a part of the teaching. Buddha answered, "No, that is not true; it is not *part* of the teaching, the development of compassion and friendliness *is* the teaching."

Compassion doesn't only have a central position in Buddhism. To Christians the life of Jesus embodies compassion and charity. In the Holy Bible, God is called "the Father of the Merciful." The Jews, too, speak of God as the Merciful One. Compassion, charity, and self-control are the three most important virtues in Hinduism. In Islam, mercy and compassion are Allah's most important qualities. All 114 chapters of the Koran, with the exception of one, start with, "In the name of God, the Merciful, the Compassionate…" Many Islamic scriptures urge the faithful to be compassionate, and *Zakat*, a tax to help the poor and the needy, is obligatory for all Muslims.

Developing compassion is an important theme in all religions and faith traditions. Compassion makes us feel connected to others and encourages us to help others or otherwise support them. Buddhism has created a form of meditation called *tonglen*, which uses compassion as a starting point for the transformation of pain and sorrow. This ancient method originated in India and came to Tibet in the eleventh century.

Tonglen

Tonglen is a loving way to open up your heart, step by step, to your own sorrow and that of others, and to transform it into light and love. There are a wide range of applications for *tonglen*, from how we handle small irritations in daily life, to the way in which we cope with pain and anger, to problems in our relationships, to caring for dying people. The feelings of friendliness and compassion you develop with these exercises also have a direct effect on the person who applies them. In this way everyone is helped.

Transforming pain and sorrow starts with accepting them. That is the basis of *tonglen*, which in Tibetan means "take and give." Receive pain and sorrow, and accept it with all its depths. It doesn't matter who or what is suffering: a fellow human being, an animal, a town, a country, the world, or you yourself. Open up your heart, take in all the pain you can contain, welcome it, breathe it in, and surround it with compassion. When you breathe out, breathe out all the joy you have—give your love to the world. This is the method for practicing compassion: Absorb pain and sorrow in your heart, and send your blessings into the world. The moment you take in the pain of the world, it is no longer suffering. Have compassion, not pity.

You do not have to take someone else's sorrow on your shoulders and carry it with you as a burden. Accept and welcome it into your heart, where it is transformed into light and love through *tonglen*.

Practicing *tonglen* helps us change our attitude toward our own pain and the pain of others. The practice asks that we open our hearts and allow ourselves to feel the pain instead of shutting it out. By doing so we soften and feel what is really going on. We become more honest and have more understanding for others.

By accepting the suffering, welcoming it into our heart, and accepting it completely, we can also gain insight into the cause. If we understand the reason why the suffering exists, we may be able to stop the suffering or free ourselves from it. This liberation and awareness is the basis of true growth and transformation.

The heart has great meaning in *tonglen*. This form of meditation is in agreement with Huna: Accept the suffering of others and free yourself of your own pain. It also corresponds to the principles of HeartMath, which suggest that an open and coherent heart works in a healing way on its surroundings. *Tonglen* is a powerful method that you can apply to yourself and to those dear to you, and also to people you have hurt and who have hurt you. Practicing it will soften your own pain and help you in the process of forgiving. How does it work?

Practicing Tonglen *for Others*

The practice of *tonglen* looks a lot like the HeartMath exercises for a coherent heart. In these exercises you visualize breathing in through your heart and exhaling through your solar plexus, the point of energy between your breastbone and your belly button. In doing so, you summon a sincere feeling of appreciation, compassion, care, or love for something or someone in your life. Keep these positive, loving feelings in mind while you radiate them to yourself and to others.

Tonglen adds to this that you connect yourself from this coherent state to a situation in which there is pain or sorrow. That situation can be about a child, a friend, a coworker, and even an animal, and can be practiced at home or at work. For that matter, do what your heart tells you. When breathing in, you take in the suffering or the pain of the person/creature chosen. When breathing out, send that person everything that can free them of the suffering, which then relaxes them and makes them happy. That can be a smile, gentleness, light, or whatever.

Pay an equal amount of attention to breathing in as you do to breathing out. Often your breathing deepens when doing this. Do this a number of times. Build up the time slowly and be well aware of how you feel when you are practicing *tonglen*. It is important that you stay loving and concentrated during the breathing, as this is the heart of this simple and powerful method. Because of this, most people find that five to ten minutes are enough in the beginning.

It is often difficult to practice *tonglen* for someone else, because your own pain and sorrow may prevail. You can be overcome with anger, resistance, sorrow, and what have you. At that moment, your compassion is directed at all living beings having the same negative emotion. You don't need to know who they are or where they are. Breathe in the collective pain and exhale relaxation, love, or happiness to everyone and everything. Feel what is necessary and send that into the world so the negative emotion(s) will be literally and figuratively "lightened." In that way, you also lighten yourself.

Tonglen *and a Burdened Past*

Tonglen can also be used to transform a burdened past. An affirmation attracts everything from the future with which it resonates. In that way your goal slowly condenses and will take shape after a certain amount of time. Just as the past and future are connected in a cyclical way, you will also continuously attract the past that you haven't dealt with. Because of the principle of resonance, you will deal with the exact same burdened past that resonates with your affirmation and blocks it with disappointments.

Our mind is connected to the future, our soul to the present, and our body to the past. A burdened past, therefore, cannot only be found in the torsion field—and with this in our surroundings—but also in our bodies. Annoying, on the one hand, because the pain in the "heart" we once had can transform into physical pain; easy, on the other hand, because you don't have to go far to find your burdened past: You have it at hand every single moment.

Everything is energy. The energy that resonates with an affirmation can be felt using the following exercise: Write an affirmation down on a blank 8½ × 11 piece of paper and draw an ellipse or oval around it. By doing this, you concentrate the energy. The next part takes some intuitive experience, but if you have any and if you are in a relaxed state of mind, you can feel the energy of the affirmation with your hand if you slowly rotate the written affirmation under it. As you do, different facets of the energy are highlighted. If that energy is free and unburdened, you experience it as relaxation. In certain positions you will experience tension or resistance, and it is at that place that there is a blocked energy resonating with a burdened past and blocking the realization of the goal you want to achieve.

If you sense the energy carefully, you can feel where the burden is stored in your body. All of a sudden you may feel pain where there wasn't any before. If, in advance, you have done exercises to relax and have prepared yourself with *tonglen*, you can now breathe in the resistance and the pain and exhale relaxation, light, love, or whatever you can think of to that place in your body. Do this for as long as it takes until you relax and the pain and the resistance are gone.

Now rotate the affirmation under your hand some more. Keep doing this until you have made a complete circle. Every time you feel resistance and/or tension, stop and welcome it into your heart. Breathe in and breathe out. A full circle can take up to an hour-and-a-half or even two hours, depending on the burden on your affirmation. Of course you can take a break, but it is more powerful if you finish it in one sitting.

Does doing this get rid of all the burdened past(s) that blocks the way to your goal? Maybe, probably. You will find out based on the way things go. Will you have good luck or bad luck? Hold the affirmation in your hand after some time and feel if it is still totally clean. If not, do the exercise again.

When you can run your hand over your affirmation and not feel any resistance, you can feel gratitude and happiness as if your goal has already been achieved. This enforces the power of the realization. It could also happen that you don't get around to that at all, because by touching your inner emotional pain all sorts of information crops up regarding the causes. Memories and events from the past may suddenly come back to mind. That is no problem, as these memories may be there because becoming aware is what this exercise is all about. In processing your experience you clear the way to your destiny. *Tonglen* helps in doing so, but sometimes another deed of the heart is necessary: forgiveness.

Forgiveness

Practicing *tonglen* softens the pain of others and in ourselves. Through *tonglen*, pain can be transformed to love and light. That doesn't always happen, however, because during *tonglen* the cause of the pain can come back to your consciousness (for instance, the reason why you were so angry at the time). This can be so powerful that you have to breathe in and out through your heart before you can look at your pain without a lot of negative burdening. Once you are able to do so, it's time for the next step—the one that is the most difficult for many people: forgiving.

Forgiving has to do with a situation in which someone did something to you that you felt was unjust. You feel you have been wronged, and that is something you cannot set aside—it haunts you. Forgiving is not easy or something that can be taken for granted. It is one of the most difficult—maybe even the most difficult of all—things we have to do in our relationships with our fellow humans.

If you forgive, you let go of all negative energy surrounding an unpleasant event. You realize that you cannot turn back time on what has happened, but forgiving is certainly not pretending nothing has happened! Forgiving is not:

- explaining away what the other person did
- forgetting or denying what has happened
- making the consequences or feelings seem less important than they are
- humiliating yourself

According to American psychiatrist Gerald Jampolsky, forgiving is to stop hoping for a better past. You cannot change what has happened, but you can decide how to cope with it now and what the effect will be on your future. Forgiving is something you do for yourself; therefore, you are the only person who can forgive the other and, with that, yourself. You don't erase the event from your memory, but you take away its negative charge. Then that negative charge changes poles in your heart and becomes positive energy.

You Forgive for Yourself

True forgiving means that you detach what the other person has done from the feelings they evoke in you. If someone literally stands on your toes, you experience physical pain. You take responsibility for experiencing that pain. It is your feeling, and you have to deal with that pain. It is your personal reaction to something that you can turn into a moment of learning, whether physical or emotional.

You can chose not to think that the person causing this moment of learning is "wrong" and to let go of the idea that the other person is guilty of doing something wrong. There is no "wrong"—"wrong" is just a label we stick on something we don't like or agree with. In the future, choose to stop labeling things and try to see as many events in your life as possible as ways to remind you of who you really are and where you are going.

Are you angry with someone because they did something to you? Try to forgive them. It is something you can do for yourself. As long as you stay angry, you are letting the other person win. Anger is a feeling that makes you unhappy. If you are very angry with someone because they have "done you wrong," you will be in a negative state of mind, day in and day out. You will be poisoning yourself with negative thoughts. This ugly feeling is something only you feel; the other person might not be troubled at all and may simply be getting on with their life. Forgive the other so you can let go of your anger. That is the only way to stop them from continuing to bother you.

"You have to forgive," Professor Dr. Ruard Ganzevoort writes in the booklet "Vergeving als opgave" (Forgiveness as a task): "If a person wants to become autonomous and free, then he has to forgive to break the spell. And to be able to break the spell, he has to get rid of not only his being a victim, but also of wanting vengeance and retribution, however justified they might be. He who cannot forgive stays a prisoner of the spell and is at risk of being a perpetrator too."

Self-Forgiveness

"Forgiveness isn't about the other, but it is about you. It is letting go of the burden you are carrying around with you," the Dalai Lama says in his book *The Essence of Happiness.* He adds that forgiving starts with self-forgiveness. According to him, we all make a mistake now and then at the cost of somebody else and then have regrets. Usually this is followed by a penalty we give ourselves or that is imposed on us by someone else. After such self-mortification, we might think everything is alright again, but that isn't true. A penalty doesn't get us there yet. After we are penalized there is another step to take: forgiving ourselves.

Self-forgiveness should not be confused with forgiveness by others. We often think that the other party will forgive us because we have paid the penalty or have said, "I am sorry," but that isn't true. It remains an active issue as long as we continue to feel guilty. Only when we forgive ourselves can we laugh again, be optimistic again, and feel love for ourselves—and therefore also give love—again, and thus leave the whole situation behind us completely. We must make it possible for others to forgive us, but as long as we persist in feeling guilty, in believing we are a culprit, others will see us that way, too.

Collective Forgiveness

The best known symbol of forgiving is probably Nelson Mandela. After twenty-seven years of imprisonment, he didn't lose himself in revenge or hatred but rather used that experience to be a good leader. He is a beautiful example of the transformation of emotions: using them as fuel for enthusiasm and willpower.

Bishop Desmond Tutu, also from South Africa, is another example. He, too, has shown how powerful compassion and forgiveness can be. At the age of sixty-two, Tutu was allowed to vote in his own country for the first time. There had been threats on his life for years, but he never gave up his fight against apartheid. The repression by the white regime in South Africa didn't make him bitter or rancorous. His motto is, "We have no future without forgiveness."

Tutu was chairman of the Commission of Truth and Reconciliation that was in charge of mapping the history of apartheid. According to him, forgiveness is the only solution, because "Revenge destroys both parties." As chairman, he wept publicly at the stories of the over twenty-one thousand victims and perpetrators, saying: "We must never forget what happened during apartheid, otherwise this country cannot be healed, but revenge and retribution are not an option. Forgiving is."

Tutu sees suffering as a possible way to achieve spiritual transformation if we are able to see the meaning in it. "Denying suffering can never lead to forgiving or to reconciliation. You must recognize what happened in the past to be able to straighten it out. You must take responsibility for your actions, otherwise your wounds will never heal." He describes the moments during the sessions of the Commission of Truth and Reconciliation, in which victims forgave their repressors, as the most spiritual experiences in his life.

Forgiveness Heals All Wounds

Sometimes it takes years before you can see the reason behind the dramatic events in your life; sometimes you never see it. You may wonder if you have dealt with all the pain you have encountered or if there is still a burdened past blocking things. There is a simple way to find out: Think back to your ex-partner, to your former job, to every moment end every encounter that you ever experienced as tedious, nasty, painful, or sad. The road to your destiny is not free if negative emotions are still evoked by those memories. Practice *tonglen* until your heart is totally relieved, and forgive what may be forgiven.

Tolerance and forgiveness heal all wounds. Once you are able to experience those feelings, you may forget. You don't have to, but you may. The words remain the same:

pain	peace
passed	present
past	promise
forgive	love
forgo	live
forget	light

The Play of Life, the Enlightened Earth, the Mystery of the Cross

13:

The Actor

Consciousness is infinite. One consequence of this is that consciousness survives death. Is there life after death? And there are other questions to answer. If everything has a consciousness, then so does the earth. If everything develops toward its higher goal, then so does the planet. Therefore, is the existing situation a developmental step of our planet toward its destiny? Have we been abusing the earth during the past twenty centuries, or was this way through matter predestined, meaning that a certain guarding, cultivating, and ennobling have taken place after all? The symbol of the cross helps solve this problem. When I found the answer to this great mystery, it made me optimistic about the future.

Everything has consciousness. Every consciousness is infinite. It is housed in the nonlocal space also known as the spiritual world. It comes and goes through gates of appearance and disappearance. If it reveals itself in space-time, it connects to a script and takes an appropriate shape that consists of life energy, information, and matter. Then, for a certain period of time, it plays its role on the stage of the world in this shape.

Every life story develops toward a goal. Every life therefore has a meaning. Every life-form's goal in life—its destiny—attracts it as if pulling it from the future. The past pushes it forward in its development, but a burdened past slows it down. During its stay on earth, consciousness gains life experience which in turn leads it to a higher level of consciousness, which is the goal of the great cosmic plan.

One can compare consciousness to an actor who chooses a part and acts in a play. The morphic field contains the script of the role. The zero-point energy field provides the energy to give the character shape, to let the actor play the part, and to enable the actor to make physical gestures that suit the language in the script. In humans, the middle self plays this role. The higher self is the director, the lower self is concerned with the shape of and your costume for the part, and the deeper self is the stage manager; it manages the stage and the archive containing your experiences of the roles played before.

As a human being, you have complete freedom to play your role in your own way and to improvise. Your free will is your highest good. You may move about the stage freely and do and say whatever you like. Because of this, the human script often has very few clear-cut lines of dialog, sometimes at best a few outlines with important events that have been agreed upon and laid out in advance.

Because other actors are involved in these important events, and other life stories cannot develop if you do not fulfill your role. Instead of starring as a leading actor, you will end up hampering someone else's development.

Work That Is Agreed Upon

In a play, it is obvious that everyone has been allowed to read his or her script in advance. This makes everyone a better actor, doesn't it? Everything and everyone on the stage benefits from it. The Universe is not interested in hell and damnation but rather in growth and becoming conscious. Everyone therefore knows what their role will be and what their destination is, but most people forget about their role once they are really into the play.

They also get distracted or seduced by other events happening on the stage. They lose their inner guidance and stray from their path. Their director often gives them directions to get them back on track, but most actors think they don't need help from the outside; they think it will hinder their freedom too much. Most directors therefore have to do their work discreetly and quietly, behind the scenes.

Becoming conscious is the goal, and therefore every actor picks a role they can really learn from and that will allow them experience a lot of (preferably) new things. As a result, many plays have difficult scenes, and sometimes there are dangerous stunts. As a player, you may have trouble finding good partners/opponents for those difficult, dangerous, and emotional moments. If there are occasionally blows to be exchanged or a lot of risk and tension, you and that person must be able to trust each other completely. Because of this, your opponents in life are often good friends with whom you have played before.

And luckily there are intermissions in every play. And every night the curtain falls, the spectators can catch their breath, and the actors see each other in the dressing room. There is consultation about how the play went: "Well that was a difficult scene today; your blow landed quite hard, and you were really yelling. What you said hurt."

Your opponent might say, "I'm sorry, I'm sorry. You know I don't really want to hurt you, but that is what the script says to do. You wanted some scenes with real action, and look, tomorrow I must hit you some more. We agreed on that before we started this show, remember?"

And then you can see in the eyes of your partner/opponent that he or she means it—that he or she really has good intentions and has a lot of trouble hurting you. Then you remember that when you read the script, you thought this role would be so interesting because you could learn a lot from it. A unique experience! You *chose* to take the part, after all. And anyway, a good play with a high level of amusement doesn't take forever—it is but a small ripple in the endless ocean of eternity.

Solving Mysteries

Before stepping onto the stage, therefore, you know what is going to happen in your play because you have read the script. Nevertheless, every scene is a mystery, and the answer is to figure out the reason why a given scene occurs in the play at a given moment. Why is this happening to you? Why is this happening in your life? This "why," this answer, is not in the script. Once you understand the reason why, you have learned the "lesson," and your consciousness has increased. This is one of the most important reasons why the play is played.

The mysteries are never so difficult that you cannot solve them. The only problem is that you have limited time. The play goes on, and many of the actors need to act in other scenes. Luckily, scenes that we haven't understood the reason for are repeated after some time. This happens for as long as it takes for you to understand the mystery—until you are no longer at a loss.

Most plays last for a very long time, sometimes up to eighty years, so there is ample time for repetition. However, after fifty or sixty years, or sometimes even after shorter periods of time, most actors have trouble remembering what was meant to happen. They have been on the stage for such a long time that they are no longer inspired. Their play becomes routine, and they forget to ask the right questions in order to solve the mysteries. This can lead to their completely forgetting what they were meant to do or say. This is difficult for the other players, because now they cannot have the experience they need due to not having a good "co-actor."

Acting Lifelike

Actors who have forgotten their lines or their inspiration could, of course, re-read their script in the dressing room, but that doesn't happen because they often, and with increasing frequency, remain seated on stage during the break because they have grown to identify themselves with the role over the years. This can happen to such an extent that they finally become stuck in the play. They forget that they are only playing a personality and believe they *are* their role. This is a shame, because then they take themselves, and life, much too seriously and can no longer see that it is just a play.

No one has much use for a spiritless personality with a rigid character who can no longer put things in perspective or improvise. Such people run around in circles and deprive themselves and others of a lot of fun and freedom of movement. We should always try to play the role of our life with heart and soul. Only then is our acting touching, convincing, and inspiring to everyone on the stage, from beginning to end.

As people live to be older and older, we can assume that we will have more roles to play in one life. We can learn a lot by playing these many roles, but only if we try to see the meaning behind them. It is alright to miss out on something; as long as you follow the thread in your script, life will make the ends meet.

The Upgrade of the "Extras"

I wrote the lines above, looked them over and thought the comparison of our daily life to a play was a good one. What about the extras?

Because of our free will, we humans are given only a little bit of script to follow, but the script for minerals, plants, and animals has always been quite fixed, with little or no room for them to move. They have played the same role for millions of years, and most of them led routine existences, which led to their consciousness developing slowly. But now, because of their encounter with humans, they have new possibilities for development. Until recently, they were extras on the human world stage, but all of a sudden plants and animals are being used for new purposes. Grasses, for instance, have acquired an important supporting role: they were ennobled to grains and from that moment on became food.

This happened to many plants and animals. Due to their contact with humans, they received a new destination, a new fate. For some that destination changed literally: Small potatoes from South America moved to far-away Europe to grow into big fat ones, which are good for cooking. Today, plants and animals have lots of experiences. Many are transported to far-off countries by car, train, boat, or plane. In that way, they travel widely and get a lot of new impressions, resulting in their consciousness developing more quickly. The problem is that most transporters only offer one-way trips. Many exotic plants and animals end up in places where they don't really belong, and unfortunately there is no way back home. This means they have to live in biotopes that are already occupied by domestic species.

Nowadays many international harbors only contain 10 to 20% of their natural flora and fauna. The water is contaminated with organisms from other parts of the world. In some countries it's now required to clean the hull of the ship offshore.

The Awareness of the Stage Manager

I looked at the actors and extras, but my question about the deeper self was not answered yet. The deeper self, the stage manager, had no part in this metaphor as of yet. What would happen if I would extend this play and bring in the stage manager?

The stage manager had an easy job, until man came on stage. Then, all of a sudden, things livened up. It took a while to get used to these changes, but in the first few centuries the development of humanity was self-restrained—it was possible to keep track of innovations. Development over the last few centuries, however, has been explosive, and there are more and more actors on the stage and they create new things all the time. The natural order is being disrupted rapidly, and the whole thing threatens to end up in total chaos.

We humans spend more time on ego trips than we do following our script. The worst aspect of this is that many "extras" have had to leave the stage ahead of their time. We have been so rough with them that some of them have had to be taken away wounded. The stage manager has often looked at the play with sorrow but has also learned a lot from it. And that was the exact intention—that is why the stage manager can live with it. Besides, the manager knew this could happen because it was in the script.

The Greatest Mystery

I had extended my comparison of life to a play. The stage manager, the deeper self, had acquired an important place in it. If this theory is true, every path in life would be inseparably connected to the development and awareness of the earth, because, before it disappears, the consciousness goes through earth, through matter, as we saw in Chapter 10

Indeed, there has never before been a period in human history that has been as materialistic as ours. Many literally dove into matter, only to find out that matter is 99.999999999999 percent void and that everything consists of energy and information, which in turn are the carriages for consciousness. The development of materialism didn't do the earth much good, but as it turns out, Mother Earth probably knew all along about what was going to happen. If we can read our script, can she too?

This was last and greatest mystery I still had to solve. I decided to look for clues that could tell me something about my role as an actor in relation to Mother Earth, the planet I live on.

The Consequence of Consciousness Beyond Life

I started by reviewing what I had learned so far. My consciousness is infinite. I am at home in the nonlocal space, also known as the spiritual world. That is where I came from, and that is where I am going back to, through a gate of appearance and one of disappearance. When I came into this world of space and time, I connected myself to a script and a body shape in which I can do as I choose and say what I have to say. I have been given a certain amount of time to do so. This time span goes quickly or slowly, depending on my lifestyle and the activity of my brain.

My life develops toward a goal. My destiny attracts me from the future. My past pushes me forward. If I have a burdened past, it hinders my development, making my life complicated. In a relaxed state, I can direct my path in life with my thoughts and my heart, and thus I can create good luck. I am helped on my path by the other parts of my being, my lower and higher selves.

During my life I have had all kinds of experiences, and through them I have gained knowledge about life. This process of becoming conscious leads to a higher consciousness. If everything has consciousness, then my life also has influence on the consciousness of the earth. This insight came from all the previous things I had thought and written. I saw the connection, and at the same time the consequences. If my consciousness is infinite, when I come and go and stay temporarily in a body on this planet, that means that my consciousness will live on after my body has died, which means there is life after death. I, with my consciousness, will live on in the spiritual world.

Now I had two questions to explore. Before looking at the influence of my path in life on the consciousness of the earth, I decided I wanted an answer to the second question—is there evidence of life after death? That question seemed simple, but finding an answer seemed impossible.

Near-Death Experiences

In our discussion of consciousness in Chapter 10, I referred to Dutch cardiologist Pim van Lommel's book *Consciousness Beyond Life*. In 2001 van Lommel published an article in the renowned medical journal *The Lancet* about his research on near-death experiences (NDEs) in 344 Dutch patients who had had cardiac arrest while in the hospital. As it turned out, 62 of them had had an NDE. Van Lommel's article was the largest and most extensive inquiry that has ever been done on this subject, and it became world news. The proof was so significant and unambiguous that all attempts to explain NDEs as something else could thereafter be refuted. Because of his study, we can no longer deny an NDE as an authentic experience that cannot be reduced to fantasy, psychosis, or lack of oxygen.

According to van Lommel, an NDE is a memory during a special state of consciousness that includes specific elements like the observation of one's own resuscitation or coming back to life from a position outside the body; the experiencing of seeing a tunnel, a light, an overview of one's life, memories of early childhood, images of the future; and meeting people who have died. This experience nearly always causes drastic and permanent changes in the life of the person involved, usually leading to the disappearance of their fear of death. Everything that is experienced during an NDE has a much greater significance and quality of reality and truth than what is experienced during normal waking consciousness.

There are more and more mentions of NDEs in the medical community, and this is because of the increased chance of surviving a traumatic health event through improved life-saving and reanimation techniques and treatments. From research in America and Germany, we know that about 4.2 percent of the population claims to have had an NDE, and it is estimated that in the last fifty years, probably 25 million people worldwide have experienced an NDE.

The Twelve Elements of a Near-Death Experience

Near-death experiences have been known about for centuries and in many cultures, and people essentially report similar experiences. Psychologist Carl Jung had an NDE in 1944 during a heart attack. American author Raymond Moody was one of the first who systematically researched these experiences. In his 1975 bestselling book, *Life After Life*, he describes twelve different elements of an NDE and the sequence in which they usually occur. Moody emphasizes that every NDE is unique and is experienced as a whole, not as a series of parts. Also, not all elements occur in every experience; most people only experience a few. The twelve elements are:

1. The nature of the experience is indescribable.
2. There is a feeling of peace and quiet—any pain felt previously is gone.
3. There is a realization of being dead.
4. There is an experience of being outside of one's body (an out-of-body experience); for example, people can see their own resuscitation from a location outside of their body.

5. This is followed by a stay in a dark place, where a bright spot of light originates at the end of a tunnel toward which one is pulled at a high speed.

6. This is followed by the perception of unearthly surroundings—a dazzling landscape with beautiful colors, flowers, and sometimes music.

7. Meeting and communicating with people who have passed occurs.

8. Meeting with a radiating light or with a creature of light occurs. An absolute acceptance and unconditional love are experienced. At the same time, one is touched by deep knowledge and wisdom.

9. There is a life review, overview, or life panorama—a retrospective of one's whole life from birth onward. Everything is experienced again. One sees one's life in one moment. Time and distance don't seem to exist. Everything is there at the same moment. The person may feel they have looked at this retrospective for days, while it turns out that it actually lasted for just a few minutes.

10. In a sort of preview, there is a vision of a part of their life that lies in the future. Here, too, there seems to be no time or distance.

11. There is a perception of a borderline that, if crossed, will not allow the person to go back to their body.

12. There is a conscious return to the body. When the person is back in their body, there is usually a feeling of disappointment, because something beautiful has been taken away.

The Life Review

In *Consciousness Beyond Life*, Van Lommel writes the following about the overview of one's life:

> Usually the overview or retrospective is experienced in the presence of the Light or of a creature of Light. During a panoramic overview one not only relives every action and every word, but also every thought of the life that has passed. One realizes that everything is an energy that influences not only oneself but others as well. The whole life, from birth to the moment of the medical crisis, may be relived, both as a spectator and as someone involved. One knows one's own feelings and thoughts as well as those of others during earlier events, because one is connected with the memories and feelings of others.
>
> During the retrospective on one's own life, one experiences the consequences of one's thoughts, words and actions on other people. This leads

to insight on whether love was given or, instead, withheld. This can be very challenging, but no one feels judged: one simply gets insight into how one has lived and how this has influenced others. There is an understanding that every thought, word or action has a lasting effect on oneself and the other. One understands that there is a "cosmic law" by which everything one does to others is also experienced by oneself, and this applies equally to love and attention as it does to violence and aggression.

Van Lommel's well-documented book, *Consciousness Beyond Life*, contains many accounts of people who have experienced an NDE. One chapter contains an extensive description of the two NDEs of a woman named Monique Hennequin. I quote her experiencing the life overview, because it is a beautiful illustration of what has been written about above:

> *The "how and why" of my actions during my life became clear because I saw, felt and knew how people felt during (and often also after) contact with me. I saw all sorts of events from my life. I recognized everything, everything felt like I had just gone back in time and was totally present at the moment at hand.*
>
> *What had I done with my life? My God, I was my own executioner and judge at the same time. If I saw that I had done something wrong, I wanted to go back and set things right. It wasn't that I had really done something wrong, but I felt the pain, the suspicion, the anger, the helplessness, the sadness of all people who felt this because of me.*
>
> *To tell you the truth, it wasn't really so much what I had done to others, but more what I had done to myself. These people mirrored my own pain, suspicion, anger and helplessness as well. In those moments I had missed out on opportunities to take full responsibility for my thoughts, words and deeds and in doing so had taken away the possibility to grow and become more conscious.*
>
> *I also saw that I could spontaneously react to someone in the "wrong" way, because the other person needed that at that moment. And I had felt guilty because I had ostensibly reacted in the "wrong" way, not knowing that the thoughts and emotions of the other person had my unintentional reaction as a consequence. Things could have gone so differently if things had been expressed and sincerely communicated.*
>
> *In events where I had difficulty seeing my responsibility, I "lingered" for as long as it took to take it in. I wanted to explain why—and say I was truly sorry—to everyone I had hurt, intentionally or unintentionally. Nobody*

condemned me and I felt the warm support of the Light behind me all the time. How could this support love me? Didn't it see how naïve my actions were in life? Out of ambition, egoism, fear and yes even out of joy or euphoria.

Luckily I also saw and felt all the nice, happy, satisfying, and joyful moments I had given to others (and therefore to myself) through my thoughts, words and deeds. Everything tumbled about, my whole life! Sometimes I even had to laugh. I didn't think for a moment where I really was and was wholly absorbed in my whole life.

I looked at my actions in the balance and I didn't do too badly. Everything had now been accounted for, all guilt (or rather all the being unconscious) had been taken away by the pain and the taking responsibility. I did think however, that there was some explaining to do to some people. I wished I could reach them. Why had I said so little during my life? Fear, but that fear had now completely gone. I was never going to be afraid again of my thoughts and feelings. Not afraid to fail in the eyes of others or to be challenged. I was and will be, my own judge. From now on I would be the one I would answer to. Everything went hazy and suddenly, with an enormously painful force, I was back in my body. What had happened?

No Purgatory and No Gateway to Hell

Van Lommel's research shows, unambiguously, that there is life after death. There is even a certain structure in the sequence of events when the soul leaves the body. But there is more: During near-death experiences, there is not only a conscious perception but also the experience that everything is energy, that everything is connected, that every thought has influence, that time and space are relative, that inner and outer are one. In essence, everything experienced fits the new view of the world described by quantum mechanics. That gives rise to hope.

The most beautiful—and certainly the most important—thing is that there is no judgment. There is no purgatory, no gateway to hell. You have finished playing, your role has ended, and you evaluate your work in the company of a loving light. You even experience the effect of your thoughts, words, and deeds, and from this you draw conclusions and explore consequences. The world after death is whole. All parts are one. There is unity. Therefore, there is no room for division and judgment. It is about insight into yourself and taking responsibility for your actions. In short, this is the process of becoming conscious. Every time, even after death, that is what it is all about.

Becoming Noble

I was now sure of the fact that my path in life contributes to my own process of becoming conscious, but does the consciousness of Mother Earth also develop because of this? That question had not yet been answered. Can I do whatever I please on earth without interference, or is there a bigger scenario I know nothing about but in which I play a part? What is the meaning of the presence of humans on earth? What do we mean to each other? What do we do to each other?

My background in biological agriculture made me think of the words *culture*, *agriculture*, and the Latin *cultura agri*. Culture points to a number of aspects of a society, ranging from cultivating the soil to activities dealing with the arts and the development of the intellect. The oldest meaning of the word, however, is cultivation of a field, *cultura agri*.

The word culture is derived from Latin *colere*, which means "to take care of," "to cultivate," and "to ennoble." "Culturing," or cultivating, a piece of land therefore literally means taking care of the earth, cultivating it and ennobling it by having compassionate contact with both the earth and nature.

Ennobling means refining something. Something noble is of a high standard. Taking care of the earth and ennobling it means refining the earth, bringing it to a higher level. In other words, refining the gross physical earth, with everything on it, to subtle matter. During antiquity, enlightening the earth by cultivating her was the goal for mankind, and agriculture was the means for doing so. To show her gratitude for this work, the earth gave us food, which in turn enabled us to do our daily work.

The basis of this daily work was an inner peace of mind. People knew that peace of mind contributes to right values and that right values lead to right thoughts. Right thoughts lead to right actions, which are in tune with what you want to achieve, and these right actions create works of quality. Quality is durable and is the basis of every trade. Always aim for an inner calmness in which you are not estranged from your surroundings. If you can manage that, everything else will proceed naturally and of its own accord.

Bringing the earth to a higher level—letting it radiate—therefore begins with us. We, too, are part of nature and are connected inseparably to the earth. There is a Dutch proverb that says, "If you want to improve upon the world, start with yourself." Taking care of, cultivating, and ennobling the earth therefore means, first and foremost, cultivating our inner selves.

That is nothing new—in the Middle Ages people wanted to be nobles. The knight in shining armor was not just seen a warrior but as someone who had risen above his temper and could control himself. He would only pull out his sword if his country and people—and therefore his culture—were threatened. Despite being brave in the face of battle, this type of noble would rather devote time to romance and love; at home, he would write poems and sing songs as a minstrel.

A noble person can ennoble their surroundings. According to tradition, Zarathustra ennobled grasses into grains. He "talked" to the grass and "motivated" the blades to make the best of themselves. His words literally made them rise to the occasion, and they transformed into proud and noble grains.

The Difference Between Culture and Civilization

In the eighteenth century the terms "culture" and "civilization" began to be used separately. "Civilization" came to be connected to outer characteristics like ownership, possessions, clothing, and good manners. "Culture," on the other hand, has to do with one's inner state and relates to things like mental development and feelings of responsibility. The distinction was made because, from the eighteenth century onward, the outside world became more important. At that time, materialism gained the upper hand. The pursuit of possessions and personal goals came first, and cultivating or ennobling the earth became less important.

According to the materialist approach, reality can only be understood and explained from matter, which is built from ever-smaller particles. The materialist is interested in the earth, not to ennoble her but rather to rule her and to develop techniques to do so. The materialistic goals are prosperity and satisfaction of want. Quantity and growth become key concepts, and nature becomes an enemy. We know what the results are: massive pollution, exhaustion of resources, extinction of plant and animal species, and global changes in climate. A small part of the world population has reached a grand level of material well-being at the cost of our natural habitat, while the greater part of humankind still lives in poverty and goes hungry. The awareness that this can no longer go on is growing worldwide, so there is possibly a glimmer of light at the end of the tunnel.

The Enlightened Earth

At first it was about *cultura agri*: taking care of, cultivating, and ennobling the earth. Bringing the earth to a higher level, letting it radiate, enlightening it. Right now our earth, which has more than seven billion people living on it, is very much out of balance, and this goal seems very far off.

Some time ago I visited an exhibition on the environment in which the growth of the world population was shown using lights. Each light represented one hundred thousand people. At the beginning of our Common Era, there were only a few lights, but over the ages you could see the number of lights growing slowly. Starting in 1850 onward, the lights began to spread across the earth faster and faster. It looked like a plague, a disease. It was frightening.

I nearly walked out in disgust before I realized that what I saw was a radiant, enlightened earth. *Cultura agri* is what it was about all those ages ago. Now there are seven billion people, and every one of them carries a spark inside! And even if every spark has just a little bit of a glow, there has never before been so much potential to cultivate the earth, to care for it, and to ennoble it.

It is about culture inside us and in the world outside: "As within, so without." If we realize that, we can make the earth shine as never before.

Ennobling Matter

Whichever way you look at it, matter has been brought to a higher level because of the development of technology. We have started ennobling and refining it; we have smelted large chunks of iron ore into pure iron, turned this into stainless steel, and used all sorts of techniques to make all sorts of shapes and compounds. From raw parts, we make functioning wholes. It doesn't get any nobler than this.

We have also done this to petroleum, which must be refined from crude oil. Refining is a way of ennobling, as it is a way to turn raw products into usable materials. The final results are fuels, plastics, textiles, and medicines. There are scores of examples; all you have to do is look at the millions of utensils in the world. In every one of them matter has been brought to a higher, more complex level, and technology helps us do this. In itself, technology is neutral—neither good nor bad. Depending on what we do with it, it can become either a friend or foe of life.

Materialism has unconsciously started the cultivation of the earth. We are on the right track, but somewhere on the way we made a leap that was too big. In early times it was more common to first evoke an inner peace of mind and a caring attitude in oneself. This is exactly the attitude that HeartMath describes (Chapter 5) as necessary to reach a coherent heart. Science has proven that such an attitude has a positive influence on both ourselves and our surroundings. The earth used to be cultivated from that basic attuned attitude; this was the origin of culture. The materialist couldn't care less about this, however. Out of self-interest, materialism immediately started with ennobling matter, and the consequences are well known.

Nevertheless, it seems that we are on the right track. Before we can continue the process of ennobling, however, we need to take a hiatus. We have to create inner peace of mind once again, shift attention inward, and return to the center of our wheel in order to retain—or regain—the awareness that everything is alive. We need to act with heart and soul, and develop a caring way of interacting with the earth.

Was a Deal Made...?

Everything has consciousness, and everything develops to a higher level. According to this line of thought, human activities are helping the earth to develop, but I wasn't yet convinced of this. Materialism had set in ages ago, developed, but is now in overdrive, and it will be just a matter of time until it will run out of track. This is quite something! If all the parties involved started this adventure deliberately, some kind of deal was made ages ago. Are there any indications of that having happened?

In his book *Conversations with God: An Uncommon Dialogue*, Neale Donald Walsch describes how much God needs humans to give divine desires a concrete shape in matter. According to him, humans, whether in the name of God or by order of God, are the designers and translators of celestial inspiration into tangible matter.

This is a beautiful thought. It made me think once again of the cycles in the Maya calendar. In it, every cycle has a particular theme and serves the purpose of developing consciousness. Had the collective consciousness of humankind come to some understanding with Gaia a few thousand years ago? In view of the disaster we have created, it might be better to call it an overly permissive agreement.

I was still looking for some sort of "proof" or a sign, something from the distant past that would support this interpretation. It was almost unthinkable that Mother Earth didn't know that the path of development she was taking would lead to overuse and exhaustion. I kept looking and thinking about it until I almost collapsed—but then the wheel caught my eye again.

The Symbolism of the Cross

In the wheel I saw the horizontal and vertical lines that form a cross together and that divide the whole world into four equal parts. The vertical line symbolizes the mind, and the horizontal line symbolizes matter. As we said in Chapter 3, the circle with the isosceles cross is a very early symbol of harmony and wholeness that is found all over the world. The Celtic cross, also known as the solar cross or the Sun Wheel (see Figure 13.1 on the next page), is an example.

FIGURE 13.1. The Celtic cross, or Sun Wheel

There are many kinds of crosses. All of them symbolize the wholeness of the world in one way or another. While we may not see this right away, the symbolism of a cross becomes easier to understand if you place it in a circle that represents the world.

Then you can see that the swastika (see Figure 13.2) is also a symbol of wholeness and harmony. Most crosses are static, but this type of cross is dynamic. At the same time, it shows, through the lines at the end of the spokes, that the whole world is in motion, is developing. The wheel turns, so you draw the lines in a certain direction, depending on what force you want to emphasize. The formative force turns the swastika to the left, and the expansive force turns it to the right. This symbol has been used since ancient times and can be found all over the world, in cultures ranging from ancient India to the native peoples of North America. Earlier it was often used as a sign for luck, but now this "hooked cross" is seen as having negative connotations because of its use by the Nazis.

The Egyptian ankh (see Figure 13.3) symbolizes the fertilization of the earth by the sun and by life. The opening in the upper half can be compared to the female vagina, which symbolizes the gate to eternal life. The lower half—which is often depicted as an obelisk—symbolizes the phallus. The two meet in the axis, where fertilization takes place. The horizontal spokes of this cross are a little bit shorter than the vertical axes. The emphasis is on the connection between heaven and earth.

FIGURE 13.2. Swastikas in the Cathedral of Amiens (France)

The Riddle of the Latin Cross

The Latin cross is the best known religious symbol of Christianity. It symbolizes the victory of Jesus over death. Christians believe that Jesus Christ, by dying on this cross, took the sins of humanity unto himself. He overcame these sins and death through his resurrection three days after his crucifixion. Because of this, suffering, reconciliation, and redemption are also symbolized by the Latin cross.

The Latin cross is called a crucifix if the body of Jesus is hanging from it. Roman Catholics usually use the cross to emphasize the sacrifice made by Jesus, while Protestants usually prefer the empty cross, which, according to them, is a better symbol for the resurrection.

The Latin cross is special because it has an important meaning to many people in this world and because it doesn't represent harmony as do most other types of crosses. If you draw a circle around it, you will not get four identical parts.

FIGURE 13.3. The Egyptian ankh

You can draw a circle around the upper part, but in that case the lower part of the vertical axis is not included. If you try to include this part, the upper part is rounded, but the lower part looks as if it is sagging strangely; there is no way to get a balanced, harmonic unity (see Figure 13.4 on the next page).

I thought this was strange; there had to be a deeper meaning and an important reason for this choice. Of course Jesus Christ had died on this type of cross—an important event—but Christianity has an abundance of symbols. Why then precisely *this* Latin cross?

The Signpost

A lot of thinking and letting your reasoning work overtime usually makes matters more complicated. That is what happened to me, and for a long time the mystery of the Latin cross remained unsolved. That was until the day I went back to the origin of the wheel. In the first division of the fertilized Cosmic Egg, mind and matter come into existence. The upper half of the wheel symbolizes the mind, the

FIGURE 13.4A. The lower part of the Latin cross goes through the wheel, and there it makes contact with the spiritual world.

FIGURE 13.4B. The Latin cross is not in balance. The lower half of the wheel (matter) is larger than the upper half (mind).

FIGURE 13.4C. The combination of both pictures shows that the Latin cross symbolizes a path where gross physical matter comes into contact with the spiritual world and so becomes subtle matter, or in other words ennobled.

 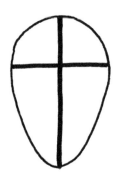 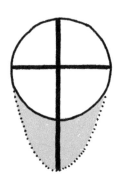

lower half, matter. Outside the wheel is the spiritual world, which looks onto her developing creation.

At a glance I was able to see the deeper meaning of the Latin cross. This cross "does something" with matter, with the earth. You can look at it in two different ways: In the second (middle) drawing, the emphasis is on the lower half, that of matter. That is represented most strongly, and here lies—literally and figuratively—the center of gravity of this cross.

In the first drawing the vertical axis goes through the circle and then comes into the spiritual world. If you superimpose the two drawings, this means that gross physical matter comes into contact with a higher vibration and turns into subtle material, as it were.

The Latin cross symbolizes the ennobling of matter. Not only that, but because of the change of the center of gravity, the cross also indicates a direction. Consciousness has a seat in the center of the wheel and accumulates along the vertical axis. The vertical line of the Latin cross therefore symbolizes a direction for consciousness into matter.

This cross is a signpost for the heart of matter. It leads consciousness into the heavy, dark matter, away from the upper half, away from the mind. It does this deeply, to a place where it has probably never been before, to the edge of the wheel, where it can go no further. There it seems to encounter a dead end. But is it really a dead end? Is the gate closed? Is this where death lurks in the deep, or is there life after death?

Yes, there is life after death. For some reason, the gate is open and the journey continues, back to the light of nonlocal space, the spiritual world. And then it turns out that not only does consciousness resume its journey, but it is accompanied by matter, or the earth, which follows in the footsteps of consciousness while vibrating at a higher frequency.

Mankind and the Cross

I was dumbfounded. I had found my first clue: The Latin cross shows the connection between matter and the consciousness of the earth, both of which are brought to a higher level. If that is true, then the next question becomes: How is the consciousness of man connected to the Latin cross?

Of course Jesus Christ is, in the deepest sense of this phrase, connected to this cross, but I wasn't looking for that connection. I was looking for a link between it and myself, my middle self, and, if possible, to the wheel. Does my consciousness literally go into the earth?

I looked once again at the Huna vision of man and saw the three circles: head, heart, and belly, with the middle and lower self. In the heart they all meet, and that is the center of our wheel.

Then I took a ruler and a pair of compasses, and I took the heart as the center and drew a circle around the three smaller circles. Next to the heart I drew extra circles for the left and right arms. Then I drew horizontal and a vertical line, and there was my wheel, and within it, a human and a harmonic, or solar, cross! The last step to create the Latin cross wasn't difficult to make: I extended the vertical line between the legs, and there it was.

Much to my disappointment, when I finished, I didn't see a deeper relationship of man with the consciousness of the Earth through this cross. This Latin cross just stood on the ground; there was nothing special about it. It didn't go through the earth and back into the spiritual world. Alas…

Until I saw that the cross was incomplete. It wasn't finished!

A Light Dawns

In a Latin cross, the part below the horizontal line is always twice as long as the part above it. In my drawing that was not true. The line to the bottom was too short. I extended it and ended up at exactly the same place as where I had previously used my intuition to draw the higher self above the head.

This line stopped under man, in the earth, at the gate of disappearance.

According to this diagram, the Latin cross ends in the gate of disappearance under our feet. In the vertical axis of the cross, consciousness accumulates, and there one can see a direct connection of the middle and lower selves originating with the consciousness of the earth. This drawing confirmed what I had found previously, but everything was now connected to a human (see Figure 13.5).

Human consciousness is literally led into matter by this Latin cross. It makes contact with the deepest layer of "hard reality," breaks through it, and connects

FIGURE 13.5. The Huna vision of man
The Huna vision of man in connection to the wheel
and the Latin cross. The lower part makes contact
with the deeper self and the gate of disappearance.

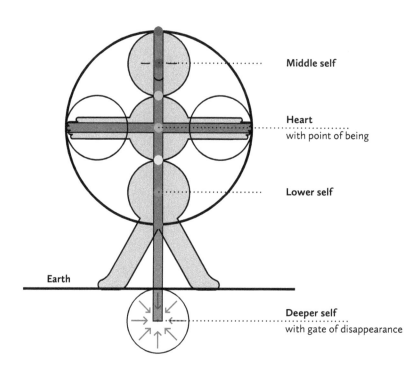

Higher self
with gate of appearance

Middle self

Heart
with point of being

Lower self

Earth

Deeper self
with gate of disappearance

to the consciousness of the earth behind the gate of disappearance. At the same time—and I found this shocking—you can see that there is no longer a connection with the higher self. The contact with the higher consciousness, with our lead, with our guide on our way to our destiny has been broken. In our connection to this cross, we are on our own.

Is that the deeper meaning of the death of Christ on the cross? That the consciousness of Christ was the first to go this way through matter, to open the gate of disappearance? Is that the deeper meaning of his words, "I am the Truth, the Light, and the Life"? Does this mean that as a human being you are cut off from your inner guidance on this material way, but that you should put your trust in him as your beacon during this dark journey?

And what about "Father, forgive them. They know not what they do"? Was that a prophesy of the following twenty centuries, with the present situation on earth as a climax? I leave these questions open. I had drawn a picture and found connections because of them, but I still felt something weak, uncertain, inside. Was this picture connected to something even greater? Something that would give me some more solid ground to stand upon?

To my surprise I found an important symbol when I least expected it. It was in the *Sacred Geometry Design Source Book*, written and illustrated by Bruce Rawles and Nancy Bolton-Rawles. The symbol was the cube of Metatron.

The Flower of Life

The cube of Metatron is one of the most complex and all-embracing geometrical shapes that exists. It is part of an even more complex pattern known as the Flower of Life (see Figure 13.6 on the next page). This six thousand-year-old symbol can be seen around the world on ancient buildings and holy monuments, including temples in Egypt and India. It consists of nineteen overlapping circles surrounded by two circles. The nineteen circles together form a unique geometrical pattern. The function of the two larger circles, however, remained unclear to me.

Over the ages, philosophers, artists, and architects have looked upon the Flower of Life as a representation of divine perfection and harmony. It is known as the ultimate symbol of sacred geometry, which includes the fundamental shapes of space and time. Many symbols have been derived from this basic pattern. The Star of David is an example, but so is the Tree of Life (see Figure 13.7 on the next page), an oblong geometrical model that has been and is used by several religious systems, among them Kaballa.

FIGURE 13.6. The Flower of Life

FIGURE 13.7. The Flower of Life with, inside it, the Tree of Life

In ancient Egypt the Flower of Life was called "Merkaba" (*mer* means "light or energy field," *ka* is "soul," and *ba* is "body") because it symbolized the field of energy of man. In the book *Ancient Secret of the Flower of Life*, Drunvalo Melchizedek describes at length the origin of the Flower of Life and its relationship to the Merkaba.

The Cube of Metatron

You can draw seven circles in the Flower of Life. If you put six more circles around that, the Fruit of Life comes into existence (see Figure 13.8 on the next page). This symbol of thirteen circles is at the base of the cube of Metatron (see Figure 13.9 on the next page). This cube originates when you connect the centers of the circles with each other. The circles are orbs in reality, and if you look closely, you will be able to see other figures within the cube as well. The cube of Metatron is known as the blueprint of material reality because, according to sacred geometry, the basic shape of every atom, every molecule, every life form, and everything that exists is stored within it.

The basic shapes of matter are represented by the five Platonic solids (see Figure 13.10 on page 196).

These bodies have very remarkable properties; even though they have different shapes, they all fit together in an orb, and like matryoshka dolls, they fit perfectly into each other. At the same time, every shape has an opposite shape that can be created from it. The opposite shape of a cube is for example the octagon. No other shapes have opposites like this.

FIGURE 13.8. The Flower of Life, and within it the thirteen circles of the Fruit of Life
The Flower of Life has been expanded with the outer circles that are necessary to construct it in this drawing.

FIGURE 13.9. The cube of Metatron
This is created by connecting the centers of the circles of the Fruit of Life.

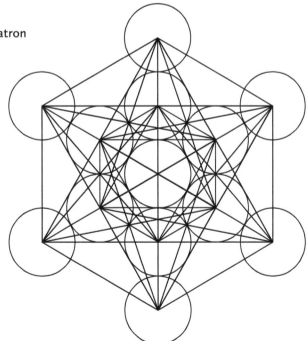

FIGURE 13.10. The five Platonic solids

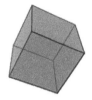

| Tetrahedron (four faces) | Cube or hexahedron (six faces) | Octahedron (eight faces) | Dodecahedron (twelve faces) | Icosahedron (twenty faces) |

Over 2,500 years ago, Pythagoras already knew at least three of these figures. Plato either learned of or found all five of them and called them the "cosmic elements of the world." He related them to the five elements: earth, water, air, fire, and celestial matter, or ether, zero-point energy, life energy. The cube of Metatron contains them all and therefore symbolizes reality in all of its essence.

Full Circle

I took my picture of the Huna vision of man with the Latin cross and put it on the cube of Metatron. They were a perfect match (see Figure 13.11 on the next page)!

The cube is seen as a blueprint of material reality. I took the heart of man as the center and drew a circle around the cube. There was the circle I had started with: the wheel, the whole, space-time. Humanity, symbolized by the middle circle, can move about freely here.

Outside the circle is the spiritual world, the non-local space. This is correct, according to the drawing: That is where the higher and the deeper selves are located. I then saw that these can probably also be depicted by one large circle containing within it three smaller ones, so I added that to the cube. Now I could clearly see that the higher and deeper selves are mediators between space-time and non-local space: One part has contact with us in the whole world, and another part reaches farther into the spiritual world.

That is when I discovered why there are always two circles around the Flower of Life. The whole world is bordered by not one but two circles; one is symbolic of the morphic field with information, and the other symbolizes the zero-point energy field containing life energy.

Consciousness connects to life energy and information when it incarnates. Literally this means "when it becomes flesh," or when it takes material shape.

FIGURE 13.11. The connection between the wheel, the Huna vision of man, the Flower of Life, the cube of Metatron, and the Latin cross
Above the head is the higher self, which has guardianship of the gate of appearance and our destiny. Under the feet, in the earth, is the deeper self, which has guardianship of the gate of disappearance and our life experience.

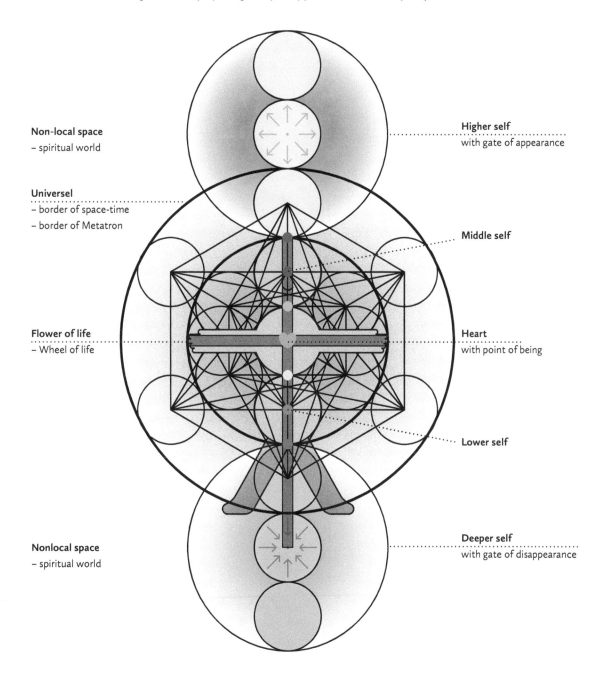

Non-local space
– spiritual world

Universel
– border of space-time
– border of Metatron

Flower of life
– Wheel of life

Nonlocal space
– spiritual world

Higher self
with gate of appearance

Middle self

Heart
with point of being

Lower self

Deeper self
with gate of disappearance

Consciousness plus life energy plus information creates a conscious formative force. A conscious formative force plus matter creates a conscious life form. The largest circle has been completed!

A Happy Ending

According to this analysis of its symbolism, Christian culture is inseparably connected to materialism; the Latin cross leads human consciousness into matter. Cut off from its spiritual source, human consciousness then went on a quest for the secret of life. In order to do so, it hacked matter into ever smaller pieces, until only tiny particles were left. In doing this it gained the knowledge and expertise from which technology developed. Because of this, matter and many life forms on earth received a new destiny. Their consciousness grew and they got to a higher level—they were ennobled.

Nevertheless, life remained a mystery. In the end, the journey came to an end at the bottom and outside of the wheel. At the greatest depth, death—but also salvation—were near: The gate opened, and once-blighted life arose in a new light. Matter and earth radiantly revealed the light from which they were once born. The journey had come to an end. The circle had come full circle. The way was predestined, the outcome was known, and somehow all involved knew this.

However, it was difficult to keep this memory alive. The Latin cross was meant as a sign of hope and as a beacon in the darkness. More often than not, however, it was associated with power, guilt, and death, and it lost its eloquence and true meaning. But we don't need a signpost anymore—matter has revealed itself and its greatest secret: In essence, everything is information and energy.

The collective consciousness of humanity doesn't yet accept this as true. We need more time for it—according to Elliot's wave another century or so because this difficult but wondrous journey started twenty centuries ago, and twenty-one are needed for inner work. After this long period of inner work perhaps thirteen centuries of outer work in the golden sunlight will follow.

We can look forward to that. We've earned it. And if our story is correct—very—maybe the whole disaster area we've created will be healed and we will be forgiven. The Universe is generous and magnanimous, but, most important of all, the Universe loves both us and a happy ending.

The Formative Force Applied—Principles of Energetic Guardianship

14 ⋮

I looked back. I had reached the end of my quest and saw the way I had come. The journey had taken longer than I had expected, but it had been worthwhile in every respect. The wheel had taken me to unknown places. My personal questions had been answered, and my goal had been attained. I knew I had found the answers; all that was left to do was put them into words: the principles of energetic guardianship.

Energetic Guardianship

If we take the position that everything consists of energy and that we shape this energy and give it meaning with our attention and intention, it is only natural to want to do this well, because it is the foundation of our daily life. In this chapter I describe the principles that make this possible. I call these the principles of energetic guardianship, and they are based on what has been discussed in the previous chapters.

In doing so, I take the stand that every organism, every organization, every house, every company, and every nature preserve is a dynamic, living whole that is constantly interacting with its surroundings. It can be compared to a wheel on its way to its destination. The wheel has a director—you—who serves as the creative force in your life or as a project leader (or the manager or as part of the board of directors of a company. In our terms these are also considered "guardians."

The foundation of health and vitality for an individual or organization is a harmonic balance between the guardian and his or her wheel. The principles of energetic guardianship help to maintain this balance. They bring the guardian back to the center and at the same time reinforce the self-healing and self-organizing powers in their wheel.

Two forces are at work in the wheel. The better known one is the centrifugal force that spins things outward—think of a centrifuge. This is experienced as an extroverted, masculine, expansive force that is connected to the intellect and the ego and is something we are all familiar with in daily life. You connect to this force by focusing your attention outward, toward material reality.

The other force is the center-seeking force that pulls you to the center. It is based on life energy and works toward vitalizing, building, self-organizing, and integrating. It is experienced as a receptive, feminine, formative force that is connected to the intuition and to us. We connect with it by focusing our attention inward on our thoughts and feelings.

The wheel will reach its destination if the guardian is in the center and these two forces are in dynamic balance. In a natural state they are in balance, but the feminine formative force is just a little more powerful, and this makes development possible. "Mind over matter" applies here: The force of the mind, when directed to the future, is always more powerful than the material force, which is connected to the past.

The Role of the Guardian

A guardian is responsible for the energetic integrity of his or her wheel. He or she balances the two forces and gives direction to the development of the whole. There may also be teams of guardians.

Management is a part of guardianship and exists in the realm of the head, the mind. True guardianship is something larger and is a state of being, of heart. It could even be considered a way of life. Guiding or "taking" the wheel in energetic guardianship is something you do consciously, and it requires inspiration and discipline. Guardians are not flashy. They have an inner peace, and it radiates. They know their job and are self-possessed. They are in control of their emotions, and in a way they are above them. Basically, nothing can disrupt their inner peace and balance.

In a wheel that is developing well, the guardian is at the center. There is no movement there, and time has come to a standstill, so to speak. Therefore a guardian has time, spare time. There is room in his or her agenda for unexpected conversations and events. All lines come together at the center. Here the guardian has an overview of the entirety, and they pull the strings. They direct the wheel and at the same time see to it that it is well charged with life energy.

Guardians do their work with heart and soul. For them, their work is not a routine job but rather more like a ritual, and they follow the voice of their heart. In this way their work also leads them to their own destiny. A good guardian is the right person in the right place in the right job. They have enthusiasm for the business and a sense of what is happening. One of their most important tasks is to listen, so that their employees feel heard and seen.

The wheel gets clear direction when the guardian has the goals clearly in mind and is fully convinced that they are able to achieve them. Expertise helps to formulate their goals in a realistic way and determine how much time it will take to attain them. New, unknown paths connect in subtle ways to tried and trusted directions taken in the past, and all those involved in the wheel can join in with processes of change.

Making the Hard Decisions

Guardianship has nothing to do with domination, which is related to power, top-down management, and hierarchy. A guardian works in a holarchy—a horizontal organization that consists of wheels within wheels and that is based on cooperation and equality. The welfare of the smallest particle is essential to the functioning of the whole, and clear communication is the most important condition for this. Decisions are made after all those concerned have been heard, and only then should the guardian make the hard decisions—"cut the knots"—that are needed.

Making proactive and difficult decisions is best done with a sharp axe. In that way one can make quick and sharp cuts. Also, it needs to be done by the guardian: Having two or more people wielding a sharp axe at the same time is not a very wise thing to do. Accidents will happen.

Guardians can therefore only function if they have the trust—which provides the sharp axe—of their coworkers. If you trust someone, you give them your confidence. We get confidence from other people, and it is difficult to give it to ourselves. When a guardian receives trust from another, their own self-confidence grows. As a guardian gets this confidence and the ability to cut through difficulties created by other people in their wheel, their axe becomes sharper, decisions can be made quicker, and the wheel develops faster.

Mutual Trust

Mutual trust is of great importance when it comes to the success of energetic guardianship. The extensive research done on the influence of intention (see Chapter 2) shows unambiguously how researchers can influence results with their personalities and inner convictions. This even happens from a distance and when the test subjects don't know the researcher.

The same applies to a company: The inner conviction of a guardian is a precondition for achieving good results. It is important that coworkers trust the guardian and that the guardian, in turn, is able to convince his or her coworkers that the goals that have been set are feasible. For their part, the guardian has to believe in their coworkers and have faith in their individual abilities and that they can get the job done as a team. That is why a wheel that is turning well needs trust—not blind trust but rather well-founded and mutual trust.

A guardian has a high level of responsibility. They can make or break, divide or unite. If the guardian privately holds the opinion that the enterprise is not going to work, it won't, and the road forward will be paved with obstacles and disappointments. If, however, they have a well-founded belief in its success, then that conviction will permeate the whole and will have a positive influence on everything, whatever it may be.

So every guardian needs to examine their own beliefs and attitudes and ask themselves these questions: Are they optimistic or pessimistic by nature? Do they see the positive or the negative side of things? Are they cautious or daring?

Choosing for a Free Conviction

The guardian's coworkers have to be conscious of the fact that they depend on the inner conviction of the guardian. Many people are not aware of this, and the moment it becomes clear to them it is the case, many of them become resistant. That is understandable and even appropriate in these modern times, when we generally like to do our own thing. It takes a good deal of acceptance and surrender to accept being a subordinate, but it can be very profitable if you are able to take this inner step. If, for instance, you doubt that you can execute a task successfully and your guardian is fully convinced that you can, accept their conviction, place yourself in their care, and benefit from it.

One day my car broke down on the motorway. AAA came along, and after some time it became clear that my car could only be repaired in a garage. The AAA man offered to take me there—for him it was a piece of cake. I, however, started sweating profusely, because it meant that my car and I would be towed along the motorway by a 15-foot-long cable while it was raining cats and dogs. On top of that, my battery was almost dead, so my windshield wipers, lights, power steering, and power brakes were hardly working.

We started out with jolts and jerks, crawling onto the highway. Then there was traffic rushing past us and rain pouring down my windshield while the wipers occasionally flipped to and fro. I felt there was no way this was going to work!

The only thing I could see were the two back lights of the tow truck, and the only thought running through my head was, "This is crazy!"

I was imagining the most terrible scenarios and doubting the ride was going to end well, when I suddenly realized that I was being towed by a man who was firmly convinced that we were fine. He was in charge of this mission, and it was his job to see to it that all ended well. At that moment I realized that he was my guardian.

I realized I had the choice of remaining fearful or giving him my trust. It wasn't difficult to choose: The second option was obviously the better one. I surrendered to his conviction, and not much later we reached our destination without a scratch.

Since that day I speak of "free" or "open" conviction. As opposed to "firm" conviction, which is always there and is sort of the basis of our lives, there is a freedom of choice in free conviction. You can choose to have a free conviction about an event or a process and place yourself in the care of a guardian at that moment.

Surrendering to Inner Conviction

Not only CEOs and senior managers of companies are guardians; daily life is full of them. A soccer coach is the guardian of his team, a teacher is the guardian of a classroom of students, a doctor is a guardian for his patients. If a teacher is convinced that certain students will flourish, then they will. If the doctor is convinced that a medicine he prescribes is a good one, and you trust him, then even a placebo will do the job—including producing side effects! The moment you get on a bus, train, or plane, the driver or the pilot is your guardian. At that moment you are in their care, and you surrender to their inner conviction.

There are people, especially men, who find surrendering like this extremely difficult. What they would like best is to sit at the front of the bus and "help" steer the whole trip. I had an acquaintance who was extreme in this regard. On one occasion, he and his wife went by bus from the Netherlands to Austria to do winter sports. A bus like that drives throughout the night, and so did he. Once they were in Austria, he insisted on getting onto his skis right away. Tired from a lack of sleep, he drifted off the slope. Everybody jumped out of his way—except a huge tree that didn't budge. He smacked into it with an enormous thud and the next morning went back to Netherlands with a broken leg. On the return trip he didn't drive, but unfortunately he didn't sleep a wink either because of the pain.

In some countries drivers hang religious symbols from the rearview mirror. Some even have their van or bus blessed by the local priest, hoping for safe traveling. As such, doing so is not a bad idea, because if the guardian brings the energy of his wheel to a higher vibration, everything and everyone in that wheel benefits.

Of course you can surrender to God or the Universe and place yourself in their care when it comes to dangerous undertakings. There are all sorts of prayers for emergencies. However, on this earthly plane the "higher" never works in a direct way but instead always works indirectly, through our fellow humans. Your guardian angel is not allowed to interfere in this free-will zone. A tug or steadying hand on the driver's wheel is not how it happens; all a guardian angel can do is inspire someone to do the right thing.

Therefore, you should wish your guardians well and let the light shine on them. They will feel better and be more awake and more aware, and in the end it is you who will benefit.

There are many forms of free conviction in daily life, in which you surrender to the conviction of somebody else at a certain moment. The more consciously you manage this, the better it works. Also, everyone is the guardian of their own wheels, because they all have people, animals, or plants in their care. It is important to be conscious of the great and formative influences we have on each other.

Hold Each Other in High Esteem

In some Buddhist orders, the abbot of a monastery is chosen by his fellow monks. Together they look for the person who is most suitable for the job. When the choice is made, the new abbot is blessed in a special ritual and "put on the throne." His fellow monks literally put him on a pedestal, where, as tradition has it, he has contact with a higher spiritual level and can therefore attain a higher insight. By doing this, the whole community benefits from this "raising" of one suitable individual.

While it is true that the other monks defer to the higher insight of the abbot, they have first looked into who was best suited for the job and have chosen who they thought was the best person. So it is an agreement that the community has made among themselves: I think your suitability is "superior," so although it is logical that I become your subordinate, I am not inferior.

In a wheel—in a holarchy—everything has equal value. By "exalting" the guardian and placing them on a pedestal, this person can come into contact with a higher energetic level and with the higher consciousness of the company or organization. And this experience is important for the development of the entirety.

Putting someone on a pedestal, however, may quickly begin to sound or feel like a form of worship. It is perhaps better to hold the guardian in high esteem, because then the mutual trust is also connected to the heart. If you hold someone in high esteem, you raise them above themselves, and they will come to a higher level of insight.

Amplifying the Unique Vibration of an Organization

A guardian uses resonance to amplify the unique vibration of their entity or organization. Every organism, every organization, every company, every community, and every nature preserve has a unique vibration. This unique vibration can be enhanced by similar vibrations as we discussed in the section on resonance in Chapter 4 (page 50), where we noted that because of resonance, one can achieve great effects with relatively little force; that to achieve this, vibrations have to be similar and coherent; and that, aside from resonance, timing is also very important.

This means that you have to give the wheel a push at the right moment. Disease, diminished vitality, disharmony, disappointing results, difficulties adapting to new circumstances, and a low state of self-organization may arise if a wheel is not in harmony with its own unique vibration. A guardian can amplify the vibration of his wheel simply by attuning to the morphic field of the company.

To recap from Chapter 1 (pages 14–15), according to English scientist Rupert Sheldrake, the basis of the development of every organism and organization is a morphic field containing experiences from the past, scenarios for solution to problems, and plans for the future. In a company we speak of a company field, a memory or script in which everything that has ever happened in the company is stored.

According to Sheldrake, things that have a similar shape resonate with each other, and he calls this "morphic resonance." A guardian tunes in to the company field by picturing the company in a positive light. The more their picture resembles reality, the better the morphic resonance and the contact with the field. If the guardian is well connected to the company field and is at the center of the wheel, he or she can amplify the unique vibration of the whole company by repeating rhythmically a few times a week using, a sound, mantra, affirmation, or color visualization.

An Example of Energetic Guardianship

A good example of energetic guardianship in the Middle Ages was Emperor Charles IV. He was King of Bohemia—the western part of the Czech Republic—from 1346 to 1378, and in 1355 he was chosen to be emperor of the Holy Roman Empire. During his reign, Prague developed into the scientific and cultural center of Europe. It was the Golden Age of Bohemia.

Charles IV was a great builder. His building projects still dominate the skyline of Prague, including the St. Vitus cathedral, the royal palace in the citadel of Prague, and the Charles Bridge across the Moldau river, which includes the Old

Town bridge tower. The first university in Eastern Europe was founded at this time, as was the fortress of Karlštejn. And the New Town made Prague one of the largest cities in Europe.

The palace in the citadel of Prague was the center of executive power, but the center of Charles' wheel was in Karlštejn; from this place he had energetic guardianship of his empire. Karlštejn, which is twenty kilometers south of Prague, is the most famous fortress in Bohemia and one of the most important medieval buildings in the Czech Republic. Charles IV founded the stronghold in 1348 as a place to keep the crown jewels, important relics, and documents of state.

The Chapel of the Holy Cross is the central room at Karlštejn, and it is where the relics were kept. Charles IV had several rooms at Karlštejn at his disposal. In a small side room inside the monastery and Church of the Virgin Mary is the Chapel of St. Catherine, which was his private chapel. The walls are decorated with a golden plaster that is inlaid with semiprecious stones from all over the Holy Roman Empire. There are paintings of the seven patron saints of Bohemia as well as a painting in which the crucifixion of Christ can be seen. In the niche of the altar is a precious statue of the Madonna with Child.

This was the chapel were Charles IV retired to make contact with his realm. We now know that the gems in the walls are resonators that resonate with the morphic fields of several parts of the empire. By relaxing into prayer, the emperor had awareness of it all and sensed what was going on. In this way he perceived what the situation was like in the north, the south, and so on. If an area didn't give the right feeling, he sent his attention and intention there, amplifying the unique vibration with the help of the patron saints.

If it still felt wrong after a while, then it was time for an envoy/ambassador to have a look. In case of an emergency he went there himself to set matters right, sometimes accompanied by a small army.

Attention and Intention

Amplifying the unique vibration of an entity or organization also gives it enough energy to prepare its wheels for take-off. As the guardian connects to it with their heart and soul, giving it positive attention and life energy, it runs faster. Through the affirmation of goals, the guardian focuses their intention; with this information he or she determines the course—the direction in which the wheel will develop. Life energy plus information generates a formative force. Practically speaking, this means that attention plus intention generates a formative force.

This formative force is the constructive, center-seeking force that amplifies the vitality and self-organization in every wheel. According to ancient Chinese knowledge, this force is based on *ch'i*, or life energy, and is connected to the "mind," spirit, or information. From the connection of life energy and information comes the left-turning formative force. This inward turning vortex is the cycle of creation, where the spirit condenses step by step via subtle matter in order to connect to gross matter at the center. From formative force and matter comes a (life) form.

The moment when a visible form originates from an invisible thought, a change of attention takes place. The attention shifts from the inner world to the outer world. The leftward-turning, center-seeking force becomes a rightward-turning, centrifugal force. The cycle of origin changes into the cycle of decay. The emphasis is no longer on mind but on matter. Still, it is always "mind over matter" and is never the other way around, because the form comes from thought.

The Ten Principles of Energetic Guardianship

Effectively applying attention and intention in a wheel can be attained by following the basic principles of energetic guardianship described below. The time you take to practice these basic principles is earned back in spare time and (financial) good fortune. Five minutes of meditating a day will bring you a two-week holiday a year plus the money to pay for it. Meditation, therefore, is a good investment.

Principle No. 1: Check Whether Your Conviction Is Free and Independent

In order to have energetic guardianship of a wheel, you must first know if you really are the guardian. Is your wheel independent, or is it part of a larger entity with another guardian? If it is indeed free, you can do as you please.

As opposed to your firm convictions, your beliefs, which are always there and form the foundation of your life, there is freedom of choice in free conviction. When you place yourself in the care of a guardian, that is a free conviction. This can have its advantages. If a teacher is convinced that certain pupils will flourish, they most likely will. If the doctor is convinced that they are prescribing the right medicine and you trust them, even a placebo will do the job.

If you are not independent, then the first thing you must do is to look at your relationship to this guardian. This is a situation you see in many companies, where you as a manager are subordinate to the inner conviction of the guardian of the company. As a teacher you are the guardian of a class, but the school as a whole is under the guardianship of someone else. A forester takes care of a part of a park or nature reserve, but they are subject to the policies and energetic guardianship of their organization (e.g., The National Trust or the Parks Department). Even in relationships it is possible that you are subordinate to each other's convictions.

The question has to do with which entity or whole your wheel is a part of. If there is mutual trust between you and the guardian of that greater entirety—if you can believe in each other, if you have warm feelings for each other, and if your goals are in agreement with the destiny of the larger wheel—then your chances of success are great. You might even rise above what you could achieve on your own.

If all of what is mentioned above is missing, then you must wonder if you are in the right place. You may find yourself swimming against the current, and there is a good chance that you will encounter obstacles and disappointments. Your guardian has not given your enterprise their blessing and doesn't believe in your success, and that is a constant hindrance. The worst case scenario is that the guardian hopes your efforts will come to nothing. The disappointments in our work often seem to come from outside, but in many cases the cause is in the wheel itself.

It is also possible that you have an excellent relationship with the guardian and that your wheel develops very well and quickly because of it. So well and so fast, perhaps, that you no longer move in pace with the slower rate of development of the other wheels in the larger organization. That is not good for the whole; it literally and figuratively causes friction. A good team clicks and ticks. Resonance and relative attuning are important, but coherence and adaption to the pace of the greater whole are also aspects that should not be underestimated. If you walk too far ahead of where the music is, it might get quiet around you at a certain moment. In that case, slow down and enjoy your spare time until the others catch up.

Principle No. 2: Develop Inner Tranquility

You must first develop inner tranquility before you can work with life energy.

In our modern Western society the emphasis is on growth and expansion and our attention is drawn outward by advertising and events in the world. Therefore we are more connected to the centrifugal, expansive force than to the center-seeking, formative force. The consequence is that we end up on the outside of the wheel. We lose perspective, and time gets away from us. We get overworked and end up burning out.

After checking whether your conviction is free, the next step is to shift your attention from the outer to the inner world in order to restore balance and once again get in touch with the formative force. Once you are reconnected with this force through focusing your attention inward and feeling inner tranquility, you are automatically taken to the center of your wheel.

Inner tranquility is also necessary if you want to use your intuition. Through inner tranquility your brain waves slow down. This brings you into a relaxed state of consciousness and concentration. The merry-go-round of your reasoning slows down, and your intuition, which is necessary to be able to contact the morphic field, is activated.

To shift your attention inward, start by sitting in a comfortable position with your eyes closed, minimizing all external distractions. After that there are many different methods you can use: breathing exercises, prayer, meditation, and so on. Everyone can do this in their own way, and it doesn't have to take long. You can use a nice book by David Harp titled *The Three Minute Meditator: 30 Simple Ways to Relax Your Mind and Enhance Your Emotional Intelligence.* Jeffrey Brantley and Wendy Millstine needed a little more time. One of their books is called *Five Good Minutes: 100 Morning Practices to Help You Stay Calm and Focused All Day Long.* If you really want to develop your intuition, then read the classic book *Intuition Magic* by Linda Keen.

Five basic exercises to get to a relaxed state of consciousness were described at the end of Chapter 4 (see pages 57–59). The first exercise is the "heart lock-in" exercise from HeartMath, and in the last one you use the analyzer, a small, virtual instrument in your head that measures the frequency of your brainwaves. Sit in an easy chair and do exercises 1 to 4. End with exercise 5, which is about the analyzer.

Principle No. 3: Become Conscious of the Whole

You can only charge your wheel of life with life energy if you internally put boundaries around it that make you conscious of the whole.

The formative force works most strongly in the inner world. Therefore you can only balance your wheel if you put boundaries around it and then check on it. Consciousness of the whole starts with knowledge of all the parts *and* a determination of their borders. Where does the inner world of your wheel end, and where does the outer world begin? Such borders include, for instance, the outer walls of your house and the fence around your garden or field, the edges of the woods in a forest, or the location and perimeter around company property and buildings.

A guardian becomes conscious of his whole by taking it in mind intuitively and having a bird's eye view, by walking the borders in his mind, or by looking at a map or a picture and then mentally visualizing this picture. The size of the entity makes no difference—the limiting factor is the consciousness of the guardian. One person may be able to visualize a house, the next a castle, another a shopping center with all of its shops. The guardian who defines their whole in this way has intuitive contact with the morphic field of their wheel through morphic resonance, and in that way they are informed about the state of the whole and its individual parts.

A good way of checking to see if a guardian has consciousness of their whole is by letting them describe it. All is well if they can picture their company clearly in their mind and "know it like the back of their hand," but there is something wrong if they can't get beyond their office, the administration floor, and the restaurant. The larger the company, the greater the consciousness of the guardian must be. Do all parts of the company have their attention? If the attention is not there, no energy will flow there, and that little wheel can block the development of the whole system.

During a hearing in the Senate about the oil disaster in the Gulf of Mexico, the CEO of BP at that time, Tony Hayward, said that he hadn't known that his company had so many oil rigs in the Gulf. That is the biggest mistake one can make in a position like that—a guardian is expected to have consciousness of the whole.

No wonder so many employees—I prefer "coworkers"—feel lost nowadays or don't feel that their guardian has their back. The guardian is absent or busy putting out fires—like the fire on the Deepwater Horizon oil rig.

Principle No. 4: Have a Sense of What Is Happening

By making intuitive contact with your wheel, you can sense what is happening inside it. Your intuition tells you who and/or what part needs attention.

The formative force consists of attention plus intention. Giving something attention means giving it life energy. Consciousness of the whole is the first condition for giving attention. This determines to "what" you are giving attention. A sense of what is happening is connected to your heart and tells you "how" to give attention. You give positive attention by having warm feelings for your wheel. The size of the entity doesn't matter; every entity that someone can take into their heart and embrace with their consciousness can be charged energetically.

By making intuitive contact with your wheel, you can sense what is happening inside. The simplest way to interpret this information from the morphic field is to pay attention to your gut feeling as you go over the various parts in a state of relaxed concentration. Is it a good or a bad feeling? Is it happy or hurtful?

It isn't easy to obtain this intuitive information clearly right away. That takes a lot of practice, because we have to learn to discern which feelings have to do with the whole and which have to do with ourselves. A sense of what is happening also means actually being there, regularly showing your face on the work floor and asking coworkers how things are going. The feeling of "being heard" gives people confirmation and in many cases proves to be problem solving. As the guardian you have to follow-up, but your presence alone will do the work; you don't have to do anything, just be there.

After hurricane Katrina destroyed large parts of New Orleans, George Bush stayed at home. He didn't think it worth the trouble to visit the disaster area. Of the mistakes he made during his presidency, this may have been one of the worst.

If something unexpected or dramatic happens in your wheel, go there. Don't be afraid that you don't know how to handle matters. You don't have to do anything; your presence and your warm interest will be enough.

Principle No. 5: Put Your Wheel in the Spotlight and Practice Tonglen

You can charge your wheel energetically with life energy by "putting it in the spotlight."

After taking your wheel into your consciousness and into your heart, you can charge it energetically by "putting it in the spotlight." You do this by starting with exercises 1 to 4 mentioned in Principle No. 2. Then connect to your wheel by taking the whole in mind and putting borders around it. Then go to your heart with your attention and breathe through it a few times using the HeartMath method.

After that, ground your wheel. A place that is suitable will spontaneously come to mind. Just like in your own grounding, imagine roots or a grounding cord of energy going into the earth at that point. You can also visualize a chain or an anchor—any image will work if it works for you.

When the grounding has been accomplished, you can then invite a strong whirlwind—or more than one—that cleans the whole and removes all the stress, blockages, and old injuries. These all disappear into the ground or go back to their source.

After that you can put the whole under a spotlight from your heart by imagining a sun above it that bathes the wheel in a beautiful, radiant light. See and feel everything radiating and imagine it as being as beautiful, lively, and full of happiness as you can. Connect this joy of living to your wheel. If your wheel or organization is so large that it is difficult for you to imagine, then take a map and ground it, clean it with the wind, and put it in the spotlight.

Through this process you will discover where or with whom in the wheel things are not well. After having put everything in the spotlight, you can practice *tonglen* with these problematic elements or with those people as "subjects." Breathe their pain, bad mood, or sadness into your heart, welcome it there, and, depending on the situation, breathe love, light, or joy of life out on them.

Principle No. 6: Affirm and Visualize Your Goals

By giving attention to your wheel, you can speed it up, and with intention you can give it direction. You can aim your intention by imagining a goal you want to attain and then affirming it.

You have now charged your wheel with life energy by giving it positive attention. The next step is to give your wheel direction into the future. The future is malleable: What is coming to us or happens to us is something we have, for the most part, in our own hands. You can create good luck by directing your intention. By giving attentive energetic charging to the wheel, you can get it to run up to speed, and by intention you can give it direction. You can aim your intention by imagining a goal you want to attain and then you affirm it.

As discussed in Chapter 6 (see page 74), affirmation is confirmation, reinforcement. With an affirmation you reinforce something you want to have or want to attain. When a guardian has a goal clearly in mind and affirms it, they throw a line with an anchor into the future, so to speak. Every repetition of the affirmation strengthens this line and fastens the anchor more securely. Then the formative force (which is attention plus intention) can roll up the line and pull the wheel forward to the goal they have in mind.

During affirmation you use the upper half of the spiral of creation. First, shift your attention inward and go into a state of relaxed concentration with the help of HeartMath exercises 1 to 4. Then, while in contact with your higher self—your sun—make contact with your wish and check if realization may be given to you.

Check if your wish comes from ego and self-interest or is "eco," good for your home, for your wheel, and for the general interest of all who live in it. Connect your wish to these two words and feel/see in your mind what makes you happy or which one lights up most brightly in your mind.

Now you can visualize your wish, your affirmation, and by doing so you direct your intention. Then you connect your affirmation to life energy by taking it into your heart. You open your heart, receive your heart's desire, and ask your lower self to send up life energy. Assume that your wish will be fulfilled completely and feel the gratitude and appreciation in your heart. In this way you evoke feelings of appreciation and compassion in your heart, with which you radiate your wish and start to attract your future.

Principle No. 7: Use Knowledge and Expertise

Knowledge and expertise ground and confirm our consciousness in matter, and our common sense makes sure that we formulate realistic goals.

Intellect and intuition, reasoning and feeling, are complementary. One cannot exist without the other. Our feeling of what is happening can be understood and explained with the intellect. The intellect sketches a plan and shows if the goal is feasible.

We discussed expertise at length in Chapter 6 (see page 77). We explored how working successfully with life energy is inseparably connected to craftsmanship and professional knowledge that is derived from the physical world, acquired with our intellect, and based on the expansive force that pulls our consciousness outward. Expertise is applied to the lower half of the spiral of creation by expressing our affirmation, researching, planning, and deciding to execute it so that it acts accordingly and perseveres in case of disappointments.

Expertise brings in an awareness of time. You need to not only estimate how long it will take to get a job done but also how long it will take for you to be ready to receive the fulfillment of your heart's desire. Both you and the time must be ready for it.

Space and time are strongly connected, two sides of the same coin. Additionally, time is money is life energy. The formative force only works if you put boundaries on the space that is on your wheel and on the time in which a goal should be attained. What is your time frame? Of course it is possible to work with an open-ended schedule, but energetic guardianship is more effective if you define both space and time boundaries.

Principle No. 8: Go with the Flow

There is a time for everything. There is a time for inner work, such as affirmations, and a time for outer work. The two forces in the wheel change places with the regularity of phi.

One moment the formative force is stronger, and the next moment the expansive force takes over. The formative force is strongest in cycles of twenty-one units of time (minutes, hours, days, weeks, months, or years), followed by thirteen time-units of outer work, during which you have the greatest chance of your affirmation becoming reality.

Through experience you know if your affirmation will be fulfilled in the short term (21 days), the middle term (21 weeks), or the long term (21 months). You adjust the frequency of your affirmations to match this knowledge. With long-term goals, there is usually also a plan of action with intermediary goals that can be attained in 21 days or weeks. You can also affirm these. Therefore you have 21 days or weeks to get your wheel up to speed.

Affirmations once a day, and thirteen times in total, are enough to boost the formative force and anchor your goal. Don't do affirmations for longer than 21 minutes, because after that the force of the affirmation diminishes for 13 minutes. If you have less time—and are able to affirm well, using your heart and soul—even

13 and 5 minutes are enough. The least amount of time you must affirm is for 2 minutes.

In the first five days or weeks (weeks/days 1, 2, 3, 4, and 5) do your affirmations once every day or week.

After that you need to do your affirmations only on uneven days or weeks (7, 9, 11, 13, 15, 17, 19, and 21). At these moments the formative force works most strongly. Together, there are exactly 5 + 8 = 13 affirmations. It is best to do affirmations at a fixed time during the day.

Principle No. 9: Transform Your Burdened Past

The past pushes and the future pulls your wheel forward. If, however, you have a burdened past that you haven't come to terms with, then the past can pull you back so strongly that you cannot go on.

We discussed the idea of a burdened past many times in the book, starting in Chapters 5 and 6 (see pages 72 and 85). I will summarize some of the discussion here: A burdened past inhibits the development of your wheel and blocks the way to your future. You are confronted with this with the regularity of *phi* because time is cyclic. If there was a drastic event in your life, when you were 13, for instance, then the circumstances of this event will be repeated every 13 × 0.618 = 8 years, or until you recognize it and consciously cope with the original experience.

As the blueprint of your affirmation becomes anchored more securely, you will be confronted even more by the burdened past that resonates with it. You can transform this by writing your affirmation on paper and phrasing it in a way that concentrates the affirmation's energy, turning the written affirmation under your hand to sense where there is tension or resistance and then practicing *tonglen* until the pain and the resistance have vanished. This can take an hour and a half to two hours, depending on the burdens on the affirmation.

Principle No. 10: Be Here Now, Consciously and with Joy

You are here on earth to learn something, to make something beautiful out of your life, and to enjoy it!

The way is the goal. However much you charge the wheel, affirm goals, and have good results, if you don't go toward your destiny with consciousness and joy, it is meaningless. Being conscious comes first. You are here, firstly, to learn something. Secondly, you are here to make something beautiful out of your life so that your fellow humans and the earth can benefit from your presence. Thirdly, you are here to enjoy this wonderful life!

Life is experiencing. The Universe is not interested in hell and damnation but in development and growing awareness. Therefore, you can always trust that there will be a happy ending, and that means there is always hope. Keep it up, walk on; sooner or later you will end up at your destiny.

Everything is one, everything is energy, and everything is possible. Reality is a waking dream come true. Everyone is a God in the depth of their thoughts, and everyone can live a happy life and start over again at any moment. We have learned to divide our world, but we know now that we can also unite and heal it on a large scale. Let that be our firm conviction for the ages to come.

Bibliography

Adams, George, and Olive Whicher. *The Plant Between Sun and Earth*. Berkeley, CA: Shambhala Publications, 1982.

Alexandersson, Olof. *Living Water: Viktor Schauberger and the Secrets of Natural Energy*, 2nd Edition. Dublin, Ireland: Gill & MacMillan, Limited, 2002.

Andeweg, Hans. *In Resonance with Nature*. Edinburgh UK: Floris Books, 2009.

———. "Institut für Resonanztherapie—Brochüre" (Institute for Resonance Therapy—Brochure). Lünen, Germany: Institute for Resonance Therapy-Cappenberg, 1994.

Andeweg, Hans, and Franz Lutz. *Resonance Therapy in Eight Steps*. Lünen, Germany: Institute for Resonance Therapy-Cappenberg, 1997.

Andrews, Ted. *Animal Speak*. St. Paul, MN: Llewellyn Publications, 2002.

Argüelles, José. *The Mayan Factor: Path Beyond Technology*. Rochester, VT: Bear and Company, 1987.

Arntz, William, Betsy Chasse, and Mark Vicente. *What the Bleep Do We Know!?* Deerfield Beach, FL: Health Communications Inc., 2007.

Backster, Cleve. "Evidence of a Primary Perception in Plant Life." *International Journal of Parapsychology* X, no. 4 (1968): 141.

———. *Primary Perception. Biocommunication with Plants, Living Foods, and Human Cells*. Anza, CA: White Rose Millennium Press, 2003.

Becker, Udo. *The Continuum Encyclopedia of Symbols*. New York: Continuum Intl. Pub Group, 1994.

Beekman, W. *Bij heldere hemel* (In a clear sky). Zeist, Netherlands: Uitgeverij Christofoor, 2002.

Benson, Herbert, and D.P. McCallie. "Angina Pectoris and the Placebo Effect." *New England Journal of Medicine* 300, no. 25 (1979): 1424–29.

Berendt, Joachim-Ernst. *The World Is Sound: Nada Brahma: Music and the Landscape of Consciousness*. Rochester, VT: Destiny Books, 1991.

Berg, J.H. van den. *The Changing Nature of Man: Introduction to a Historical Psychology*. New York: W.W. Norton & Co., 1983.

———. *Het menselijk lichaam* (The human body). Nijkerk, Netherlands: Uitgeverij G.F. Callenbach, 1961.

Bischof, Marco. *Biophotonen: Das Licht in unseren Zellen* (Biophotons: The light in our cells). Frankurt am Main, Germany: Zweitausendeins, 1995.

——. *Tachyonen, Orgonenergie, Skalarwellen—Feinstoffliche Felder zwischen Mythos en Wissenschaft* (Tachyon, orgone energy, scalar ways—subtle matter between myth and science). Aarau, Germany: AT Verlag, 2002.

Blavatsky, Helena P. *The Secret Doctrine.* New York: Tarcher, 2009.

Bohm, David. *Wholeness and the Implicate Order.* New York: Routledge and Kegan Paul, 1980.

Braden, Gregg. *The Divine Matrix.* Carlsbad, CA: Hay House, 2008.

——. *Fractal Time.* Carlsbad, CA: Hay House, 2009.

——. *Walking Between the Worlds.* Belleview, WA: Radio Bookstore Press, 1997.

Brantley, Jeffrey, and Wendy Millstine. *Five Good Minutes: 100 Morning Practices to Help You Stay Calm and Focused All Day Long.* Oakland, CA: New Harbinger Publications, 2005.

Brennan, Barbara. *Hands of Light: A Guide to Healing Through the Human Energy Field.* New York: Bantam Books, 1987.

——. *Light Emerging.* New York: Bantam Books, 1993.

Bruyn, Renny de. *Pijn als positieve boodschap* (Pain as a positive message). Deventer, Netherlands: Ankh-Hermes, 2007.

Calleman, Carl J. *The Mayan Calendar and the Transformation of Consciousness.* Rochester, VT: Bear & Company, 2004.

Capra, Fritjof. *The Tao of Physics: An Exploration of the Parallels Between Modern Physics and Eastern Mysticism*, 5th Edition. Berkeley, CA: Shambhala, 2010.

Chödrön, Pema. *Tonglen: The Path of Transformation.* Halifax, NS, Canada: Vajradhatu Publications, 2001.

Chopra, Deepak. *Ageless Body, Timeless Mind: The Quantum Alternative to Growing Old.* New York: Harmony Books, 1994.

——. *The Seven Spiritual Laws of Success.* Novato, CA: New World Library, 1994.

Coats, Callum. *Living Energies*, 2nd Edition. Dublin, Ireland: Gill & MacMillan, Ltd., 2001.

Cooperrider, David L., and Suresh Srivastva. *Appreciative Management and Leadership. The Power of Positive Thought and Action in Organizations.* San Francisco, CA: Jossey-Bass, 1990.

Crawley, Jacyntha. *The Biorhythm Kit.* North Clarendon, Vermont: Journey Editions, 1996.

Csikszentmihalyi, Mihaly. *Beyond Boredom and Anxiety.* San Francisco, CA: Jossey-Bass, 1975.

——. *Creativity: The Psychology of Discovery and Invention.* New York: Harper Perennial, 1998.

——. *Flow: The Psychology of Optimal Experience.* New York: Harper Perennial Modern Classics, 1990.

Dahlke, Rudiger. *Mandalas of the World.* New York: Sterling, 1992.

Dalai Lama. *The Path to Tranquility: Daily Meditations.* New York: Viking Books, 1999.

Dalai Lama and Howard C. Cutler. *The Art of Happiness: A Handbook for Living.* London: Hodder, 1998.

———. *The Essence of Happiness.* New York: Riverhead Books, 2010.

Dale, Cyndi. *The Subtle Body.* Louisville, CO: Sounds True, 2009.

Däniken von, Erich. *Chariots of the Gods.* New York: Berkley Books, 1984.

Dossey, Larry. *Recovering the Soul. A Scientific and Spiritual Search.* New York: Bantam Books, 1989.

———. *Reinventing Medicine. Beyond Mind-Body to a New Era of Healing.* San Francisco: HarperOne, 2000.

Dunne, B.J., Y.H. Dobyns, and S.M. Intner. "Precognitive Remote Perception III: Complete Binary Data Base with Analytical Refinements." Princeton Engineering Anomalies Research. PEAR Technical Note 89002. Princeton, NJ: Princeton University, August 1989.

Dunne, B.J., and R.G. Jahn. "Experiments in Remote Human/Machine Interaction." *Journal of Scientific Exploration* 6, no. 4 (1992): 311–32.

Dunne, B.J., R.G. Jahn, and R.D. Nelson. "Precognitive Remote Perception." Princeton Engineering Anomalies Research, School of Engineering/Applied Science. PEAR Technical Note 83003. Princeton, NJ: Princeton University, 1983.

Dunne, B.J. "Gender Differences in Human/Machine Anomalies." *Journal of Scientific Exploration* 12, no. 1 (1998): 3–55.

Dyson, Freeman, *Infinite in All Directions.* Harper & Row, New York 1988.

Friedman, Norman. *Bridging Science and Spirit: Common Elements in David Bohm's Physics, the Perennial Philosophy and Seth.* Needham, MA: Moment Point Press, 1997 Reissue.

———. *The Hidden Domain. Home of the Quantum Wave Function, Nature's Creative Force.* Needham, MA: Moment Point Press Inc., 1997.

Frost, A.J., and Robert R. Prechter. *Elliott Wave Principle: Key to Market Behavior*, 10th Edition. Gainesville, GA: New Classics Library, 2005.

Ganzevoort, Ruard, Piet Verhagen, Wim Ter Horst, and Marjoleine de Vos. *Vergeving als opgave: Psychologische realiteit of onmogelijkheid?* (Forgiveness as a task: Psychological reality or impossibility). Serie Geestelijke Volksgezondheid 2-62. Tilburg, Netherlands: KSGV, 2003. 17–33.

Gawain, Shakti. *Creative Visualisation.* Berkeley, CA: Whatever Publishing, 1978.

Gleick, James. *Chaos: Making a New Science.* New York: Penguin Books, 1987.

Goswami, Amit. *Physics of the Soul: The Quantum Book of Living, Dying, Reincarnation and Immortality.* Charlottesville, VA: Hampton Roads Publishing Company, 2001.

———. *The Self-Aware Universe: How Consciousness Creates the Material World.* New York: Penguin Putnam, 1993.

Hawking, Stephen. *The Universe in a Nutshell.* New York: Bantam Books, 2001.

Heisenberg, Werner. *Physics and Beyond.* New York: Harper and Row, 1971.

———. *Physics and Philosophy.* New York: Harper and Row, 1958.

Hill, Napoleon. *Think and Grow Rich*. New York: Random House, 1960.

Honorton, Charles, and Warren Barksdale. "PK Performance with Waking Suggestions for Muscle Tension Versus Relaxation." *Journal of the American Society for Psychical Research* 66 (1972): 208–212.

Hunt, Valerie. "Bioscalar Energy: The Healing Power." 2000; http://www.bioenergyfields .org.

———. "The Human Energy Field and Sound Therapy." 2001; http://www.bioenergyfields .org.

———. *Infinite Mind: Science of the Human Vibrations of Consciousness,* 2nd Edition. Malibu, CA: Malibu Publishing Company, 1996.

Jahn, Robert G., and Brenda J. Dunne. *Margins of Reality. The Role of Consciousness in the Physical World*. Princeton, NJ: ICRL Press, 2009.

———. "The Science of the Subjective." *Journal of Scientific Exploration* 11, no. 2 (1997): 201–224.

Jahn, Robert G., Brenda J. Dunne, R.D. Nelson, Y.H. Dobyns, and G.J. Bradish. "Correlations of Random Binary Sequences with Prestated Operator Intention: A Review of a 12-Year Program." *Journal of Scientific Exploration* 11 (1997): 345–67.

Jampolsky, Gerald G. *Forgiveness: The Greatest Healer of All*. Hillsboro, OR: Beyond Words Publishing, 1999.

Jantsch, Erich. *The Self-Organizing Universe*. New York: Pergamon, 1980.

Jenny, Hans. *Cymatics: A Study of Wave Phenomena and Vibration*. Newmarket, NH: MACROmedia Publishing, 2001.

Jung, Carl Gustav. *Man and His Symbols*. New York: Dell, 1968.

———. *Memories, Dreams, Reflections,* Reissue Edition. New York: Vintage 1989.

Kamp, Jurriann. "Een verandering in je hart verandert alles" (A change in your heart changes everything). *Ode* magazine (June, 2005).

Kamalashila. *Meditation: The Buddhist Way of Tranquillity and Insight*. Birmingham, UK: Windhorse Publications, 1996.

Keen, Linda. *Intuition Magic*. Charlottesville, VA: Hampton Roads Publishing, 1998.

Keen, Linda, and Aart de Waard. *Intuitie in je vingers* (Intuition in your fingers). Deventer, Netherlands: Ankh-Hermes, 1994.

Kennedy, J.E., and Judith L. Taddonio. "Experimenter Effects in Parapsychological Research." *Journal of Parapsychology* 40 (1976): 1–33.

Kern, Hermann. *Through the Labyrinth: Designs and Meanings over 5,000 Years*. New York: Prestel Publishing, 2000.

Kerner, Dagny, and Imre Kerner. *Der Ruf der Rose—Was Pflanzen fühlen und wie sie mit uns kommunizieren* (The call of the rose—What plants feel and how they communicate with us). Cologne, Germany: Kiepenheuer & Witsch, 1992.

Koestler, Arthur. *The Act of Creation*. New York: Penguin, 1964/1990.

Knoope, Marinus. *De creatiespiraal* (The creation spiral). Nijmegen, Netherlands: KIC, 1998.

———. *De ontknooping* (The denouement). Nijmegen, Netherlands: KIC, 2007.

Kotzan, Anne, and Marianne Mehling. *Praag en Bohemen* (Prague and Bohemia). Amsterdam: Uitgeversmaatschappij Agon bv, 1993.

Kübler-Ross, Elisabeth. *The Wheel of Life.* New York: Scribner, 1998.

Kuhn, Thomas. *The Structure of Scientific Revolutions.* Chicago: University of Chicago Press, 1962.

Lao Tzu. *The Illustrated Tao Te Ching.* Translated by Man-Ho Kwok, Martin Palmer, and Jay Ramsay. New York: Barnes & Noble, 2002.

László, Ervin. *Science and the Akashic Field: An Integral Theory of Everything.* Rochester, VT: Inner Traditions, 2007.

László, Ervin. *The Self-Actualizing Cosmos.* Rochester, VT: Inner Traditions, 2005.

Lauterwasser, Alexander. Water Sound Images. Newmarket, NH: MACROmedia Publishing, 2006.

Lawlor, Robert. *Sacred Geometry: Philosophy and Practice.* New York: Thames and Hudson, 1982.

Lievegoed, Bernard. *Phases: The Spiritual Rhythms of Adult Life.* London: Rudolf Steiner Press, 1997.

Lipton, Bruce. *The Biology of Belief.* Santa Rosa, CA: Mountain of Love-Elite Books, 2005.

Lommel van, Pim. *Consciousness Beyond Life.* New York: HarperOne, 2010.

Lommel, Pim van, Ruud van Wees, Vincent Meyers, and Ingrid Elfferich. "Near-Death Experiences in Survivors of Cardiac Arrest: A Prospective Study in the Netherlands." *The Lancet* 358 (2001): 2039–2045.

Lonegren, Sig. *Labyrinths: Ancient Myths & Modern Uses*, 4th Edition. Glastonbury, UK: Gothic Image Publications, 2015.

Lovelock, James. *The Ages of Gaia.* New York: W.W. Norton, 1995.

Lovelock, James. *Gaia: A New Look at Life on Earth.* New York: Oxford Paperbacks, 2002.

Long, Barry. *Making Love: Sexual Love the Divine Way.* Ocean Shores, NSW, Australia: Barry Long Books, 2006.

Luczack, H. *Signale aus dem Reich der Mitte, Geo –Das neue Bild der Erde* (Signals from the belly, geo—The new image of the earth). No. 11 (November 2000).

McCraty, Rollin, Raymond Trevor Bradley, and Dana Tomasino. "The Resonant Heart." *Shift: At the Frontiers of Consciousness* 5 (Dec. 2004/Feb. 2005): 15–19.

McTaggart, Lynne. *The Field: The Quest for the Secret Force of the Universe,* Updated Edition. New York: Harper Perennial, 2008.

———. *The Intention Experiment: Using Your Thoughts to Change Your Life and the World.* New York: Atria Books, 2008.

Melchizedek, Drunvalo. *The Ancient Secret of the Flower of Life, Volume 1.* Flagstaff, AZ: Light Technology Publishing, 1999.

———. *The Ancient Secret of the Flower of Life, Volume 2.* Flagstaff, AZ: Light Technology Publishing, 2000.

Messing, Marcel. *Van levensboom tot kruis* (From tree of life to cross). Deventer, Netherlands: Ankh-Hermes, 1994.

Moody, Raymond. *Life After Life*. New York: HarperOne, 2001.

Nau, Erika. *Huna Self-Awareness*. San Francisco, CA: Red Wheel/Weiser, 1992.

Nelson, R.D., B.J. Dunne, Y.H. Dobyns, and R.G. Jahn. "Precognitive Remote Perception: Replication of Remote Viewing." *Journal of Scientific Exploration* 10, no. 1 (1996): 109–110.

Peoc'h, René. "Psychokinetic Action of Young Chicks on the Path of an Illuminated Source." *Journal of Scientific Exploration* 9, no. 2 (1995): 223.

Pirsig, Robert M. *Zen and the Art of Motorcycle Maintenance*. New York: HarperTorch, 1981.

Pogge, R.C. "The Toxic Placebo." *Medical Times* 91 (1963): 773–81.

Prechter, Robert R., Editor. *R.N. Elliott's Masterworks: The Definitive Collection*, 2nd Edition. Gainesville, GA: New Classic Library, 2005.

Prigogine, Ilya, and Isabelle Strengers. *Order Out of Chaos: Man's New Dialogue with Nature*. New York: Bantam New Age Books, 1984.

Puthoff, Harold E. "CIA-Initiated Remote Viewing Program at Stanford Research Institute." *Journal of Scientific Exploration* 10, no. 1 (1996): 63–76.

———. "The Energetic Vacuum: Implications for Energy Research." *Speculations in Science and Technology* 13 (1990): 247–57.

———. "Ground State of Hydrogen as a Zero-Point-Fluctuation-Determined State." *Physical Review D* 35, no. 10 (1987): 3266–70.

———. "Searching for Universal Matrix in Metaphysics." *Research News and Opportunities in Science and Theology* 2, no. 8 (April 2002): 22.

———. "Source of Vacuum Electromagnetic Zero-Point-Energy." *Physical Review A* 40 (1989): 4857–62.

———. "Where Does the Zero-Point-Energy Come From?" *New Scientist* 2 (December 1989): 36.

Puthoff, H.E., and Russell Targ. "A Perceptual Channel for Information Transfer over Kilometer Distances: Historical Perspective and Recent Research." *Proceedings of the IEEE* 64, no. 3 (1976): 329–54.

Radin, Dean. *The Conscious Universe. The Science Truth of Psychic Phenomena.* New York: Harper Edge, 1997.

———. "Dishing Up Entanglement." *Shift: At the Frontiers of Consciousness* 10 (March–May 2006): 36–38.

———. "The Emperor's New Media: Sciences, Psi and Skeptics: Breaking the Silence." *Shift: At the Frontiers of Consciousness* 2 (March–May 2004): 34–37.

———. *Entangled Minds: Extrasensory Experiences in a Quantum Reality*. New York: Paraview Pocket Books, 2006.

Rawles, Bruce. *Sacred Geometry Design Sourcebook*. Nevada City, CA: Elysian Publishing, 1997.

Richardson, Diana. *The Heart of Tantric Sex*. Bandung, Indonesia: Mantra Books, 2003.

———. *Tantric Orgasm for Women*. Rochester, VT: Destiny Books, 2004.

Richardson, Diana, and Michael Richardson. *Tantric Love: Feeling vs Emotion*. Bandung, Indonesia: Mantra Books, 2010.

Rijswijk, Richard van. *De taal van het licht* (The language of light). Deventer, Netherlands: Ankh-Hermes, 2009.

Roob, Alexander, Wilhelmus Hubertus, Piere Boesten, and Elke Doelman. *Het Hermetische Museum, Alchemie & Mystiek* (The Hermetic Museum, alchemy & mystics). Keulen, Germany: Taschen, 2006.

Rosenthal, Robert. "Covert Communications in Classrooms, Clinics and Courtrooms." *Eye on Psi Chi* 3, no. 1 (1998): 18–22.

———. *Experimenter Effects in Behavioral Research.* New York: John Wiley & Sons, 1976.

———. "Teacher Expectancy Effects: A Brief Update 25 Years after the Pygmalion Experiment." *Journal of Research and Education* 1 (1991): 3–12.

Rosenthal, Robert, and Lenore Jacobson. *Pygmalion in the Classroom.* New York: Holt, Rinehart & Winston, 1968.

Russel, Peter. *From Science to God: A Physicist's Journey into the Mystery of Consciousness.* Novato, CA: New World Library, 2002.

Sadat, Anwar A. *In Search of Identity.* New York: Harper Collins, 1979.

Schneider, Michael S. *A Beginner's Guide to Constructing the Universe.* New York: Harper Collins, 1994.

Schmidt, Helmut. "Mental Influence on Random Events." *New Scientist and Science Journal* 24 (June 1971): 757–58.

———. "Quantum Processes Predicted?" *New Scientist and Science Journal* 16 (Oct. 1969): 114–15.

Sheldrake, Rupert. *Dogs That Know When Their Owners Are Coming Home,* Fully Updated and Revised. New York: Broadway Books, 2011.

———. *A New Science of Life.* Rochester, VT: Park Street Press, 1995.

———. *The Presence of the Past.* New York: Vintage, 1989.

———. *The Rebirth of Nature.* Rochester, VT: Park Street Press, 1994.

———. *Seven Experiments That Could Change the World,* Second Edition. Rochester, VT: Park Street Press, 2002.

Sheldrake, Rupert, and Matthew Fox. *The Physics of Angels,* Reissue. Rhinebeck, NY: Monkfish Book Publishing, 2014.

Sheldrake, Rupert, Terence McKenna, and Ralph Abraham. *Chaos, Creativity, and Cosmic Consciousness.* Rochester, VT: Park Street Press, 1992/2001.

Sogyal, Rinpoche. *The Tibetan Book of Living and Dying,* Revised Edition. San Francisco: HarperSanFrancisco, 2012.

Stam, Jan Jacob. *Het verbindende veld* (The connecting field). Groningen, Netherlands: Uitgeverij Het Noorderlicht, 2004.

Steiner, Rudolf. *Knowledge of the Higher Worlds and Its Attainment: An Esoteric Spiritualism Initiation.* Leicester, UK: Forgotten Books, 2008.

———. *An Outline of Occult Science.* CreateSpace Independent Publishing Platform, 2010.

———. *The Philosophy of Freedom.* Morrisville, NC: Lulu.com, 2011.

———. *Über Gesundheit und Krankheit* (Health and disease). Dornach, Switzerland: Rudolf Steiner Verlag, 1923.

Taylor, Steve. *Making Time.* London: Icon Books, 2005.

Tolle, Eckhart. *The Power of Now.* Vancouver: Namaste Publishing, 2004.

Toonen, Peter. *De natuurlijke tijd* (Natural time). Tiel, Netherlands: Uitgeverij Petiet, 2002.

———. *Wat wisten de Maya's?* (What did the Mayas know?). Tiel, Netherlands: Uitgeverij Petiet, 1997.

Touber, Tijn. *Spoedcursus Verlichting* (Crashcourse enlightenment). Utrecht, Netherlands: A.W. Bruna Uitgevers, 2009.

Trungpa, Chögyam. *Training the Mind and Cultivating Loving-Kindness.* Boston: Shambhala, 1993.

Vries de, Marja. *The Whole Elephant Revealed.* London: Axis Mundi Books, 2012.

Weber, Gunthard. *Zweierlei Glück: Das Familienstellen Bert Hellingers* (Two kinds of happiness: Bert Hellinger's family constellations). Heidelberg, Germany: Carl-Auer Verlag, 1993.

Waddington, C.H. *The Strategy of the Genes.* London: Allen and Unwin, 1957.

Walsch, Neale Donald. *Conversations with God: An Uncommon Dialogue.* Charlottesville, VA: Hampton Roads Publishing Company, 2005.

Whitehead, Alfred North, *Process and Reality.* Cambridge University Press Cambrigde (VK) 1929.

Wicherink, Jan. *Souls of Distortion Awakening.* www.soulsofdistortion.nl/SODA_toc.html (2006).

Wijk, Roeland van. "Bio-Photons and Bio-Communication." *Journal of Physics* 31, no. 6 (2001).

Wilber, Ken. *The Holographic Paradigm and Other Paradoxes.* Boulder, CO: Shambhala Publications 1982.

———. *No Boundary.* Boulder, CO: Shambhala Publications, 1981.

Winter, Daniel. *Implosion's Grand Attractor. Sacred Geometry & Coherent Emotion.* http://www.soulinvitation.com/newbook.

Wolf, Fred A. *Mind into Matter: A New Alchemy of Science and Spirit.* Needham, MA: Moment Point Press, 2001.

———. *The Spiritual Universe: One Physicist's Vision of Spirit, Soul, Matter, and Self.* Needham, MA: Moment Point Press, Inc., 1996.

———. *Taking the Quantum Leap: The New Physics for Nonscientists,* Revised Edition. New York: Harper & Row Publishers, 1989. 87–93.

Zohar, Danah. *The Quantum Self: Human Nature and Consciousness Defined by the New Physics.* New York: William Morrow, 1990.

center for
ECO intention

Mind Moves Matter

Everything is energy, and people can strengthen and direct this energy with their attention and intention. This principle is the foundation of ECOintention. The practice of ECOintention connects modern science and ancient wisdom in practical techniques that can stimulate vitality and improve the ecological balance of ecosystems and organizations from a distance.

The Center for ECOintention was cofounded in 2000 by Hans Andeweg and Rijk Bols to further research, teach, and apply these techniques. It offers a four-year vocational training course for those who want to become ECOintention Practitioners. The Center also works on eco-balancing and energy vitalization in over one hundred projects each year.

ECOintention is unique. The application of ECOintention achieves the following results: increased health, vitality, and work; higher turnover; greater profit; better product quality; and improved collaboration between people. Currently there is no other method that both coaches the client in the Principles of Energetic Guardianship and at the same time brings healthy energy and balance back into the whole ecosystem or organization.

www.ecointention.com

Printed in the USA
CPSIA information can be obtained
at www.ICGtesting.com
LVHW060950290124
770139LV00005B/149